The Practice

Almost four hundred years
of legal practice in a
Welsh county town

QUENTIN DODD

To Dave
With best wishes
Quentin.

First published in 2003
on behalf of the author
by
BRIDGE BOOKS
61 Park Avenue, Wrexham,
LL12 7AW
Wales, UK

ISBN 1-872424-72-4

A CIP entry for this book is available from the British Library

Printed and bound by
Bridge Books, Wrexham

Contents

For all the support and encouragement she gave me in this project in her lifetime, I dedicate this book to my late sister Rosemary Jones.

Introduction and Acknowledgements

The late John Cwyfan Hughes was always very proud to tell both his friends and clients that Keene & Kelly was a very old firm which went back to before the French Revolution.

On my retirement, I was asked by the continuing partners to authenticate this statement, a task that I expected to take a little time. When I commenced my research I was pleasantly surprised at the amount of material and information available. I thought then that I might have sufficient information for a couple of talks — but like Topsy the project grew and grew.

I must thank Elizabeth Pettitt and Paul Mason of the Flintshire Record Office, Hawarden and David Casteldine of the Denbighshire Record Office, Ruthin for their help and advice over the last eighteen months. In addition, I must acknowledge the support that I have received from all the staff of the following archives departments (in alphabetical order): Cheshire, Gwynedd, Isle of Anglesey, Kent, Lincolnshire, Liverpool, Shropshire and Wrexham, as well as school archives, various libraries (both national and local) and the Law Society. The Council Tax payer does not realize what wonderful value is the service provided by the county record offices.

I would like to thank the descendants of Alfred Thomas Keene and Thomas Thelwell Kelly who have allowed me access to papers which had not seen the light of day for many years.

I must thank my daughter Gemma and Marian Gregory for their recognition and interpretation of my distinctive style of handwriting and for their many hours of word-processing.

I unearthed a fascinating story and whether I have been adequately able to tell it only you, the reader, can judge.

Chapter 1
Where did it all start?

When Tom Kelly died in January 1901, it signalled the start of the end of an era for the 'Practice'. That era came to a close with the death of his partner Alfred Keene in 1904. The death of Tom Kelly occurred only days after that of Queen Victoria: his funeral took place before hers. Locally there was a clear conflict within town and the local press as to which was most to be mourned. One press report confirmed:

> On Sunday morning at the Parish Church, Mold, a touching pulpit reference was made to the late Mr Kelly. The preacher was the Rev J. P. Poole Hughes (Vicar). After a brief reference to the death of our late Queen, the Vicar alluded to the death of Mr Kelly remarking that, that gentleman held a prominent position in the County and was one of the kindest and most sympathetic of men as well as one of the most generous and it would no doubt be a comfort to his bereaved family to know how well he was loved and respected by his fellow men.

In the *Wrexham Advertiser* it was said:

> There was no other firm of solicitors in the town — at least of any note — and all the legal business of the town together with that of the greater part of the County was conducted at the offices of this firm and Mr Kelly was generally looked up to as the dispenser of the fortune of the high and low. Nothing scarcely could be done without him and his force of character and almost incomparable tact Mr Kelly reigned supreme.

Neither Kelly nor Keene were native to Mold. Kelly's family were Irish exiles in Chester whilst Keene was a native of south-east England. They established a position in the town that meant that the forty years from 1863 were their years. Kelly gave over fifty years to the town and lived at Bryn Coch for forty of them. His death and the consequent loss of income to the family meant that Bryn Coch had to be sold along with many of the contents. At the time of the 1881 Census, he employed seven people at Bryn Coch including a coachman.

The contents sold comprised very many oil paintings (including 'Boy with Basket of fruit' by Frans Hals and others by Alfred Taylor, John Breughel and Molinaur), Chippendale furniture and thirty-seven old pewter plates and twelve hallmarked dishes. The books included many originals from the seventeenth and eighteenth century such as *Tryal of Thomas Earl of Macclesfield* [1725] and Goldsmith's *History of Greece* [1805] and *History of Rome* [1805]. The dining table is described as 'Massive Spanish Mahogany Extending Dining Table on fluted pillar supports and brass castors admitting 6 extra leaves'.

The Duke of Westminster always dropped in to see him if he was passing. We have to realise what Mold represented. It was the county town of a small Welsh county with large mineral deposits. People much better qualified than I have chronicled the history of the coal, lead and limestone industries.

The influence of the railway in the late nineteenth century has been told. Mold was a town that, for the most part, had to provide its own entertainment. The only real way in and out of the town was through the railway station particularly that serving the Chester line. Other railways were developing all the time. Direct passenger trains to Wrexham, Connah's Quay and Rhyl all came into being during Tom Kelly's time. The station was the way in and out of the town as this story from the *Chester Chronicle* in 1891 shows

AMUSING ADVENTURES OF A MOLD LOVER
A PAINFUL DILEMMA

Within the last few days an incident has come to light which is affording a rare fund of amusement to a great many people both in Mold and Chester. A well known gentleman of middle age, residing in the former town, has for some time been paying his addresses to a lady in the suburbs of Chester, and lest the regularity of his visits to that city should arouse the curiosity of the Mold people he latterly took some trouble to throw them off their scent by walking to the station beyond Mold and starting thence for Chester. A week or so ago he entered the train at that place to keep an appointment with his lady love. He had hardly seated himself, however, when he was attacked ferociously at all points by some insects and it dawned upon him that he had been sitting upon an ant's nest by the side of the platform; there could be no doubt about it, the little creatures were swarming all over him, and apparently protesting against being carried off. He could resist their combined attack no longer, so he appealed to the other passenger to allow him to undress. Sanction was of course given, and in his eagerness to get rid of the enemy he pulled down the carriage window and proceeded to shake his unmentionables outside. Horrors on horrors head! He had dropped them! The train was rolling along, and in a few minutes would be in Chester. Fortunately the good Samaritan who travelled with him had a rug by means of which a kind of kilt was improvised, and the unfortunate man was thus smuggled into the waiting room.

The course was apparently clear now. A man who had volunteered his services was despatched with a sovereign to buy a garment to replace that missing. Time went on, but he did not return. At last, it forced itself upon the unhappy man that his commissioner had appropriated the money, and did not intend to return. Another and more reliable one having been found, a pair of indispensables were at length forthcoming, but they were about twelve inches too short. Although they hardly formed correct attire in which to parade the Rows with his intended, at least they were enough to help him to return to Mold. That course he took as soon as dusk set in, declining to be no longer the plaything of a tantalising fate, even if he had to leave the disconsolate lady who expected him parading the city alone.

The time of the railway's arrival in Mold coincided with the high peak of influence for the Practice: but I go too far ahead. There are small beginnings, as we shall see.

Certainly, in the mists of time it did start. I have come to the conclusion that it was about 1630. The practice remained in the same building for over one hundred and forty years. During this time inherited papers were allowed to accumulate. Keene never seems to have thrown anything away. This is why so many intimate details about the personalities of the people involved are known.

Shortly after I came to the practice in 1955, when we were already based at The Limes in Upper High Street, Mold, a request was received to remove papers from the old office in Earl Road. A great many old metal boxes still full of documents were removed and put in that part of The Limes office not then in use. A few years later pressure on space there meant further action was necessary. So, all that had been collected was shipped off to the then Flintshire County Archives and other items were deported later. Under County Archivist Geoffrey Veysey, all these papers were sorted and classified and there are over fifteen hundred items alone in the Keene & Kelly archives. These are both personal and legal and have to be considered alongside official records from many other sources.

In the law, there are two standards of proof. In the criminal courts the case must be proved beyond all reasonable doubt. In the civil courts cases are decided on the balance of probabilities. In this work, in coming to my conclusions, I have adopted both standards of proof and I leave my readers to draw their own conclusions as to which test has been applied in which circumstance. Most of the events after William Wynne the Elder are beyond all reasonable doubt and some before, whilst even some arguments adopted later do have the civil standard.

It is the task of the researcher or biographer to establish facts and he is then at liberty to interpret those facts. He can draw reasonable conclusions. In this way, I feel I got to know many of the personalities involved intimately. But to understand and follow events some knowledge of how the profession of the lawyer developed is necessary. For those who wish to be deep students in this matter, I recommend they read *Portrait of a Profession — A History of the Solicitors Profession 1100 to the Present Day*, by Harry Kirk.

The term 'lawyer' is convenient to describe all the various dabblers in the law from attorneys, proctors, advocates, solicitors, barristers and pleaders. Educated men could become solicitors. It comes from the Latin *solicitare* which means to agitate, to urge or solicit. In medieval times, the common man had no rights and certainly no reason to get involved with the law. The large houses, the Crown but no one else needed lawyers. The large estates, therefore, employed a servant to facilitate their business. If he was clever he became the estate solicitor but he had no status or qualification. He was a menial servant. Private practice did not exist and he was employed as an in-house lawyer.

An attorney was one who argued his employers case. The barons when they forced King John to sign Magna Carta recognised this. They enshrined in Magna Carta a right to have a person to argue your case for you — the attorney.

As time passed, feudal systems were allowed to die and the common man acquired rights. Lawyers of one sort or another became licensed to be involved in certain types of dispute. London, as the focus of the legal courts, became a centre for lawyers.

But in the provinces, the Assize system and the development of other courts gave plenty of opportunity to demonstrate the skills of a lawyer. There were criminal courts and civil courts. But land was owned by a very small number of people. The itinerant lawyer who had challenged the estate solicitor began to settle in a locality and practice from there. He was still involved with the London courts but more and more with a local connection.

The property owning democracy was a thing of the future. The land was still part of the large estates. Probate and wills were jealously retained by the Church. Ordinary litigation that we see today did not exist.

In an area such as north Wales, the mineral deposits were a new opportunity and it would not necessarily be the mineral owner who would exploit the deposits. There would have to be agreements to record the terms on which they were to be worked. The mining lease became a feature of local activity as, from the sixteenth century, coal and other minerals were extracted. Those acting for the mineral owners had more legal work than those acting for the mineral extractors. The lease of land to build houses or places to make goods (factories) became commonplace but actual ownership was retained by the original estate owners.

A county such as Flintshire had a county town where its justice was dispensed and where the provisions of local services could be co-ordinated.

One of the posts most sought after in the sixteenth, seventeenth and eighteenth centuries was the post of vestry clerk. What was the vestry?

By the end of the Middle Ages (signalled by the succession of Henry VII in 1485), there was a steady breakdown and erosion of all civil authorities that existed. The posts of sheriff and under-sheriff continued to exist and be effective. But the authority of the feudal system and the old manorial courts were no more. How was some form of local government or responsibility locally to be achieved? After the dissolution of the monasteries in 1536, Henry VIII found he had created a void that had to be filled. The one permanent feature of every locality, of every parish, was its church. Parliament passed local service provisions to it. It was only in the nineteenth century that the reduction of the powers and responsibilities started to take place, until, early in the twentieth century, the secular power was removed altogether. The secretary to the Parochial Church Council is, now, a post that is only responsible to church members for management matters. When Thomas Hardy would write of the parish clerk in his novels there was civil power.

So the vestry and churchwarden's were responsible for the highways surveyor, the overseer of the poor and the constable. They had care of the pound, the maintenance of the stocks, the appointment of Hayward Tything Men. They could discharge various functions for the civil power. As other courts waned they waxed more powerful. The parish became a deliverer for the community. To the lawyer, therefore, it was a post to be coveted. The larger the parish the larger the salary was the order of the day. After 1815, new bodies such as the Board of Guardians, Local Highway Board and the Local Board were created before the advent of the Council and Urban District Council.

At his death, Alfred Thomas Keene was the oldest vestry clerk in the county and both Arthur Troughton Roberts and his father Hugh Roberts had held the post before him.

This explains what happened in April 1893. There had been rumours going around the town that the Non-conformists were going to come to the Easter Vestry and select the Peoples Warden. So there was a way above-average attendance. The rumours were unfounded and the Non-conformists did not attend. It was a threat to the wielding of civil power.

A press report of 1896 of Mold Urban District Council illustrates the reduced powers that still existed.

Councillor Parry, in seconding, endorsed all that had been said, and a long discussion ensued as to who shall be clerk for the urban Parish of Mold

— Mr Bradley contended that the Council having obtained the powers of the parish council, and he being the Clerk, was the proper person to act, but Mr Keene, the vestry clerk maintained that when the new authorities came into operation the offices were still vested in him under the 81st section of the Act. He, (the Clerk) entirely differed from the views expressed, and declined to do work unless he was paid — Mr Keene had been asked by the overseers to do the work for one year, and, as he still contended he was the officer of the Council, he ought to have been present. He had given him notice to attend. The vestry had no power now except in ecclesiastical matters and he felt certain that Non-conformists visiting the vestry would be looked upon as outsiders It was more quibbling, — Councillor Simon said he was an overseer only by name, and asked to be removed from the duties of that office in future. The Chairman asked if it was necessary to appoint overseers, — The Clerk: Yes. He could not see why he should do the work and Mr Keene get paid for it. — Councillor Eaton proposed that no overseer be appointed. — The Clerk stated that if the Council did not do so the guardians had the power, and it would not be nice for them to see the Holywell people appointing persons whom the council would have no control over. He suggested the overseers be appointed, and that they be instructed to do nothing. — Councillor Simon then asked if they did not do anything would the overseers be liable to an action. — The Clerk asked them to empower him to make the poor rate. The overseers had appointed him their clerk. He never got any accounts on the adjustment of rateable value between the urban and rural parishes. — Councillor Eaton moved that the vestry clerk's salary be eliminated from the account, and he objected to the use of the term of vestry in the accounts. Councillor Morris said the council ought to know its strength and what they could do, and bring the matter to an end. It appeared to become more or less a personal matter between their Clerk and Mr Keene. — The Clerk said he had made an offer to pay Mr Keene his compensation out of his own pocket if he was allowed to do the work. — The Chairman suggested the better course to adopt was to appoint the old overseers, and for another meeting to be called, when all the facts and details could be gone into, as at present it was neither fair to Mr Keene or their clerk. — Councillor Lloyd Jones supported, and after some further remarks the recommendation was carried.

Besides the fact that Keene the lawyer was clearly right, it shows the piecemeal nature of the reforms that had been carried out by Parliament.

The attorney or solicitor became a necessary feature of the community. The land was still owned by very few. The developed communities had to have certain people appointed to do legal jobs; officials such as the clerk of the peace, the vestry clerk, the under-sheriff, the coroner and clerk to Turnpike Trustees, Board of Guardians, *etc.*

From the sixteenth century, these posts were created and expanded over the next four hundred years until we see the arrival of the County Council. Without these posts, Mold, as Flintshire's county town, could not have supported a solicitor. They were posts that would not occupy all the time of the holder but would provide the salary and, therefore, a regular income. The holding of a part-time appointment was essential for success.

Training was very haphazard and, certainly in Wales and the provinces, there were no organisations in full control of the licensing and control of the lawyer.

It was the latter part of the nineteenth century before effective checks on the general education of articled clerks in the effectiveness of their training and, therefore, professional skills on qualifying were introduced. Thomas Kelly and Alfred Keene were both admitted after the Solicitors Act 1843 had brought order out of chaos. Fortunately their training had been very successful. This Act was the real assertion of control after many years of ineffective drift the Law Society had been founded in 1825.

The articled clerk became as good a solicitor as the training he had received from his principal. No outside examination had existed. Good lawyers were as good as their teachers. He was no better than a trade apprentice.

Kirk tells us:

> If the training which the articled clerk got from his master was defective there was until 1833 no other means by which he could acquire a knowledge of the laws which he was subsequently to assist in administering than the study of the manuals which from the beginning of the century poured from the Press.
>
> Before 1729 the ordinances, rule and statutes relating to the admissions of attorneys had referred to the judges admitting only those who were apt for the profession and the elimination of those who were not. But in practice there was no test of any sort as to the applicants legal knowledge.
>
> The verbal certification by the clerk to the judge before whom the affidavit of due service is sworn that he knows the party to have been in the habit of transacting professional business during a considerable time was together with the affidavit usually deemed sufficient.

Let us now return to the tin boxes recovered from the Earl Road Offices of Keene & Kelly in the late 1950s. There is a profusion of documents prepared during the period from the succession of Charles I in 1625 for the next fifteen years.

Firstly, there are deeds of feoffment. This was originally the only way by which a freehold estate could be conveyed in England. It required writing. It consists in the livery of seisin *i.e.* the Feoffment for expresses on the land.

Tithing	0:8:8
Bro: do: gd: or do forecal	0:2:0
figd indo	0:7:0
bob	0:12:6
	0:2:0
Composition	0:18:0
Marshall	0:2:0
Cryor	0:13:6
Councel	
Proffon	1:9:8
ffees Atty Wass' Attorn	0:3:4
Cramerly.l	0:11:0
ffees Attorn	0:9:14
	4:1:0

Socos the Contents of this Bill
of Mr. Charles ffoulkes

(livery in deed) or in the sight of it (livery in law), his intention to convey the land to the feoffee. He usually handed him a key or a clod of earth as a symbol of possession but this was not essential. The livery was generally accompanied by a charter of feoffment. This clearly was a very important document, necessary to prove ownership.

Secondly, there are quitclaims. These are deeds of renunciation of rights especially to land. These are very important documents and ones that having been entered into, need to be kept safe. What safer place could there be than with the lawyer?

There are, also, documents from between 1630 and 1750 which, I would maintain, show the continuity of the Practice. We have the attorney John Humphries in 1649; we have two copy bills of Robert Davies the Fourth of Gwysaney who was known to practice as an attorney, dated 1684 and 1685. We can see the increase in the importance of the Vestry clerk in the creation of bonds for the bastards in the parish.

The contents that would be expected of a lawyer's strong boxes for this period are present in the Keene & Kelly deposits in the archives. The names of the early participants in the practice, with the exception of Robert Davies the Fourth, may be lost but the continuity of the practice is clearly shown and the starting date of 1630 is not unreasonable. Very little information is available of the holders of public office during this period. We do not know the names of the clerks of the peace, under-sheriffs or vestry clerks before 1700. But they existed. They were an essential part of the fabric of society. We know the names of the sheriffs: they include Robert Davies. But only those who could afford it trained as lawyers.

Facing: Two copy bills of Robert Davies IV, 1684 and 1685   [FRO D/KK/499 & 501]

Chapter 2
More Modern Times (1750–1860) and the troubles of William Wynne the Younger

In the early part of the eighteenth century a family called Wynne take over the Practice. Their ancestral home is at Plassau Cwm and traditionally they have been baptized in Cwm and buried at Trelawynydd. Their estate was half in each parish. Their tombs are immediately adjacent to the church.

The first who concerns us is Peter Wynne. He clearly in 1719 engrosses a bastardy bond and acts as a witness as well. The significance and importance of the post of Vestry clerk are demonstrated. They are responsible for these, a parish responsibility. He was the son of William Wynne of Plassau and Peter Wynne, though he married, he died childless in 1739. He had a younger brother William who also died childless. There is a deed witnessed by a clerk to Willy Wynne, attorney, Mold in 1750 amongst Keene & Kelly papers, which could be referring to him.

A third brother was John Wynne the eldest of the brothers who was born on 20th July 1695. He had two sons. The eldest was also named John and achieved prominence as agent to the Mostyn Estate for very many years, dying in 1782 without issue.

It is his younger brother William who concerns us. He was born on 11th July 1730 and is known as William Wynne the Elder. He rose to be Clerk of the Peace for Flintshire holding the post until his death in March 1792. He always, as his son did later, signed Wm Wynne.

He married Anne, daughter of George Leach of Pentre Hobyn who appears to have been a surgeon. He acted as Deputy Clerk for many years before becoming Clerk in 1765. He held the post until his death. His time is marked by a long-standing disagreement with Ralph Griffiths of Chester, which included litigation. His eldest son John was also a solicitor but he died unmarried at the early age of 24 in 1787. Another interesting aspect of the work of William Wynne the Elder is shown when in 1786 he is advising the Bankes estate on the exercise of a right of turbary. This is defined as a right of digging out turf on common or another's ground or it is a place where turf or peat is dug. It is a right that can go back to medieval times.

Com' Flint

Vicecom

Com. pred.

A° 1771

[Thomas Eyton Arm.
fuper Comput fu determinat
pro Uno Anno integro finito
dia Aprilis
Anno Regni Domini noftri nunc Regis
Georgij Tertij ———— Magnæ | Quos liberav
Britanniæ, &c. Duodecimo ———— | ad man'
Annoq; Domini 1772 — Debet— | Cotton Ar.]

Receptoris Generalis Revencon' dicti Domini Regis
ibidem ex recognitione fua inde fuper hunc Com-
putum coram Auditore. Et fic de fumma præd'
receff Quiet'. Thomas Wynn Auditor

Appointment of Sheriff, 1772

He seems to have been Clerk to the Court Leete. 'This usually refers to a manorial court. It dealt with petty offences such as common nuisance, highway or ditch disrepair, breaking the Assize bread and ale.' It was also a Court of Record and had public jurisdiction with the lord or steward meeting twice a year.

William Wynne writes on 22nd April 1750: 'I hold Court Leete at Mold. I have adjourned it to Monday 5th May'.

In the major mineral case between Grosvenor and Swymmer (Lord of Mold who died in 1760), the Court Leete records show witness Willy Wynne Arbitrator. Wynne tells Bankes:

I think the present one may answer under the general word of Turbary. It appertains to Waen Ddofn late in the holding of Rice Jones and now of his widow. The description I gave you of the Turbary was from my own survey of it acceded to by Mr R. Williams so that there can be no difference about it hereafter.

In the records in the accounts in 1784, is a claim for a payment of £3 4s. 6d. to reimburse William Wynne the Elder, Clerk of the Peace, for money he had spent with Mr Poole the bookseller for Burn's *Justice* and for books for the use of in the gaol at Flint.

His youngest son was also William who was known as William Wynne the Younger. He was also given the post of County Treasurer to go with the post of Clerk of the Peace on his father's death in 1792. He held both posts until his very sudden death in August 1820. He married in 1794 Mary Roden of Gwernle, St Asaph, at Christleton Parish Church. They had several children. He was involved in the launch of the Mold Savings Bank.

Hugh Roberts is the next name to concern us. He came from Glan Menai a home in the parish of Llandegfan on Anglesey. He returned there on his retirement from practice in 1844 dying in 1857.

He had married in 1814 Anne Hughes, the daughter of John Hughes of Chester. She was the mother of Arthur Troughton Roberts and Llewellyn Lloyd Roberts of whom we shall hear further. She died in 1847 and is buried at Cilcain (Rhydymwyn Church had not been built then).

In 1811 the *Chester Chronicle* carried an advert:

> A freehold estate called Coed Du situate in the Parish of Cilcain in the County of Flint consisting of a fashionable and very substantially built House with about 82 acres of land — the House is in an unfinished state but may be completed at small expense as most of the materials for that purpose are ready and upon the spot. Inquire amongst other Mr Wynne Solicitor, Mold. Hugh Roberts bought and is shown practicing from there in the 1819 *Digest*.

Within three weeks of the death of William Wynne the Younger, Hugh Roberts, the new Clerk of the Peace, is issuing the statutory adverts in that capacity.

Arthur Troughton Roberts was the eldest son, born 28th November, 1815. When his father retired in 1844 he was twenty-nine years old with an abundance of legal experience. He married in 1849. There is no evidence that either father or son, as leading mineral lawyers, gave evidence to the 1842 inquiry into the employment of children in the mines. This is a surprise.

The tradition of the Practice holding the post of under-sheriff had started by then. Hugh was the holder of the post in 1835 and 1839 and Arthur from 1843 until 1864 with one break in 1847. The *Chronicle* of 12th January, 1844 reports his appointment by the Marquis of Westminster (Lord Lieutenant) as Clerk of the Peace in the place of his father. He was elected the first chairman of the Mold Local Board when it was established in 1859. We have some reports of their deliberations.

> At a meeting of the Mold Local Board held on the 1st December 1859, when Mr A. T. Roberts was in the chair, it was ordered: 'That the lamp opposite the Crown Surveyor's office be placed on the opposite side of the street under the superintendence of the committee'.

ALSO, TO BE SOLD,

A Freehold Estate, called Coed du, situate in the parish of Cilcen, in the said county of Flint, consisting of a fashionable and very substantially built House, with about 82 acres of Land, statute measure.

The House is in an unfinished state, but may be completed at a small expense, as most of the materials for that purpose are ready and upon the spot. The building is commodious, and contains a handsome entrance hall, and stair case, dining room 27 feet by 19; drawing room, 21 feet by 18; breakfast parlour, 21 by 15; and another parlour, 16 by 11; all on the first floor, with servants' hall, large kitchen, pantry, scullery, and good cellaring. The House is two stories high, and contains ten very excellent bed rooms, the extent in front is 18 yards, and in depth 22.

These premises are distant about three miles from the market town of Mold; Ruthin, seven; Denbigh, eleven; Holywell, seven; and Chester, fifteen.

Advert for the sale of Coed Du, 1811   [FRO NT/1874]

The motion of Mr Jones (see last week's *Gleanings*) for rescinding the two resolutions of the meeting of the 27th October, was negatived by a majority of ten votes to three.

Ordered: That the Gas Co. from this date be at liberty in lighting the gas lamps to take advantage of the moon in all its stages, and that a new contract be entered into with the Gas Co. from the 1st January next on the new principle.

This principle of 'allowing for the moon' in the street lighting of Mold lasted for nearly sixty years, and was only abolished after an agitation when electricity became the illuminant — an instance of how strong is the hold of local tradition.

At the same meeting,

It was proposed by Mr Wm Jones, and seconded by Mr Craig: That the tender and estimate of Mr Dykins, amounting to £31 for putting up new lamps, *etc.* as stated in the specification annexed to such tender, be accepted conditionally on his giving an undertaking to have the while completed to the satisfaction of the Board on or before the 31st inst.; and on his agreeing to an alteration of the position of the lamp in King Street.

Resolved: That the clerk's salary be £25 *per annum*, to date from the 1st January last (irrespective of any remuneration he may be entitled to receive for professional services.

Mold Gleanings — The Origin of 'Moon' Lighting (By 'Penman')

Again on 5th January, 1859

At a meeting held on January 5th when Mr A. T. Roberts was in the chair. It was 'Resolved: That the salary of Mr Musgrave (the treasurer), for the year commencing January 1st be £15, to include interest, commission, and all expenses.' The accounts passed at this meeting show something of the Board's activities. Mr Cain Parry, the clerk received £14 16s. for 'drafting the bye-laws'; also £25, a years salary. The Gas Co. were paid for lighting the streets the sum of £51 12s. 6d. There is an item of £1 paid 'to Mrs Powell for looking after the Board's Room' — not an exorbitant amount for a year's work.

Mold Gleanings — Names Out Of A Hat (By 'Penman')

Cain Parry was a black sheep. He was a local solicitor who disappeared overnight to Australia with other people's money, to be followed a couple of years later by his wife and daughter with more of other people's money. He was described in a digest of the time as 'Clerk to the Local Board and perpetual Commissioner for taking acknowledgments of deeds by married women and to administer Oaths in Chancery'. He was also solicitor to the Hawarden Association for prosecution of felons and the Conservative Association. This is a curious feature as we shall see from Keene that authority to administer Oaths was given by individual courts.

We also have this habit of lawyers being party to documents never describing themselves as attorneys or solicitors but always as gentleman. Spotting the lawyers is therefore difficult, but perish the thought that they would be other than gentlemen. When I came to Mold in 1955, Charles Sydney Moore, who took over the practice of H. G. Roberts always, if he was a party to a deed, described himself as 'gentleman'.

The value of the public appointment is really evident now. In the seventeenth century the lawyer would probably do all the work himself. In the eighteenth century a public appointment would enable him to employ clerks that in turn meant he could have more clients.

How did they know when to hold Quarter Sessions? The times were prescribed four times a year. One for example was held in the first week after the feast of the Translation of St Thomas the Martyr.

You will say that this has been a description of a very uneventful century in the life of the Practice but the discerning reader will suspect that something has been held back. You would be right. The *Chester Chronicle* has over the years found a local inhabitant with a good memory and produced these recollections as a feature article. The year 1885 was such a year. Joseph Eaton was a well-known local man aged about eighty, god-fearing and a Liberal. Throughout this year a series of articles dealt with the 1820s and described which families were in various houses in the High Street.

One such article on 27th June, 1885, under the title 'Old Mold' helps us. Joseph Eaton had a style all of his own and I quote his article in full.

Mr Joseph Eaton continues: A tombstone in Mold churchyard, which attracted the greatest notice about 65 years ago, was that of William Wynne, Esq., clerk of the peace, and agent for most of the gentry in the country - a man of great power and influence in his day. Whom he would he would raise up, and whom he would he would cast down. He was the general trustee for the labourer, the mechanic, the artisan, and all others who by dint of economy had been able to put a little of their savings on one side. All went invariably to Mr Wynne to have their little sums invested in his hands. In fact, he was the chancellor of the exchequer for them, and it was admitted he paid a good interest, but unfortunately for the depositors they never had anything but the interest. He also had an unlimited power given to him by the gentry and by the country in general, but having a rather large and expensive family to keep up an appearance he overbalanced himself, and at last ventured to draw mortgages on some properties for which he was agent. So after shouldering it for a considerable time the burden of his iniquity became so great that it was impossible to conceal it any longer, and rather than be tried at the bar as a felon he slipped out of the house one afternoon in February 1820, and in a place called the Wern, about a mile from the Mold Cross, he committed suicide by shooting himself through the head at the age of 49, thereby fulfilling to the very letter a passage from the Old Book — 'As the partridge sitteth on eggs and hatcheth them not, so he that getteth riches and not by right, shall leave them in the midst of his days, and at his end shall be a fool'. When the shades of evening appeared and there was no return of Mr Wynne there was great anxiety and uneasiness respecting him, and as night rolled in parties were dispatched in different ways with lanterns in search of him. Some of the party had a clue of him walking through the lower part of New Street towards Pen-y-Ffordd on the Ruthin Road — going at a very sharp pace. Black despair having seized its victim hurled him away to go, 'Anywhere — anywhere out of the world'.

So about 10 or 11 o'clock that night he was found by Tom Wynne the doctor and Watkin Jones (after that of the Bank). When Tom Wynne, who was a relative, saw what had taken place, he threw his pocket handkerchief over the deceased's face and called out 'All right', in order to keep others from approaching too near to witness the awful tragedy. The fact of his death could not be concealed, but there was an attempt to conceal the cause thereof, and the event was so incredible in the sight of many that they could not be brought to believe it possible that the high and mighty Mr Wynne could ever do such a thing, and some held out for a long time that he was not dead, but had made his escape out of the country, and that his burial was only a sham. But the evidence of the coroner and his jurymen, together with the testimony of old Edward Bill, the plumber, who made his leaden coffin, and who assisted to put the body in, was of too stubborn a nature to be shaken.

Mr Wynne's residence was that large house in the centre of the town, now used as offices by Messrs. Kelly and Keene, solicitors, and Mr Wynne's offices were those rooms where the volunteers meet. Mr James Knight, of Rhual, banker, had married one of Mr Wynne's daughters, but both families are now extinct. The last of the Wynnes — Llywelyn — died some years ago in Manchester. It is an old saying that mighty men never last long, and the more I think of it the more I am convinced of its reality; and herein we see another awful specimen added to the long black list, showing that they who will be rich fall into temptation and a snare, and into many foolish and hurtful lusts, which drown men in perdition. But I should not have mentioned this deplorable and awful case had I not known that several wished me to do it: and as I am perfectly satisfied that the whole family of the Wynnes are now extinct, it cannot hurt anyone.

The surrounding evidence does support Eaton's account. There are no reports of the death or the inquest. There is only a death announcement. The local establishment did get together to cover up what had happened. Hugh Roberts was the instrument chosen to achieve this. He was appointed Clerk of the Peace with undue speed. He takes over the practice run by William Wynne the Younger.

Joseph Eaton was right that William Wynne the Younger had got himself into an enormous financial mess, but in choosing James Knight as his executor he made a very wise choice. If there had been regulation of the profession in his time, his tricks and other schemes would have been difficult to unravel. He does admit his problems were all of his own making.

We have to remember there was no real regulation of solicitors at this time. The Law Society was formed later. There was no real control over admission to the profession. Until the Solicitors Act of 1888 authorized the establishment of a disciplinary committee consisting entirely of solicitors, the responsibility for the discipline of the profession had rested with the courts Kirk tells us. Originally the attorney was in precisely the same position as the litigant whom he was representing and the courts exercised control over his conduct in the same way and on the same basis as they would have done over that of his client had the client been in court.

If as Joseph Eaton says he had unlimited power given to him by the gentry they had to sort it out — but some were outside that circle. The public office of Clerk of the Peace and the legal practice were only part of William Wynne. We do not know if there was a shortfall on the Quarter Sessions account, but the local establishment would have dealt with this and quietly as Joseph Eaton suggests.

The legal practice was safe in the hands of Hugh Roberts but we have to look at Wynne's own financial position and on this Eaton was wrong. This was subject to litigation. In the Court of Chancery there was heard in 1825 the case of William Matthews, on behalf of himself and all other creditors of William Wynne, late of Mold, in the county of Flint, gentleman deceased, who should come in and contribute to the expense of this suit plaintiff and James Knight, Llewelyn Wynne 10 years and Richard Gamons defendants.

William Wynne the Younger had made a will in March 1820 appointing James Knight, a banker, and husband of his daughter Anne, as his executor. Llewelyn Wynne was his only son and only 10 years of age but his heir-at-law.

The case came before the vice chancellor of the Chancery Court on 4th July 1825 but sitting at the summer Assize of Salop. The pleadings were copious and, if you think modern law, are long winded in saying the obvious and go back almost 200 years:

> That in or about the month of October 1810, the said William Wynne who carried on the business of an Attorney and Solicitor at Mold aforesaid, being indebted to Plaintiff in the sum of £600 for money lent and advanced to him by Plaintiff he the said William Wynne for securing the said sum to the Plaintiff with interest duly executed a bond or obligation in writing bearing date the 10th day of the said month of October 1810 whereby he became bonded to the Plaintiff in the sum of £1200 and by the condition of the said bond it was declared that the same should be void on payment by the said William Wynne, his heirs, executors or administrators unto Plaintiff, his executors, administrators or assigns of the said sum of £600 with lawful interest for the same upon the 10th day of April then next as by the said bond to which Plaintiff for his certainty as to the date and purport or effect thereof craved leave to refer when produced would appear.

It goes on to say abbreviating as much as possible that, in 1814, £200 was repaid and the balance of £400 unpaid at Wynne's death and owed to the other plaintiffs as well and the Wynne owned much property in Flintshire and Denbighshire and that the court should order all to be sold to pay and discharge all his debts. Wynne was involved in working a slate quarry in Caernarfon with Richard Gamons but there was no deed of partnership or lease of any nature, but Wynne's wife, Mary, was to have an annual allowance from Gamons to support their children after paying Gamons and his debtors.

Wynne says in his will 'and in case any surplus should remain afterwards, he gave the same equally between his wife and children trusting they would forgive him for having reduced them (by his unfortunate mineral speculations) to their situation'. James Knight proved the will in the proper ecclesiastical court which would be St Asaph.

The plaintiffs wanted the estate to pay what was owed. The executor, James Knight, was required to make a full disclosure of all assets. Gamons claimed money from the estate as well. By a mortgage dated the 1st January 1820, he alleged Wynne charged a large number of properties to secure £10,000 he owed to Gamons (*e.g.* he claimed a charge on all Wynne's real estate).

The plaintiffs in turn alleged such mortgage was fraudulent — an attempt for Gamons to be a secured creditor and that it had not been completely and perfectly executed by the testator in his lifetime. Other allegations were:

that the said Indenture attest it bore date the 1st January 1820 was in fact signed by the testator and attested in the month of April following and that the said testator did not disclose the existence of such Indenture to any person in his lifetime and on the contrary used his interest and endeavours to keep the same secret for which purpose he privately proposed and engrossed the same himself without the existence or knowledge of his clerks and the said Indenture was attested by a young lady, a niece of the testator, who was ignorant both of the nature of the deed itself and of what was necessary for the perfect execution (deeds by the parties thereto and no other persons was present at the time when she attested the same although he had four clerks in his office at the same and the said testator delivered the said deeds with other deeds included in a brown paper parcel to Elizabeth Wynne, his sister, but he did not desire her to deliver the same to the said defendant or inform her what were the deeds contained in the said parcel).

and

That after the said deed was not delivered by the said Elizabeth Wynne to the said defendant Richard Gamons during the lifetime of the said testator nor did she inform that any deed of parcel had been delivered to her for him by the said Testator but in fact the said Elizabeth Wynne held the same subject only to the order and disposition of the said testator which he caused was the same until his death and accordingly sometime after he had delivered unto her the said testator applied to her to deliver said parcel to him who thereupon delivered it to him and he kept it in his possession two or three weeks and having taken out one of more of the deeds contained therein returned the said parcel such deed or deeds having been taken thereon to his said sister.

and the Gamons should deliver the mortgage to the court.

It would have been a fascinating case to hear argued. There were two decisions on 4th July, 1825, and the 19th January, 1826, and the judgments of the Vice Chancellor are set out below:

> The cause coming on to be heard and debated before council on both sides after stating the substance of the said bill as before abstracts and answers of the several defendants and hearing the said bond dated the 13th October 1810 the Will of the said William Wynne dated the 18th March 1820 and the said indenture dated the 1st January 1820 and the proofs taken in the cause read and what was alleged by the council on both sides the court ordered that the said defendant Richard Gamons should bring an action for ejectment to be tried at the then next Assize for the County of Salop for the recovery of the possession of the estate comprised in the mortgage to the said defendant Richard Gamons in the pleadings mentioned and the said William Matthews was to be a liberty to defend the said ejectment in the name of the said defendant James Knight the devisee in trust of the said estate who was to admit proper for the purpose of trying such ejectment and to be restrained from setting up any prior mortgage on any other legal estate as opposed to the estate conveyed to the said defendant Richard Gamons.
>
> 4th July, 1825
>
> By a decree of Court after reciting the said bill and answers and the said order of the 4th July 1825, and after stating that in pursuance of the said order the said parties proceeded to a trial of the said action of the summer Assize for the said County of Salop for 1825 when the jury found a verdict for the plaintiff in the said action. It was ORDERED that the Plaintiff bill should be dismissed out of that Court and against the said defendant Richard Gamons with costs and that it should be referred to the Master in rotation to tax such costs and that such costs and also the costs of the said action should be reimbursed to the said plaintiff out of the estate of the said testator and the court did declare the will of the said William Wynne (the testator) dated the 18th March 1820 well proved and that the same might be established and the trusts thereof performed and carried into execution and did order and decree the same accordingly and it was ordered that the real estate of the said testator should be sold to the best purchaser or purchasers and it now ordered that the said estates should be sold subject to the mortgage of the said Richard Gamons in the pleadings mentioned and that the defendant Llewelyn Wynne (the infant heir-at-law) of the said testator should also join in such sale when he should attain his age of 21 years unless on being served with a Spa to show cause against the now reciting decree should within 6 months after he should attain such age good cause to the contrary.
>
> 19th January, 1826

By November 1830, Wynne's widow Mary and the other executor James Knight were able to transfer the mansion house to Hugh Roberts. When Hugh Roberts went back to Anglesey he transferred to Arthur Troughton Roberts, on Christmas Day 1853, his Mold land and buildings which included:

> All that capital messuage or dwelling house, Solicitors Offices, Coach House, Stables and other buildings courtyards gardens. And also all that pew or seat or sitting place now forming two pews or sitting places situate on the south side of Mold Church belonging to the said capital Messuage or dwelling house under one of the windows of the said church and opposite to the pews or sitting places belonging to Llwynegrin. All which said premises were in the holding of William Wynne deceased afterwards of Hugh Roberts and are now in the occupation and holding of the said Arthur Troughton Roberts his under tenants or assigns.

Now let me say a few words about the property itself. It is three storeys. The house was not built all at the same time. The ground floor is now five shops. The last shop, Paul Williams the butcher, is built where the entrance was. You went up stairs to go in a first floor level. The strongroom was on the ground floor. My initial thoughts were that it had been built by William Wynne the Elder. But whilst a conservation expert thought that possibly a building date around 1800 to be more likely. It is a Grade II listed building which it is a shame was not better protected in the 1960s. Some of the sash windows are beautiful, particularly the large one to the rear which is best seen from the car park behind.

The old Trustee Savings Bank building (built c.1868) is one part of the front garden whilst Earl Road (not created until around 1900) is on the other part. There was a circle that carriages could turn around on from an entrance in High Street. There was a beautiful red hawthorn tree at the front. A collection of outbuildings including shippons was where Earl Road is now. The staircase between the first and second floor is typical of the 1800–20 period. The floors were stone so the building could be cold in winter. I find it a real shame that such a property was not subject to painting or engraving before the days of photography which also seems to have forgotten it.

Is it surprising that the building of the property drained William Wynne the Younger's resources and more? From the description in the deeds, William Wynne the Younger had real status in the community. His means could not enable him to live up to these and build such a splendid property. The property was obviously the security for the money that had to be found. In 1830 it passed to the Roberts family who owned it for over eighty years. The field behind was the origin of the name Meadow Place that leads out of New Street. The rooms on the first floor are spacious and ideal for a set of nineteenth century solicitors' offices.

It was during the time of the early Wynne's that the first involvement of the practice with a Parliamentary Bill that becomes an Act occurs. In 1736 when the Act was passed many changes that would now be made by application to the Court had to be the subject of a private Act passed by Parliament. We have in that year 'An Act to enable the Guardians of Anthony Langley Swymmer, an infant, to join in making leases of certain mines in the county of Flint with the other owners thereof, during the minority of the said infant'. This Act relates to the lords of Mold long standing clients of the practice of whom we shall hear more.

Then there is the Mold Enclosure Act of 1792. Penman who drew together historical notes in the 1920s for the *Chronicle* which he edited tells us when he comments on it that he is very indebted to R. S. Kelly of the Practice for allowing him to peruse the only copy in existence (except he says) there may be a copy in the British Museum. It is called,

> An Act for Dividing Alloting and Enclosing the Commons and Wastelands within the Manor and Parish of Mold in the County of Flint certain Common and Wastelands containing in the whole four thousand acres and upwards.

> And whereas Thomas Swymmer [we had heard that name before] of Penton Lodge Southampton is the Lord of the said Manor of Mold and of the said commons and Wastelands within the said Manor and is also owner and proprietor of divers. Messuages Cottages lands Tenements and Hereditaments within the said Manor of Mold.

It then lists other interested parties and how the Act shall be implemented and provisions for arbitrators.

It says finally, 'That all Orders and Proceedings of the said Commissioners at their respective meetings shall be entered in a book or books to be provided for that purpose'. That book is in existence, and I have been permitted to inspect it. The Commissioners held their first meeting on 14th September 1792, 'at the dwelling house of Mary Rogers, known by the sign of the Griffin of Mold'.

The first meeting is to take place.' The meeting had been advertised (as the Act prescribes) in the 'Two Chester newspapers'. These were *Adams' Weekly Courant* and the *Chester Chronicle* — so this fact ought to assure present day advertised of our antiquity. At this first meeting, I see that William Wynne, gentleman, of Mold was appointed clerk. This appeared to have been the only business, except to arrange to meet on 4th October (at the hour of eight in the forenoon) at Carreg Carne March Arthur and, from thence to perambulate the limits or boundaries of the said Manor of Mold'. Advertisements were again issued for this purpose in the two Chester papers, and by notices on the principal door of the Parish church of Mold, and on the south doors of the chapels of Nerquis and Trythin, and on the principal doors of the parish churches of Hope, Llanarmon, Llanverras, Kilken, Northop and Hawarden of the intention of such a meeting. The Commissioners also decided to hold the first public meeting for carrying into execution the powers of the Act on the 17th day of October 'at the dwelling house of Mary Rogers known by the sign of the Griffin.' On the 4th October that appear to have duly met for their early walk and the record says that it occupied 'this and the following two days.

We then have a report of the Public Meeting:

At the first public meeting aforementioned, the claims began to come in. These were received and numbered. I only have space for a few of the largest. Alexander Denten claimed 1,000 Acres; Trevor Lloyd, Esq., claimed 582 acres; Mrs Puleston (by her agent, John Williams) claimed 1299 acres; Sir Roger Mostyn, Bart (by his agent, William Wynne), claimed 46 acres; John Giffard claimed 1,394 acres; and the rev. Thomas Wynne (by William Wynne, his agent) 154 acres. At the same meeting it was ordered that the clerk 'be empowered to borrow the sum of £700 towards defraying the expenses of obtaining the said Act and carrying the same into execution.

The Second Public meeting was ordered to be held on 23rd of the next April. It was also ordered that the clerk 'be empowered to obtain 200 Meer stones with the letters 'M.C.' cut there in, upon the lowest terms he can, to ascertain the boundary between the present enclosed lands and the Common.' Mr Edward Matthews, of the Parish of Mold, was appointed surveyor of the roads to be made through the commons and waste lands at a salary of £42. Mr Matthews was empowered to 'employ any number of men he may find it necessary to raise stone and gravel for the above purpose, and to cover the road which is now in part formed from Pont Blythin to Bala, Dolgelle, *etc.*' This resolution is dated 13th November, 1792. On 16th December, the Commissioners arranged for a survey measurement and map of the commons, the same to be made 'with as much dispatch as the season of the year and the extent of the undertaking will admit.' Another minute in the record show how this was done, for we read:

I, Josiah Potts, a commissioner appointed by the above named Act of Parliament, do order and consent to the above named James Calveley and John Matthews, do survey map and produce the same at, or before, the third meeting of the said commissioners.

Calveley and Matthews were, of course, the other two commissioners.

On 17th December the three commissioners (Jas. Calveley, Josiah Potts and John Matthews) viewed the part-made road already mentioned (Pontblyddyn to Bala) and marked out as far as the manor of Mold extended towards Llandegla. The commissioners met again on 23rd April for the second public meeting, but adjourned to 27th May. They then further adjourned to the 24th June, when further claims were received and numbered. I see that Thomas Swimmer Champneys, Lord of the Manor, claimed 1,399 acres, and a Mr Berks, on behalf of Lord Grey de Wilton, claimed 60 acres. The Rev Thomas Roberts and others (by Thomas Roberts, their agent) claimed 67 acres, Robert Wynne claimed 15 acres; John Lloyd (by his agent, Thomas Williams) claimed 1,130 acres, and there was a claim by Mr Whitley of Aston in respect of 60 acres. Sir Edward Lloyd, Bart claimed 46 acres, and there is a claim by a Mr David Samule of London, for 27 acres. Peter Williams of Llwynegren, 14 acres; Mr Robert Knight (by his agent, James Davies) claimed 84 acres, and Mr Gwllym Lloyd Wardle claimed 606 acres. I fancy the Mr Knight referred to is the banker of Mold, who was connected with the Cotton Mills, and at one time was owner of Rhual. His daughter married Charles Blancy Trevor Roper, of Plas Teg, in 1821.

It can be seen that this Act had one very major outcome. It generated a lot of work for the Practice and for William Wynne the Younger. Having continually throughout my professional life had to review carefully any potential conflict of interest, I am somewhat surprised that William Wynne can act as Clerk to the Inquiry and represent persons interested in the outcome. Whilst it does appear there was a high level of consensus on the outcome at the start, when Wynne was multi-instructed this was not a certain conclusion.

The enclosing of the land created ownership which could be sold to repay the costs of the procedure. Auctions took place on 1st November 1794 and 27th November 1795 and who do we find buying part of the land — why of course William Wynne, gentleman of Mold — our old friend William Wynne the Younger again.

The inquiry had the effect of identifying land not subject to specific ownership but which was available and unused at the time. It was almost the equivalent to a grant to an early settler in the colonies but it had to be paid for. It did of course only relate to the surface of the land. The Lords of Mold had their interests in the mineral deposits protected.

Complaints are made about the level of Stamp Duty now levied on the purchase of a house. It must be remembered that the politician of yesteryear regarded stamp duty as an important source of revenue. Indeed it contributed to the American War of Independence. But they were not alone in having a grievance. When I started in 1955 all receipts given for money paid over two pounds had to have a 2d stamp cancelled out on them — probably equivalent to 25p today.

The Bastardy Bonds given to a parish for indemnity for illegitimate children in the eighteenth century attracted 8d. The document said at the signature of duty had already been paid. All legal documents other than wills attracted duty of some sort.

There was an office for the enrolment of certificates such as those where two magistrates certified that a married women 'acknowledged a deed to be her Act and Deed and at the same time of her acknowledging was of full age completed understanding and was examined by his apart from her husband touching her knowledge of the contents of the deed and that she freely and voluntarily consented to the same.'

That level of protection protracts the period required to complete the transaction and benefit the lawyers.

The Lower Kingsferry Turnpike Roads Act 1860 sees the appointment of Alfred Troughton Roberts as a trustee. Railways were putting great pressure on the turnpikes. The executors of Hugh Roberts are owed £250.

The Practice finishes this period in the hands of Arthur Troughton Roberts, a solid respectable lawyer with impeccable connections comfortable with his peers but was ready for its participation in the industrial and commercial revolution that took off in Flintshire in the second half of the ninteenth century.

Chapter 3
Enter Thomas Thelwell Kelly

As his surname suggests, Thomas Thelwell Kelly was of Irish extraction, although his parents had settled in Chester. It is even thought the family may have come via the Isle of Man.

He was born on 14th January 1830: his father was Robert Stewart Kelly who worked in a managerial position for the *Chester Chronicle* who owned a coaching business as well. His mother was Martha Thelwell: she was born in 1804 and was three years younger than her husband. She lived until 1890: her husband died in 1864. Thomas had a brother Robert Steward Kelly, who died age 22, and two sisters Sophia and Elizabeth.

He was a man of enormous energy and extrovert personality. He was educated at King's School, Chester, but no information is available of his career there. He did clearly enjoy school and in later years was a regular attender of the annual dinner of the Old King's Scholars' Association.

On leaving school, he joined the offices of John Finchett Maddock who, besides being a solicitor, held the post of Clerk of the Peace in Cheshire. He went there as a trainee law clerk, not as an articled clerk, to qualify as a solicitor. Somewhere around 1850, at the age of twenty, he moved to work in Mold for Arthur Troughton Roberts, the Clerk of the Peace for Flintshire, with an office in the High Street.

He left a large office for a smaller one and there must be a suspicion that he came to Mold because he had met Elizabeth Griffiths. The year 1850 is given as that of his move, but it may have been a little later. He married Elizabeth Griffiths at Mold Parish Church on the 11th July, 1854: he is described as an 'Attorney Clerk' while she had no occupation. Her father was dead but is described as an 'innkeeper'. She is described as a lady nurtured amid the picturesque surroundings of the far-famed Loggerheads. She was intelligent and in December 1864 the *Wrexham Telegraph* informs us she attends with her husband a lecture on the 'North Wales Coal Field'. They lived first at Rhydygaled, then Penyffordd (a house in Mold) and finally at Bryn Coch. She was clearly a gentle creature with a lovely disposition, ideally suited to the young love of Kelly. When he explains to Keene, in later years, that he and his wife are to holiday in 1863 at the

Waterhead Hotel, near Ambleside in the Lake District, there is a warmth and comfort that radiates from the relationship. They were married for fifteen years. We do not know how often she was unsuccessfully with child but, in October 1869, at the age of thirty-nine, she died in childbirth. Kelly was devastated and threw his enormous energies into his work.

We are told that in his early days he used to attend, periodically, the English Wesleyan Church. Indeed he is described as a staunch churchman of the Evangelical School. This leads one to believe that, although her father was an innkeeper, Elizabeth Kelly was originally a Methodist. Kelly certainly put his energies into helping to pay for the new chapel built in Wrexham Street.

Being settled into marriage at 24, Kelly formed his lifelong friendship with another of Arthur Troughton Roberts' clerks, William Theophilus Thomas. This lasted until Thomas' death in 1899. Thomas, a poet, writer, part-time congregational minister and legal clerk, dedicated a set of poems published in 1857 to Kelly. By then, Roberts had recognised the qualities of Kelly, the clerk, and had given him articles of clerkship. Although it was traditional for a premium to be paid, I suspect that Roberts waived it and we shall see more on this point later. Five years articles would have been required and examinations passed at the end. All went well and, in 1861, Kelly was admitted as a solicitor and started to work for Arthur Troughton Roberts.

The local *Chester Chronicle* Mold correspondent tells us that Kelly:

... by diligence and application to his business, combined with tact and courtesy, gained many friends and his legal advice was eagerly sought. Even those who had grievances or imaginary ones and had not the wherewithal to pay legal fees adopted means of waiting outside his house to meet him on his way to business to get advice *gratis* and he earned himself the appellation of the poor man's friend.

THESE

POETICAL EFFUSIONS

ARE

RESPECTFULLY DEDICATED

TO

MR. THOMAS THELWELL KELLY :

THE

ESTEEMED FRIEND

OF THE

AUTHOR.

Book dedication to Kelly from
W. T. Thomas

When the town decided to give a dinner for Wynne-Eaton of Leeswood Hall (he had been treasurer for the Clerk of the Peace) it was Kelly who was given the task of organising it.

The only photograph that we have of him, supplied by his great grand-daughter, shows him in middle-age, completely be-whiskered and stern in overall appearance. As we shall see, he could be strict with the children but, as *Bygones* (a local magazine) tells us: '... of Irish descent and to this fact only be attributed the never failing good humour which distinguished him and his buoyancy of spirits'.

Thomas Thelwall Kelly

In other words, he was extremely good company.

In 1867, the local unit of the Volunteers was reformed, the equivalent of a local Territorial Army platoon. Kelly, though 37, joined, as did John Scott Bankes of Sychdyn Hall. Whether this was the start of their friendship, that lasted until Bankes' death in 1898, or a continuation of a longer-standing one, we shall never know. They both joined the ranks, spurning the commissions that could have been available to them. An interesting twist to this is that, in January 1872, Captain Lake, the commanding officer, was court-martialled on charges of irregularities in recruitment. The officer was defended at the court martial by one of his privates, Tom Kelly, who instructed Swetenham, the same barrister as had defended the original Leeswood miners. Captain Lake was acquitted on all charges.

The formation of the corps was taken up with such avidity that Mold was the first Flintshire town to apply to the Lord Lieutenant to form a Volunteer Corps under the provisions of the Volunteer Act 1873 with the results that the company earned the title and was originally known as the lst Flintshire Rifle Volunteers. Increasing business commitments led Kelly to leave after a few years.

He threw himself into the affairs of the town. When, in 1870, Lord Mostyn, who owned the Bailey Hill, decided to sell it, Kelly organised a

National Provincial Bank,

Mold, 8th June, 1870.

I have much pleasure in informing you, that the

BAILEY HILL

has now been purchased by means of a Public Subscription, for the moderate sum of £400, and as the purchase money will shortly be required, the Committee will feel much obliged if you will pay the amount you kindly promised, before the end of this month, to either of the Banks here, for the credit of the "BAILEY HILL ACCOUNT."

I am, Yours Faithfully,

J. W. DALTON,

Hon. Sec.

Amount Promised £ *15*

P.S.—When all the Subscriptions have been paid in, a General Meeting of the Subscribers will be held, of which due Notice will be given.

J. W. D.

Call for Bailey Hill
[FRO D/DM/716/3]

public subscription list to raise money to purchase it. Having secured the necessary financial backing, he went to the auction to bid and bought it. The manager of the National Provincial Bank collected in the promises and it was conveyed to the trustees, of whom Kelly was one. The trustees immediately conveyed the Bailey Hill to the Mold Local Board (the then form of local government) for posterity as an open space.

Kelly's position of influence in the town cannot now be understated. The *Observer* says

Mr Kelly was generally looked up to as the dispenser of the fortunes of the high and low. Nothing could scarcely be done without him and by his force of character and almost incomparable tact Mr Kelly reigned supreme.

One of the Practice's responsibilities was to act as agents for Bankes' Estate and there were properties in the area of Maentwrog east of Porthmadog. This was an area which railways had not fully penetrated. A visit to the area, once or twice a year, to collect the rents, was necessary. The trip involved going to the Royal Oak in Betws-y-Coed for lunch before passing on to the Oakley Arms at Maentwrog. We have receipts showing their arrival there on 16th August, 1870: the 17th was spent collecting the rents involved, the landlord buying drinks and lunch for the tenants (thirty-nine in number): on 18th August, lunch and a bottle of chablis was taken at the Royal Goat Hotel in Beddgelet before posting on to the Royal Victoria Hotel in Llanberis then back to Mold via the Bee Hotel in Abergele. The task involved at least one clerk as well.

Was it on such a trip that Kelly first met Margaret Agnes Jones of Caernarfon, the daughter of a local doctor, whose brother was a solicitor? They married at Christ Church, Caernarfon, on 13th August, 1874. She was

25, he was 44. After his almost five years of widowerhood, there was great joy in the town. The office staff rejoiced as much as the town. The dinner they had to celebrate the event was fully reported in the papers.

MARRIAGE OF T. T. KELLY, ESQ. The Clerks of Messrs. Kelly, Keene and Roper solicitors, partook of a sumptuous dinner, on Thursday, the 13th inst., at the Lion Hotel, which was catered by Miss Dean, in a most satisfactory manner. The repast was given by the principal partner of this respectable firm, on the occasion of his marriage that day at Caernarvon. Mr Goodman Roberts, articled clerk, occupied the president's chair, and Mr W. T. Thomas that of the vice. After doing ample justice to the viands abundantly provided, and the cloth being removed the evening was spent happily with toasts and songs. The president, besides acquitting himself most creditably with most excellent remarks on the toasts he had to propose, kept the company lively with witty hits. The 'Army' coupled with the Mold volunteers, was responded to briefly by Mr John Jones; 'The Firm' in very appropriate terms, was responded to by Mr Rothwell; concluding his observations by saying — 'I certainly must add my tribute for the kind manner in which I have been always treated by the firm, and from nine years' experience, I can speak something for the treatment other clerks have received. Mr R. Williams gave 'The

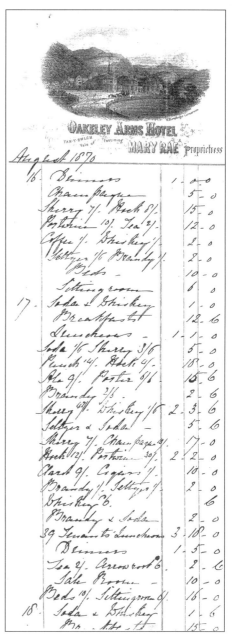

Invoice for the Oakley Arms
[FRO D/DM/716/2]

Clerks' in a very appropriate manner, which was ably responded to by Mr Ollive. The Vice-chairman, in giving the toast of the evening, said he felt inadequate to propose the toast that was entrusted to him, after the very excellent speeches that had already been delivered. He could say that although they might widely differ in many matters, he was certain that they all agreed with unmingled pleasure to sit together on such an auspicious occasion, namely, the marriage of Mr Kelly, one of their respected employers, and to wish him and his dear wife a long life of happiness. They all knew that Mr Kelly would make a good husband; he was a good employer, a good townsman, a good neighbour and a good lawyer (cheers); and from 'information received' he believed Mrs Kelly would make a good kind and affectionate wife. After some observations on married life, the speaker added that he had been in the same office as Mr Kelly for a long period — he was rather afraid to name the length of that period — twenty years, and he was ready to endorse what Mr Rothwell and the President had said about Mr Kelly. He had always found him generous and forbearing. Things had not always run smoothly at their office more than at others. The storm at times agitates the placid surface of the sleeping lake, and circumstances occasionally cause some commotion at places of business, but as the storm purifies the atmos-phere and gives firmness to trees, so bits of excitement in an office chase away mischievous imps and bring about a better understanding between the clerks and their employers. He could say without flattery that he believed Mr Kelly was more tender hearted at times than he would have people believe. Though his long experience as magistrates' clerk had given him a chance to see human nature in its many unfavourable phases, his feelings had not been blunted nor his bosom closed to charity and kindness, and when not pressed by overwork his cheerful spirit and racy wit showed to advantage his agreeable disposition. He would wish Mr and Mrs Kelly a long life of health and happiness (applause). Other toasts were given, and responded to, by Messrs Lloyd Hughes, Thomas Hughes, Parsonage, Joseph Roberts and Mr Dean.

This reveals the style and type of dinner for people such as Clerks: it has a formality about it.

However, the town wished to have its own celebration. The Black Hotel had a very large function room (where Woolworths is now). Miss Dean, the licensee, was a formidable cáterer. Estimates vary that between one hundred and fifty and two hundred people sat down to honour Kelly on his return from honeymoon. In the fashion of the time it was *his* marriage that was celebrated and therefore his wife was not there. It was an all male gathering and was a hearty welcome home.

The room was decorated with banners, crests and appropriate mottoes — another report says bayonets as well. Anybody who was anybody in the town was there. Goodman Roberts and William Theophilus Thomas had their second dinner. But the latter had to sing for his supper and recited some lines as bard in honour of the occasion. Kelly's own speech was very fully recorded and demonstrates the goodwill that existed towards him. It is worth reading what he said.

I am sure you will believe me when I say that I feel myself totally unable to return, in adequate terms, thanks for the extreme kindness which you have shown to me this evening. There are occasions in the lives of most men when they have cause to be grateful to their friends and neighbours.

I have had cause on many occasions to be grateful to my friends and neighbours, but I never remember when I had greater cause than I have on the present occasion, and I tender you my thanks most sincerely and most heartily for the great favour you have conferred upon me this evening, not only by asking me to this sumptuous entertainment, but also for the hearty manner in which you have responded to the toast proposed to you by the chairman in such flattering terms. When the gentlemen who waited upon me asked me to attend the dinner this evening, I confess I felt considerable diffidence in accepting the invitation, for although I have had the pleasure of, I may say, placing many people in a position somewhat similar to that in which I now stand, it is one thing to place others in it, but quite another thing to be in it yourself. (Laughter) I also had great doubts whether I was entitled to so much consideration, and I had also to consider whether my position in the neighbourhood would justify me in receiving such a handsome testimonial at your hands, but when I found who the gentlemen were who were originating the movement, and who the gentlemen were who were supporting — finding that it was totally devoid of political feeling — (Applause) — finding that church and chapel people, Whig, Tory and Radical, for once, as it ought to be more frequently — (hear, hear) — have agreed to sink their differences and meet around the festive board, I felt it to be a duty I owed to myself and to those dear to me, to accept the invitation. (Cheers) And I feel a pride, and I mean by that an honest pride, in being able to stand up and return thanks to so many for whom I entertain the highest possible respect. The toast which Mr Bankes has proposed is necessarily a personal one, and I know of nothing more difficult than to speak to such a one. I shall, however, avoid speaking of myself, except to this extent, that more than twenty years ago I came into this neighbourhood a perfect stranger, and from that day to this I have received the utmost consideration and kindness from all classes in the neighbourhood — (hear, hear) — from magistrates, from trades people, who have always been good friends of mine, from farmers, from the labouring classes — in fact from every class of persons with whom I have come in contact. (Applause) In return for that it has always been my desire to endeavour to do unto others as I would have them do unto me, and though I know it is sometimes difficult to carry out that golden rule, owing to the weakness and infirmities of human nature, still it has always been my wish that my conduct should be regulated by that principle, and I believe the more determined we are to do that, the more likely we are, whatever may be our standing, to succeed in what we undertake. (Cheers) Gentlemen, there was one other subject to which allusion was made in the toast, and that is my wife. (Laughter and applause) I have already said that I had great difficulty in speaking of myself, but I have still greater difficulty in speaking of my wife. All that I can say is that I believe I have been a lucky individual in securing such a prize. She is a stranger at present in the neighbourhood, but I think I may venture to express the opinion that the better she is known the more favourable will be the opinion entertained of her. (Cheers) I may also add one other fact in respect to her. In these days of Welsh-speaking judges, I thought, as a naturalized Welshman, I could not do better than select a Welsh wife. (Laughter) I have not only secured a wife who is Welsh and born in Wales, but, judging her ability in connection with the Welsh language, I am able to say that she is exceedingly proficient in it. Gentlemen, in conclusion, I beg to thank you most sincerely for your extreme kindness as displayed this evening. I never shall forget it. What I now see will never be effaced from my memory as long as live, and if I ever require a spur to help me continue in the path in which heretofore I have sought to tread, my mind will recur to the banquet this evening, in attending which I have derived so much pleasure and satisfaction. Gentlemen, I beg to thank you from the bottom of my heart for the cordiality with which you drunk the toast. (Loud cheering)

But the town was not finished yet. Magistrates had their own presentation: the *Advertiser* tells us:

The Chairman said it was his next place to perform a duty, which was a gratifying to him as it would be pleasing to the recipient — that of presenting Mr Kelly on the occasion of his marriage a silver salver, in acknowledgement of the regard and esteem in which he was held by them. A few days previously the tradesmen of Mold had given Mr Kelly a dinner in honour of the same event, at which he had been requested to fill the chair. At that dinner he had to descant on the merits of Mr Kelly, so it could not be expected of him to make a second speech on the same subject. Besides on the salver there were words more eloquent than he could utter, as proof of the regard and esteem in which Mr Kelly was held by the magistrates of Flintshire. (hear, hear) He hoped Mr Kelly would live to enjoy the respect of those among whom he lived, and to persevere in that unswerving rectitude which had won him the position he occupied. He (Mr Bankes) disclaimed all credit originating the scheme, that owed its existence to the fertile brain of Colonel Cooke, and to whom their thanks were due for the trouble he took in the matter. He concluded by wishing Mr & Mrs Kelly every happiness.

Mr Kelly begged to thank them for the additional compliment they had done him, and that he had been considered worthy of having it presented to him in open court. He had been connected with that court, in various positions for twenty years, it had always been his desire to serve them with the best ability, and he was proud that those services had met with the approval of gentleman who were so competent to form an opinion upon it. (Hear, hear)

The salver was a magnificent one of solid silver, on which was engraved 'Present by the magistrates of the County of Flint to T. T. Kelly, Esq., deputy clerk of the peace on the occasion of his marriage August 18th, 1874, as a mark of their respect and esteem.' The salver was valued at 74 guineas.

This is only an introduction to the flavour and character of the man and his incredible drive.

You, my reader, are already asking yourself how this man Kelly can have ended up in such a successful partnership with Alfred Thomas Keene but that is, as they say, another story.

Chapter 4
Alfred Thomas Keene

If it is possible in a story like this, to have a hero then it must be Alfred Thomas Keene. His inability to throw anything away has given us many of the minor details, which help to explain this amazing man. In so many cases we only have the letters sent to him but their detail does assist in the preparation of the overall picture.

Superficially, he was the archetypical Englishman who ended up in practice in a Welsh county town but this is an oversimplification of one who is part of a rather special family. To try to understand, we have to go back in time and see from where the family came.

The Keenes were a very well established family and the first name to examine is Henry Keene who was born in 1726 and died in 1776. His own father was also named Henry and, like him, was an architect, but Henry Junior acquired fame. From 1750 he was employed at Magdalen College Oxford and in 1769 designed the buildings at the south-west corner of Balliol College. He also completed additional buildings on the west side of the Worcester College quadrangle. He designed the Radcliffe Infirmary in Oxford as well as the Radcliffe Observatory, which was incomplete at the time of his death. It was completed in 1795 on an elevation prepared by him. In 1775, in his capacity as surveyor to the Dean and Chapter, he designed fittings for the choir of Westminster Abbey

Alfred Thomas Keene, c.1862
[FRO D/KK/35]

that could be removed for public occasions. He had a London town house and a county seat at Drayton Green, Ealing.

Keene had married, in 1762, Anne Desvalles, a French Huguenot refugee, by whom he had many offspring but only two survived, a son Thomas, and a daughter: the latter married the son of William Parry, the blind harpist to George III. This was John Parry a noted painter, member and exhibitor at the Royal Academy. He was Alfred Thomas Keene's only Welsh connection. Elizabeth died in 1779. Thomas became a solicitor and Freeman of the City of London and ultimately died in India. He married Jane, the daughter of George Harris, who was curate at Brasted in Kent. His brother-in-law was George Harris, first Lord Harris of Seringapatam and Mysore, of whom we shall hear more later.

Thomas Keene had only one son, Henry George Keene, a combination of Keene and Harris, christian names, of which we shall also hear more.

On 30th September, 1781, Henry George was born and the only picture we have of him is a pencil sketch drawn in the year before his death in 1864 which somehow has ended up in the Flintshire County Archives. He looks very academic and perhaps humourless but he, the family tell me, definitely had the Keene nose. The artist cannot be identified, but, I suspect, was one of the daughters. Katherine had several portraits of members of the family when she died and is the probable artist.

Henry George was privately educated, at one time by Menon, who later became one of Napoleon's generals. The family's love affair with India started when young Henry joined the Madras Army as a cadet around 1798. He became the adjutant of a sepoy regiment that formed part of the brigade commanded by Arthur Wellesley (who later became the Duke

Freedom of the City of London certificate of Alfred's grandfather, Thomas Keene

of Wellington). He, therefore, had a unique connection with both sides in the Napoleonic Wars. In May 1799, he led the company carrying the scaling ladders for the storming party of Seringapatam, the battle from which his uncle took his title in later years. The storming party were very brave men and were described as the 'Forlorn Hope'.

The fatigues of Indian campaigning affected his health and in 1801, with the influence of his uncle, by then Commander-in-Chief, he obtained an appointment in the Madras Civil Service. After a short visit to England, he entered the college at Fort William in Calcutta, then newly created by Wellington's brother for the training of young civil officers. In January 1804, he passed out in the first class with honours in Persian and Arabic, with prizes in classics, English composition and French and gold medals in Mohammedan law, having held public disputations in Arabic and Persian.

He clearly established himself as a brilliant academic, but it was his area of specialism that laid the foundations for his later problems. Joining the service at Madras, he became, in turn, registrar of a district court and assistant registrar to the Sudder courts at the Presidency. He wrote a book in Arabic on law for which the government awarded him 10,000 rupees. He was in Europe between 1805 and 1809, but, on his return to India, incurred the displeasure of Sir George Barlow the Governor and he returned to England, finally retiring from the Indian Civil Service in 1815. On the 13th November, 1811, he matriculated at Sidney Sussex College, Cambridge, and graduated from there in 1815 as eighth *optime*. He became a college Fellow in 1817 and took holy orders.

Henry George met and started a friendship with Lord Stanhope and Baron von Hammer, the famous orientalists, that was maintained by correspondence for many years. He unsuccessfully contested the professorship in Arabic at Cambridge University in 1819. In 1824, he became professor of Arabic and Persian at the East India College at Haileybury and afterwards became its Registrar. At Haileybury, he received visits from many famous men and enjoyed his leisure in literary

Henry George Keene, the elder
[FRO PR/?/74]]

work, among other things, assisting his friend Dr Adam Clarke in the philological part of his commentary on the Bible. He had written a Persian grammar but destroyed the manuscript on learning his assistant had prepared a similar document. This picture is important, I think, because of what happened later.

Sarah Apthorpe was a single lady, who, in the early 1820s, was given the task of taking three nieces into society. Their father was a loyalist who had left America after the War of Independence and, indeed, one of the girls, Anne had been born in Boston, Massachusetts. One can only assume both parents were dead as Sarah was now responsible for them. She succeeded in marrying

Jane Harris, Alfred's grandmother.
Attributed to Gainsborough

off two of them. One married a clergyman from Durham le Chevalier. In later years Alfred clearly valued advice from his uncle who took a great interest in his career. Another daughter remained unmarried.

Anne, who probably had some American bounce and personality, married the somewhat dour but brilliant professor of Arabic and Persian. Henry George Keene was forty-three when he married Anne Wheelwright who was in her early to middle twenties. They had four children: Henry George (the Second), of whom we will hear more; Jane who was 24 in 1851; Alfred three years younger, born 28th April, 1829, and, finally, Katherine, a year younger. It was a dangerous match and ended in disaster when they separated in 1842 entering into a deed of separation.

We will call our 'hero' Alfred for convenience, as there are other Thomases in this story. The problems between his parents occurred in Alfred's formulative years and had a severe effect upon him. He kept on good terms with both of his parents but more and more he had to shoulder family responsibility. Despite the marriage settlement between his parents, once they had separated two establishments had to be maintained. His mother went off to live in Hastings and Brighton on the south coast and his father remained in Tunbridge Wells to where the family had moved in 1834 after he had resigned from Haileybury. There, Henry George spent the rest of his life in local work and in writing much on the ancient history of Persia that he never published. The Civic Centre of Tunbridge Wells is now built on the site of that home in Calverly Terrace.

Although he was in holy orders, Henry George never appears to have had a parish responsibility. He was a brilliant man but it does not appear that Tunbridge Wells ever accepted his separation from his wife and, for all the information in the reference library and local papers of the time, he may as well have died in India.

All the male Keenes liked to have a grumble and Alfred's father was no exception. After the separation deed, in which he agreed to his wife living separate and apart as if they had not been married, he then grumbles when she does precisely that.

He smoked Mild Old Amsterdam tobacco and published several books including *Persian Fables* in 1833 which was translated into Tamil in 1840. A new edition was published in 1880 under the care of his daughter, Katherine. To do this, she must have had qualifications for the project.

After his parents separated, Alfred was sent to Marlborough College and was one of the first 199 boys to attend the school. Marlborough was founded with the primary purpose of providing good, cheap boarding education for the sons of clergy (the initial fees for clergy sons were only 30 guineas a year, with no extras). This was clearly an attraction for a school apparently far away. After the Indian Service, as will be seen, distance was never a problem.

He was there until December 1845 when he left aged 16. Alfred, I am told, would appear to have been pretty bright, for, in midsummer 1844, he was in the Upper V Form and was top of it in mathematics. In his half, Christmas 1845, he was in the Lower VI Form, was tenth out of thirteenth overall and third in mathematics. He remained very fond of his links with Marlborough and was a regular contributor to the scholarship fund that was maintained by the school.

He started to train as a solicitor: at first articled to Charles James Abbott of 8 New Inn, Strand, London, but transferred his articles in December 1851 to Fowler, Walker & Thomas. He passed all his exams, was admitted as a solicitor in 1853 and worked as an assistant solicitor in London until 1857. We do not know where, but it does appear that it was a firm that did London agency work, particularly involving parliamentary procedure. When he came to Mold this experience proved invaluable. In those days, all provincial solicitors had London agents to whom they could send papers for any court hearing that was to take place in London. Even when I was in articles, it was good practice for five years students to serve the last six months of their articles with the firm's London agents.

Alfred decided to go into practice on his own account in London and obtained a practising certificate from the Law Society (he had not needed one as an assistant solicitor). He remained in practice for three years and for five years there is available his personal account book that gives us a real picture of his life at this time. His elder brother Henry George had, by this time, gone to India having entered Haileybury and the East India College in 1847. He served as a magistrate and a judge for thirty-five years until his retirement in 1882. He wrote many articles and books on India in great historical detail, including a *History of India from the earliest times until the present day*. The *Times* described this book 'as a fair-minded presentment of Indian History like that contained in Mr Keene's two volumes is at this moment peculiarly welcome.' He married twice, on both occasions to daughters of army men; Fanny in 1862 and Emilee in 1868. He was father to four sons and six daughters and died in 1915. He achieved a mention in the *Law's Who was Who 1897–1915* which seems very harsh on Alfred who was a much more able lawyer.

Henry was the arch grumbler in the Keene clan. We have much correspondence from him and, financially, he was always in trouble. In 1847, he borrowed £1,800 under a bond from his father that was witnessed by Alfred's friend Vincent Nelson, of whom we shall hear more. He owed money in India and did not achieve the promotion to which he thought he was entitled, only acting as relief. He always seemed to feel he was owed success. At times he could be very sanctimonious. In 1875, when he writes to Alfred to try and get more money from his father's estate he writes:

> Thank goodness nothing depresses a man long who knows he is honourably trying to do his best and living an unselfish life. One's fellow men are generally doing the same I hope but they are rather hard and stupid folks and we must learn to be indifferent to their opinion.

We must give him credit that, when Alfred was very low in 1860, he gave clear advice for him not to follow him to India. Alfred would not have survived. Besides, Alfred was useful to him in London.

There was, for example, the Himalayan Club that was formed where Henry George was stationed. They wanted to avoid the prices of the Calcutta importers. Why not ask for Alfred's help? Alfred never knew how to say 'No'. Starting from scratch, Alfred bought cutlery from Joseph Morton, knives with ivory handles, stationery and all the china from the Wedgwood Hare rooms of W. P. & G. Phillips in Oxford Street (including 120 dinner, pudding and soup plates and everything else for a major dinner). The firms were by appointment to the King of the Belgians and the Duchess of Kent (Queen Victoria's mother). Alfred was under instruction to have the Himalayan Club's coat of arms put on all cutlery, crockery and glassware. They also supplied the glasses: over one hundred of each, including finger cups. Then there was the alcohol. Alfred was put in funds and spent almost £1,000 — 168 gallons of brandy at a guinea a gallon, 30 gallons of Irish and 30 gallons of Scotch whisky at 7/6d a bottle, claret, champagne, Moselle, hock, port, two butts of sherry at £70 a butt. Oh yes, Alfred had his uses! Henry was committee chair and Alfred did the work, although he does not seem to have received any commission.

Alfred had to act as literary editor for his brother in London, trying to get his articles and books published, he was prepared to put pen to paper on any Indian subject.

Henry is the enigma of all the Keene's. He was the elder son who chose his career in India. He was clearly a poor personal financial manager and Alfred was always involved in loans or raising funds for him. His own belief in his legal ability did not match that of his superiors. We have a picture of him sending articles home in the hope Alfred could persuade some magazine to buy them. In one letter he instructs Alfred, 'Pray like a good fellow, keep all my papers on the rebellion that may not be published by *The Times* or *Saturday Review* and tell *Blackwood* I shall be very happy to write a long and exhaustive article on the whole subject.'

Whether it was his service in India or not, he clearly had a coarseness of character that shows in his letters home to Alfred. Is that why so many letters were at the office rather than at home where Mary would see them? She would not have approved. They include comments like 'What a very prolific pair of old boys we are! No danger of the family becoming untried through a good deal of them becoming costermongers'. In another Mary has not replied to his wife, 'Do jog your good lady's elbow.' Did Mary get on with Henry?

He was clearly a man's man. Unlike Vincent Nelson, he was a real imperialist and he was owed his living. It matters to him who he knows: when he writes to Alfred in 1896:

> Lady Harris has asked me to go to Belmont in Sept but I am afraid I shall not have the means. She tells me her niece Violet Pawson has made a marriage in all respects good with young Lord Guildford (whose grandfather was a friend of our father's). There were five hundred people at the wedding. Her ladyship had a stall at the fair on behalf of the Soldiers and Sailors Fund on which my Dora and Daisy also assisted. The gross takings exceeded £20,000.

But while all this is true, it is not the whole picture: we must take his writings more seriously. He wrote many books essentially about the Moslem empire in India — a different sphere to that in which his father was such a specialist. I secured a copy of his *The Turks in India*. It shows the depths of his research and has his coarseness as when he writes:

> The wife of this chief was a woman of the utmost spirit and resolution, who cut to pieces, with the help of her maids, a bridegroom who had been forced upon her by the fortune of war.

My copy is, however, a 1972 reprint from India and sold for 28 rupees. Their publication of his works in post imperial India must be an acknowledgement of his scholarship.

Henry came home on leave with instructions to obtain canaries. Again, Alfred comes to the rescue. In January 1863, he went into a shop between Covent Garden and Leicester Square to buy some and purchased and paid. Henry said no particular birds were chosen and for them to be sent to Calcutta. They never arrived and the shopkeeper claimed that certain birds had been chosen and had died. We have Henry's statutory declaration on the subject.

Alfred's sister Jane was twenty in 1847. The Keene girls did not seem to marry — neither of Alfred's sisters did, nor his three daughters. Maybe they moved in circles where a dowry was expected and money was never available. Either that or they attracted impecunious suitors. A young anonymous solicitor or barrister only known as 'H.M.S.' was much smitten with her charms and addressed her in at least two poems.

A Voice from the Temple
Dedicated (without permission) to Miss J Keene

Forgive me, Lady, if I claim
The lustre of a maiden's name
To grace my worthless strain
Embolden'd by a conscious tie
Of sadly blended sympathy
And too congenial pain
For you like me must learn to part
With one the brother of your heart.
It shall our spirits turn away
From converse kind and laughter gay
And love from tangling cares released
To muse upon the burning East
And think that every Western breeze
That strays o'er dark dividing seas
Perchance to those we love may come
With whispered messages of Home
And if I seem in idle song
To praise the City's noisy throng
'Tis only that my lot is here
For Nature's every sound and scene
Have ever from my childhood been
Familiar to mine eye and ear
And Nature's smile can still impart
A gleam of boyhood to my heart

Then one who loves her well as thou
May twine a chaplet for my brow
For minstrels from the older days
Have sought that beauty's partial praise
Should consecrate their lowliest rays

Inner Temple, April 15, 1847

A Voice from The Temple

Ten thousand minstrels sing
Of incense-breathing Spring
Of the soft spell of Summer Evening's sigh
Of visions pure that bless
The Muses' loneliness
'Neath the stile presence of the starlit sky.

I know that spirits high
Drink dreams of Melody
From the wild voice of mountain storm and sea
That strike a deeper tone
Of rapture from their own
Till all the listening world entranced be.

But he who must abide
Mid Life's swift circling tide
Where toil and care and schemes tumultuous meet
May with attentive ear
'Mid that strange discord hear
Snatches of Music Eloquent and Sweet.

Within the human breast
Doth living glory rest
That o'er dull Earth a radiant mantle flings
In that mysterious cell
The pain and sorrow dwell
Which Fancy mourns in mute material things.

In days that ne'er may come
Each hath his promised Home
welcome waiting at his door
And faces full of glee
To cluster round his knee
And songs to soothe when day's dull toil is o'er.

None would grow old alone
Strong arms to lean upon
Kind words to cheer the failing flesh will crave
And in death's chill repose
Soft hands our eyes to close
And gentle tears to dew a Father's grave

As this the shouting throng
Silent he passed along
What bade his cheek with deepest crimson burn?
In some Agean Isles
A dark eyed maiden's smiles
Would proudly greet her chosen one's return.

We win from musty page
Frosts of untimely age
Yet not for Fortune or for Fame we sigh,
The loneliest will not part
With dreams that haunt his heart
Of one whose love will bless him e're he dies

No sympathetic glass
For its brief-lived compass
Sheds the pale languor o'er the Lily's brow
Though maiden blushes speak
In the young Rose's cheek
It hath not listened to Love's whispered vow.

Senseless to mortal woe
The streams complaining flow
No poet's doom the greenwood's sigh deplore
And mean waves whose tone
Might seem Creation's moan
Beat passionless on dull unheeding shores.

But in you living wave
Is purpose pure and brave
Victorious patience — Noblest poverty
There are true hearts whose beat
Makes melodies more sweet
Than wandered thro' the woods of Arcady
And thoughts that cannot die
Of happy days gone by
Live in lone hearts amid those crowded ways

As some serenest star
On waters cold and far
The livelong night it's pitying look delays.

Nor doth Love ever dwell
In sylvan grove or dell
The priest of Nature's holy solitude
Into the sunless room
Mid the tall city's gloom
It will the gentle visitor intrude.

No costly prize of yore
The Olympic victor bore
Yet none believe he strove for empty praise
Braved danger toil or death
To win a parsley wreath
Or twine a weary brow with withering Bays.

I wonder what was the whole story — did the poet die — go to India — or was he just impecunious and inspired?

Alfred decided to practice on his own account in London in 1857 but did not set the world on fire! It did not help that on his mother's side a trustee of a family trust had embezzled the funds. He was not naturally an outgoing fellow but, when he made friends, he gave deep, lasting friendship. Vincent Nelson was a boyhood friend from Tunbridge Wells who qualified as a vet and went out to India. We have three long letters from him to Alfred, the last written only a few weeks before Vincent became one of the British victims of the Indian Mutiny.

In 1853, when Alfred was still in articles, he wrote to Vincent, on office paper, to a place in India that Vincent had left: the letter, however, found him. Although mail went by sea, it seems to have its cost assessed by weight. Vincent wrote his letter on a kind of rice paper with the paper being turned through ninety degrees for another page to be written across on the same side.

In his letter he makes considerable fun of Alfred that could only be allowed because of his lasting friendship:

Your mind must have been pre-occupied with John Doe and Richard Doe' (characters regularly used in legal exam questions) 'that you forgot not only the address of your correspondent but all circumstances connected with him except that you had to acknowledge the draft I ordered the Oriental Bank to forward to you.
I am not so well known in India as you give me credit.

Then my dear fellow why select the very thickest paper in your office to write that specimen of a lawyers letter — one individual date on two pages four times. If all your clients are going to get no more for their 6/8, I pity them. Seriously my dear fellow you must have been wool gathering all the time. I begin to suspect that there is more than Law in your head since I left you.

Alfred was given a passport in 1857 and we still have it. It was Vincent that tells us Alfred went to Davos, the only record he ever left the United Kingdom. Vincent's letters contained serious protests about conditions in India and this information did not fall on deaf ears, Alfred being a very caring and considerate man. Vincent writes:

I came out here later in life than most people landing in India for the first time and like me a man has had opportunities of seeing other countries. He is a better prospect that the less experienced.

I cannot say that the perfect undeveloped and neglected state of this vast country struck me very forcibly. The country is a century behind any other half civilised part of the world in every respect.

Had the American's such country as this what would they have made of it. Even France would have made more of it.

In damp weather you can drive a side half quarter of a mile out of cantonments.

You have large opened holes in every compound and near every barrack receptacles for every sewage.

No wonder we have fevers and agues and that the hospitals in Bengal are always full.

Now surely a state of apathy in this service and country would soon cease if the Old Ladies in Leadenhall Street would see their interest in letting their services progress with the age.

Vincent Nelson's death so far away was a severe blow to Alfred.

Another friend he made at this time was a young solicitor, Thomas Vaughan Roberts, who became a trustee of his marriage settlement.

Alfred did not throw anything away and this is a great help to any researcher.

We have five years personal account books which show how he lived from day to day. He was interested in cricket and went to Lords on 9th July 1860. It cost him sixpence. He was interested in culture, going to the Royal Academy Exhibition on 8th May, 1860, Crystal Palace on 21st July, 1860, and he buys K A S, Volume I, on 26th July, no doubt part of his later very large book collection. On 1st August of the same year he went to the Kensington Museum. He played cards and lost regularly, anything between three

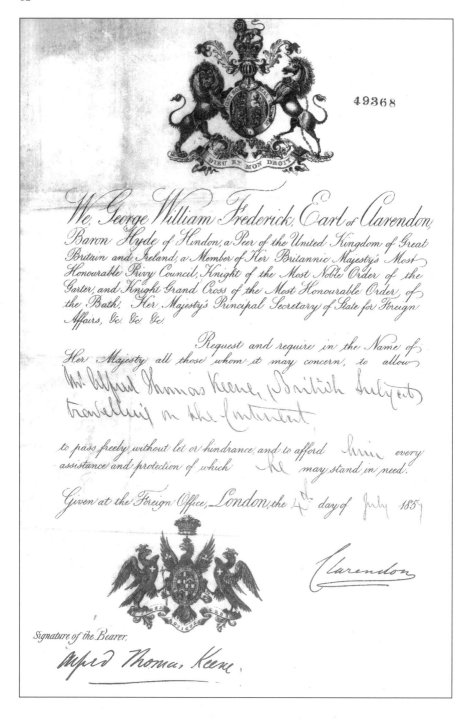

49368

We, George William Frederick, Earl of Clarendon, Baron Hyde of Hindon, a Peer of the United Kingdom of Great Britain and Ireland; a Member of Her Britannic Majesty's Most Honourable Privy Council, Knight of the Most Noble Order of the Garter, and Knight Grand Cross of the Most Honourable Order, of the Bath, Her Majesty's Principal Secretary of State for Foreign Affairs, &c. &c. &c.

Request and require in the Name of Her Majesty all those whom it may concern, to allow Mr. Alfred Thomas Keene, (British Subject) travelling on the Continent,

to pass freely, without let or hindrance; and to afford him every assistance and protection of which he may stand in need.

Given at the Foreign Office, London, the 4th day of July 1857

Clarendon

Signature of the Bearer.

Alfred Thomas Keene,

shillings and a pound. His colleagues were either more competent or a bit sharp. He made many gifts to charity. We see evidence of his real passion — marmalade. To Alfred this was the staff of life: that and tea! At the beginning of 1862, he paid ten pence for a pot on 1st, 6th, 18th, 25th of January, 5th, 11th, 15th and 26th February. He visited his father and mother regularly. In July 1860, he paid four shillings to have his watch cleaned but further examination does not reveal fussy efficiency.

Alfred had a problem with gloves. He bought many pairs, even out of season, which suggests a high level of mislaying them. Only Alfred would buy a scarf in June or receive a bill for Christmas in August.

Postage is recorded, particularly overseas. He writes to India and one assumes this is to his brother Henry. But running through 1860 are letters to Italy as though they are following someone around — Verona, Lucea, Rome Florence. Vincent Nelsons' comments lead you to suspect a lady. In Victorian times, young ladies were taken to the dry climate of Italy to try and recover from consumption. Anyway, Alfred decides to leave his practice and leave London as well. Uncle Chevalier, based in Durham, even asks him if he wished him to look out for an opportunity in the north. Alfred had not been very successful in practice on his own but what were the extra reasons for leaving London?

This remarkable family, thanks to the efforts of Alfred and his father, can trace their ancestry back to Edward I (not to the time of Edward I) and his eldest son by his second marriage. They achieve this through two separate lines of inheritance.

At the start of 1861, Alfred is found in Grantham (Thelwell Kelly became a G.P. there in later years) where he works as an assistant solicitor, I think, to a man called Beaumont. His first action is to join the local cricket club and he stops playing cards. He has his photograph taken in a local studio, presumably for his parents and his sisters to whom he shows great responsibility all his life. I believe he left London because he wanted to move away from memories. He could have found employment in the south.

So, how does a man who comes from distinguished lineage and connections arrive in Mold and practice very successfully for over forty years? How does a man who is such an outstanding lawyer end up in a small Welsh county town? His ability in the law far outstrips his ability to manage his own affairs but how he came to Mold is another story.

Facing: Alfred's passport [FRO D/KK/56]

Chapter 5
The Start of the Partnerships

The reader will by now be wondering how the shy, diffident Keene met the flamboyant Kelly and came to go into partnership. This question has been the most challenging aspect of this matter.' I must go to Mold!' was not the first thought that sprung to the Londoner's tongue first thing in the morning.

The first clue was an entry in Alfred's cashbook showing that between the eleventh and twenty-eighth of August 1860 he visited Mold and Leamington Spa. He pays for his dinner both before and after these dates but has no expenditure between them.

Clearly, therefore, he is staying with friends for his holidays. There were no former schoolmates living in the Mold area and no events to attract him.

Two names did feature in his life. Alfred originally practised from N° 1 Lincoln's Inn Field then in Moorgate Street. In 1 Lincoln's Inn Field was, also, Thomas Vaughan Roberts who, until 1864, was practising on his own: he was, later, to be trustee of Alfred's marriage settlement. Another solicitor who practised from 62 Moorgate Street was part of the firm Simpson, Roberts & Simpson. He was one Llewellyn Lloyd Roberts, a single man who died in 1864. The three solicitors got on well together. Simpson, Roberts & Simpson acted as London agents to solicitors outside London. Lo and behold, Arthur Troughton Roberts was one of their clients. Then, who is Llewellyn Lloyd Roberts? He is, in fact, Arthur's brother.

Alfred was feeling low because of what was happening in Italy or he just needed a holiday. Coed Du Hall at Rhydymwyn would have been an ideal place for a holiday as the composer Felix Mendelssohn found out, but Arthur Roberts was living at either Colomendy or The Tower at the time — probably the latter, I believe Keene was hosted there. While in Mold, he got to know his host reasonably well and at some time also met the rising Thomas Thelwell Kelly and his sweet wife Elizabeth.

We move on to the middle of 1862. Kelly, newly qualified, is working with Arthur Troughton Roberts. Roberts decides he wants to retire from private practice. He has a good practice but, at the age of forty-seven, he has had enough. He will keep the post of Clerk of the Peace and the Practice is doing well. He will drive a hard bargain.

Having worked with Tom Kelly for over ten years Roberts knows his strengths and weaknesses. So when Kelly asks him how he is to manage, he will need help, Roberts remembers Alfred Keene of whom his brother has spoken so highly of as a lawyer.

Alfred kept many of the letters written to him by Kelly concerning the purchase and some from Roberts himself and we have a unique look inside the negotiations that are to take place. Kelly writes in a formal nature while Roberts has a little freer handwriting like his brother and Thomas Roberts. Alfred has not the strength of personality but has strength as a lawyer and starts to assert himself over Kelly in protecting the new partners in the deal. He is, of course, still working in Grantham. Roberts is, in effect, acting as a 'marriage broker'. With two such opposites, it is such an unlikely choice. As we shall see, it was a marriage made in heaven! Arthur Roberts protected his own interests and gave to the town a duo whose impact was considerable.

The price negotiated for the practice was £5,000 which was to be paid at the rate of £125 a quarter. It would take ten years if all instalments were paid. He would also keep the post of Clerk of the Peace until he was ready

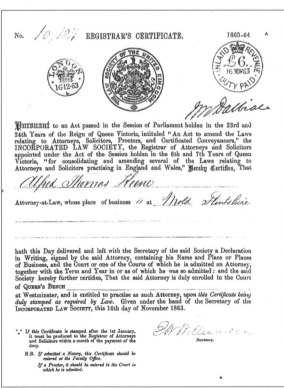

Alfred's first Practicing Certificate in Mold [FRO D/DK/35]

to give it up. As deputies, Kelly & Keene were to do all the day-to-day work. No guarantee was given of Kelly's succession to the clerkship as Roberts insisted this was in the gift of the lord lieutenant and not him. The use of the Roberts name in the firm title had to be negotiated.

Keene readily agreed to Kelly being senior on the paper. Roberts' name was still to be shown. He was also happy for Kelly's initial share to be larger than his. In case of the early death of either of them, Roberts wanted a life insurance policy, as an addition, for ten years. Counsel was asked to help settle the deeds of partnership and acquisitions. The correspondence between Kelly and Keene goes on for two months from July to September 1862.

It is not all achieved by correspondence. They calculate a half-way point in a cross-country journey between Mold and Grantham and arrive at a choice of Tamworth. Railway enthusiasts will confirm or challenge their calculations. The three way nature of the correspondence is shown by the two letters below from Kelly to Keene. As Kelly starts to appreciate him more, the 'Dear Sir' becomes 'My Dear Sir' and by the end, the correspondence concludes, 'Yours very truly'.

Mold

July 12 1863

Dear Sir

I am obliged for yours of the 10th.

Mr Roberts has communicated to me the purpose of your correspondence and I must confess that your proposal is an improvement on the terms he and I had agreed upon. The principle you seem to content for is, I think, a sound one, and in this case peculiarly applicable because for the reasons I gave you we have no positive means of testing the figures given, although I do not for one moment suggest they are not accurate yet if owing to the mode of book keeping we have here there should happen to be a mistake we must inevitably be the losers if the annuity is a fixed one, whereas by the plan you propose no such event can happen and besides it possess the further advantage that for ten years at least it will be Mr Roberts' interest to do what he can for the office. Your proposal is not objected to but the difficulty Mr Roberts seems to have is that inasmuch as the amount of his annuity will be dependant on the amount of net profits he would if the necessity arose be held to be a partner which is just what he wants to avoid. There certainly is something in this but we must endeavour to find out some plan which will remove his objections for it is important to us to have your proposals adopted.

If there are any points upon which you want information pray let me know as I am most anxious you should, to prevent any disappointment hereafter, be furnished with the amplest details. The terms Mr Roberts and I agreed to are reduced into writing and these you ought either to see or to have explained although there is nothing much in them.

My position in the office and the excessive hard work I have undergone for several years justified me as I conceived in making one or two special stipulations.

Yours faithfully,
Thos. T. Kelly.

A. T. Keene, Esq.

Mold
July 19 1863

My Dear Sir,

My terms with Mr Roberts are in substance these —

1. He is to retain the appointments of Clerk of the Peace, Clerk to the Lieutenancy and Clerk to the Trustees of the Turnpike Roads worth together £600 a year allowing £100 a year for working them.
2. A firm is to be constituted. Mr Roberts' name appearing first mine second and another gentleman third — Mr Roberts not to be considered a partner and if he thinks proper he can remove his name from the style of the firm at the expiration of two years.
3. The firm (for I will so describe myself and third party) to take the appointments of Clerk to the Magistrates, Vestry Clerk and Clerk to Commissioner of Taxes now worth together £485 a year.
4. The firm to pay Mr Roberts £500 a year for 15 years and £100 a year afterwards for his life if he shall then be living but an account shall be taken at the end of the first 7 years and if the net profits received by the firm from appointments held by them to the value of £485 a year and of private business shall not have averaged £900 a year a reduction in the annuity shall be made to the extent of one half of the deficiency.

The balance of the profits to be divided between the firm but I am to receive a larger proportion than the third partner.

The firm to give security by Life Policy or otherwise for payment of the annuity.

The arrangement will work out thus

Appointments taken by firm	£485
Allowance by Mr Roberts for working the appointments retained by him	£100
	£585

from which sum Mr Roberts is to take £500 for 15 years and there will be £85 a year left for you and I. Practically, we shall have to work the appointments for nothing to secure the private business — it is essential however for the carrying out of any arrangement that the appointments are secured but under any circumstance this will have to be managed and by a joint appointment in your name.

Mr Roberts will appoint a deputy as Clerk of the Peace but we cannot rely upon securing the appointment after his death — it is impossible to say who will be Lord Lieutenant then — we may however get it.

At present there is a considerable amount of conveyancing in the office which will keep you fully employed for a time and if the Mold and Denbigh project goes on we shall have I expect that.

Our ordinary conveyancing however is not extensive but I have no doubt with the mining leases you will always be well employed.

I regret very much I was prevented seeing Mr V Roberts.

Yours truly
Thos T. Kelly

A. T. Keene, Esq.

P.S. What are your movements during the next week? Would you like to see me? I am going to town tomorrow and I have to call at Stafford on my way back towards the end of the week.

K

My address in Town will be at The New Himman.

Keene readily agrees to Kelly having an extra £100 per year (his suggestion indeed). Keene relates Roberts' annuity to income, not a fixed sum. They have to accept a very general assurance from Roberts on the post of clerk of the peace. In actual fact, he keeps the office until 1888, which is a very long time after Kelly & Keene, had anticipated.

No lawyer decides to go into partnership with someone he does not know. Roberts clearly set this up and Kelly found more and more affinity with Keene throughout the correspondence and the various meetings they had.

I would take the analogy that the Practice was a ship. From the outset Kelly with his personality was the captain on the bridge and at whose table people need to sit. Keene was the chief engineer and he was in charge of the legal engines. The captain never goes to the engine room but the chief engineer does come onto the bridge. After 1885 Keene was on the bridge and in the engine room keeping the practice at full steam ahead.

At the end of 1863 and the beginning of 1864 the partnership commenced and lasted until Kelly's death in 1901. But Keene's share of the profit was always a little below that of Kelly.

Keene had found the right opening for himself, at last, and never looked back. The law and his deep knowledge and comprehension of it could be two main assets. Kelly was the P.R. at the front and we shall see the superb value of this to the practice. We shall also see what happened when other solicitors in the town tried to challenge Keene, the lawyer supreme. Professionally Keene was happily settled in a working environment of a Welsh market town, which may have surprised him, but he then had another enormous slice of good fortune.

Somewhere, he met Mary Bradburne, a remarkable woman and by the standards of her time even more so. She was the eldest of the three daughters of William Sutton Bradburne, a Northwich solicitor. Her grand-daughter tells me there was a painting in the old home of her and she was a very beautiful woman. The photograph of Alfred Keene shows him a grim mid-Victorian. Mary, however, clearly saw his virtues. He was compassionate, kind and considerate of her views. He needed the stability in a marriage after his childhood. She had no intentions of entering marriage as an escape from spinsterhood, which was the plight of so many of her contempories. She had every intention of contributing. I suspect that she knew she was going to marry this shy, brilliant lawyer before Alfred did himself. Even though 1864 was a leap year, she would not have proposed but I am sure she had by subtle means made clear to Alfred what her answer would be.

She was twenty-three and Alfred thirty-five when they married at Witton parish church Northwich in June, 1865. The reporter, writing in the style of the time, tells us he recognised amongst the guests Mr T. Beaumont, Grantham, Mr J. Irving, London, and many others when he is unlikely to have met them. It is a very full report describing bridesmaids' dresses, *etc.* He also tells us the music they had chosen. I know that the Victorians usually chose contempory music but her choice tells us more I think. Mendelssohn's 'Wedding March' to enter is usual but I had not heard of the music she chose to leave the church. It was the 'Coronation March' from the opera *La Prophete* by Meyerheer composed in 1849. I have since learnt that it is a short piece with two distinct separate periods of positive loud music and then of quiet music. My wife's reaction was 'she didn't come down the aisle to that'. Her pride and pleasure in Alfred is evident. They spent their honeymoon in London.

Mary bore him seven children who survived infancy, four boys and three girls. The census returns show that whilst she had domestic help for the cooking and cleaning she was directly involved in child-care herself.

We soon see her passionate concerns for education and the poor. Education comes first. She has seven children to educate. The boys are sent away to school but, unusually for Victorian times, so are the daughters. We know that at the time of the 1881 Census, Benedicta is away at school in London. I suspect that Frances and Rose were also sent away.

There is no evidence of any musical skills, which is surprising when the Keene's were such a multi-talented family. Mary Keene is not the sort of woman to take her card around and leave it where it mattered. Indeed, there is little evidence that they were involved in the social side of the town they did go to a fancy dress ball given by Henry Raikes (the Postmaster General) at his home Llwynegrin clearly to chaperone a daughter.

The parish church and worship there was very important without Alfred holding office there. When the church required decorations for Christmas and Easter, it was the daughters who generally got involved but, if they were unavailable, Mary was involved. By the time the youngest, Rose, was about 9 or 10, the early start of Mary's political career were showing. She had already visited the Church school in Gwernymynydd. It is interesting to see how she changed in emphasis from Mrs A. T. Keene to become her own woman, Mrs Mary Keene. In January 1891, there was a meeting of the ladies for the purpose of considering the propriety of establishing a cookery class in the town in connection with the Technical Society of the Welsh Intermediate Education Acts which took place in the ante-room of the Town Hall. The chair was taken by the cvcar and those present included Mrs Raikes (M.P.'s wife) Mrs Phillips (Rhual) Mrs Webber (Chief Constable's wife). Mrs Buddicom (Penbedw) and Mrs Bankes (Sychdyn Hall) apologised. A lady instructress was also present — decided to commence classes — very strong committee. Mrs A. T. Keene was elected secretary — classes to start on 23rd January. It was reported to the County Council that Mold has 75–80 students in physiography and 60–70 in cookery, as high as anywhere in the county.

In February she is at the annual general meeting at the Cottage Hospital and, a little later, Mary Keene is appointed lady patroness of the Mold Benefit & Assurance Society for Ladies. She becomes a school governor and is present at the laying of the foundation stone for the new County Technical School. Alfred is not. The date is 22nd June, 1897. The Chairman, Johnson (male), lays a stone as the chairman, the vice-chairman, Parry (male), lays a stone. Their names and position are on the stone with the date. There is a stone to commemorate the opening by the Duchess of Westminster in 1899 of the extension. And immediately to the left of the Duchess's stone is another stone as three were laid in 1897. It says simply 'Mary Keene, 22nd June 1897': she is not described as wife of Alfred Thomas Keene, as so many stones would have recorded in this era. She lays it in her own right and, clearly, the governors felt they could not ignore her contribution to the school and chose her in no capacity other than as a governor to lay a stone. Bryn Coch Primary School now occupies the old school site. The four stones, although weathered, look out across the school field to Alexandra Road.

She plays a major part the growth of education and the plight of the poor in Mold until Alfred's death in April 1904. Alfred was very proud of her achievement and involvement. There is a newspaper cutting in the archives, which is entered as being about a sewage scheme in Holywell. Turn it over and there in the middle of the page is Mary's attendance at an Alun County School governors meeting 26th October 1900. 'Decided on proposition of Mrs Keene to have a bazaar in May or October 1902 to raise a fund for reduction of the debt in connection with the local intermediate education and to ask Stanley Weyman the author to distribute the prizes on prize day.'

On 17th October 1899, she was present when the Duchess of Westminster opened the new building at the Alun County School in her capacity as governor. It was an evening programme from 7 to 10. Amongst the events at 8.30 Practical Chemistry by the boys in the laboratory! The building is still there!

In 1895 there died John Corbett who was a member of the Mold Urban District Council and the Holywell Board of Guardians. This latter body was responsible for administering the Poor Law. Mary was not qualified to stand for the Urban District Council but what about the Board of Guardians? The posters advertising the election went up — 'Election of Guardian'.

The section 'how qualified' read:

1. If the candidate is a Parochial Elector of some parish within the Union.
2. If the candidate is not a Parochial Elector of some parish in the union but he or she has during the whole of the twelve months preceding the election resided in the union

If in the case of a Parish or united parishes wholly or partly within the area of the borough the candidate is qualified to be elected a councillor for that borough.

Mary qualified under (2) above and stood. Married women did not do that in Victorian Times! Here, men stood against her. The result of the ballot was:

Commemorative stone at the County Technical School

Mary Keene	242
John Price	135
Robert Morris	82
Rev Thomas Roberts	26

She is only one vote short of an absolute majority. The winning candidate for the Urban District Council seat only polled 252 votes in a three cornered contest. The *Chronicle* in reporting the result showed its pleasure:

Mrs Keene is well known for her interest in the poorer classes and besides having a practical knowledge of their wants it is the general opinion that the electors could not have made a better selection.

She was re-elected at least twice and there is no evidence of her place being challenged. The meetings were generally held in Holywell and the minutes show she was not there to make up the numbers.

The appointments of overseers was an important part and she knew the sort of person she wanted. One candidate seeking a post only secured two votes on one occasion (one of which was Mary Keene) but was successful next time. She retired on Alfred's death but was still full of good works.

In 1900, Mrs Roberts, Bromfield Hall, called important people together to consider the families of the volunteers in South Africa. Her own son was there. Mary was there playing a full part immediately.

Her family was distributed all over the place — three of her sons abroad. So her home Bryn Hyfryd, Pwllglas was in effect the family base. Her grandson Ralph came home there on holiday from Marlborough College, during the First World War. There is one small mystery. Bryn Hyfryd was tenanted while Mary Keene owned Tŷ Brith at Llanarmon. This was a substantial property with four bedrooms and still is. How had she come to own it? It is referred to in her will in detail without telling us anything.

When she died, her obituarists remembered her with fondness. Of the guardians, they wrote:

She brought to bear upon the discharge of the duties of that office clearness of outlook, combined with much human sympathy which were ever prominent traits in a personality long to be remembered with affection and veneration.

She was a devoted church worker and philanthropist a most remarkable woman who was way ahead of her time.

Alfred was so lucky in his wife and in his legal partner.

His brother Henry George who was a real Victorian chauvinist felt compelled to write to Alfred of Mary in glowing terms in 1897 for choosing 'an excellent woman' to be their mother (Alfred's children).

Chapter 6
The Mold Riots

This chapter is not an attempt to tell the story or comment on the political aspects of this event. It is an attempt to present the part played by the Practice in the event and to enumerate the legal opportunities and restrictions that prevailed.

What is meant by 'the Riot Act'? It is an expression that has become part of the English language. Parents will use it to explain how they disciplined children. They 'read them the Riot Act'; they laid down the law; they set out the perimeters in which the children's behaviour had to be contained.

In 1714, Queen Anne, an English born Queen, died. She could not be succeeded by her father, James II (deposed 1688), or his son James Edward (the Old Pretender) because they were Catholics. Parliament would not allow a Catholic to succeed. George I, a German, became King, succeeding through his great-grandmother who had been daughter of James I. He spoke no English and lacked charisma.

The government of the day feared unrest and disturbances and so passed the Riot Act to deal with Jacobite protesters. The purpose of the Act was to give the authorities a free hand to deal with rioters and not to be accountable to society.

If twelve or more persons gathered together to make trouble and the authorities feared they could not contain the disturbance, they could use the Riot Act. A magistrate had to give instructions for the Riot Act to be read. The reader had to read the Act in its entirety in the clear hearing of the rioters: it was essential to complete its reading. The theory was, therefore, that, first of all, the rioters would know exactly what was happening and by reading the whole Act would have time to disperse. To stand up in front of an angry mob to read a long document written in early eighteenth century English was obviously a real ordeal for the reader.

Once read, the authorities could take any action at all to suppress the disturbance including indiscriminate arms fire. The rules of self-defence had been well established in the courts by this time. Such action as was reasonably necessary to protect yourself or others could be taken to resist an assault or a reasonably anticipated assault or attack.

The Riot Act remained on the statute book until 1986 when it was repealed by the Public Order Act 1986.

This created the criminal offence of riot: it could be committed in private as well as public places. It needed twelve or more who used or threaten unlawful violence for a common purpose. No reading is ever involved and proving a common purpose between all defendants was difficult. The lesser offence of affray was a more likely charge. Improved crowd or mob control by police was thought to render the Riot Act obsolete. It had not been used for many years.

At the time of the Mold riots in 1869, Thomas Thelwell Kelly was the Clerk to the Mold magistrates but on this occasion his partner George Edward Trevor Roper was acting as Clerk. If Kelly had been the Clerk on this occasion, I do not believe the riots would have happened. He would have been pro-active and was respected by all, including the miners themselves.

The incident started with the routine hearing of a case by the magistrates of a charge of assault by eight men upon a colliery manager. The police had instructed a Wrexham solicitor, Joseph Acton, to prosecute on their behalf and a barrister, Swetenham, instructed by another Wrexham solicitor, Sherratt, appeared for the defendants. Kelly had instructed the same barrister for other cases. It will help if we read, at this stage, a letter sent by Kelly, Keene & Roper to the Home Office.

Mold
June 11, 1869

Sir,
Mold Riots

We regret to have to inform you that some evil disposed persons are still endeavouring to keep up the excitement in this district, — a notice of which we beg to enclose a copy herewith was posted on Friday last at the Pit Head at the Leeswood Green Colliery.

Will you oblige us by saying for the information of the Magistrates of this district whether you feel disposed to offer a Reward for the apprehension of the writer and poster of such a dangerous notice.

We have the honour to be,
Sir,
Your obedient Servants

Kelly, Keene & Roper
Clerks to the Justices.

To the Right Hon.
The Sec of State, Home Office.

At the start of the hearing, the men surrendered to their bail. In other words, they took themselves to the court voluntarily and surrendered to the police. The magistrates who heard the case were representative of those appointed in the area. They were persons of influence and it has been suggested that they were mine owners, particularly Trevor Roper. They were not. There were some mineral owners: there is a distinct difference. Minerals were let to people to exploit in return for a ground rent and royalty per ton extracted. The mineral owners had no part to play and the mine owners managed their mining lease as they thought fit. Trevor Roper was, in fact, one of the lords of Mold who have been defined and explained elsewhere.

The complainant, Young, was arrogant and clearly had no idea about man management and the men had tried to expel him from the area. The case had been heard in a reasonable and rational way with both advocates contributing to a balanced hearing. The hearing had taken all day. The charges of assault were clearly proved and the prosecution was seeking the imprisonment of some. The two ring leaders, Ishmael Jones and John Jones, were given one month gaol sentences and the other six were fined.

The magistrates knew that this case was important, in principle, to the miners who had called for support from other collieries. Many had gathered at the time the verdict was due but their behaviour was satisfactory. The verdict was correct on the evidence. Were there agitators at work? We do not know. The mining community was law abiding if not in drink. The magistrates expected trouble: why else did they send for the military? Fifty officers and men arrived during the hearing. They had, presumably, consulted with the Chief Constable before doing so. The entire Flintshire Constabulary (about 40 officers) appears to have also been present. But the crowd waiting the result of the hearing was over 1,000, some reports put it as high as 3,000.

No thought had been given as to how to use the troops and police. No course of events had been mapped out *i.e.*

Appeal to the crowd
Threat of action
Reading the Riot Act
Firing over their heads
Firing at the crowd.

These were all courses available before the gaoled prisoners had been brought outside the courthouse.

The stones that were thrown at the police and the militia were in a pile near the court at the entrance to a quarry. The police knew they were seeking imprisonment and should have taken precautionary steps. The stones should have been removed.

Prisoners were normally taken by road to Flint gaol but someone decided to use the train. They would have to go to Chester first. On any view, to try to take two prisoners through such a large mob of people to a train was foolhardy. Chester was also an unknown world for the miners. The Chief Constable should not have attempted it. Stones were thrown at the group moving through them and the Chief Constable panicked. Nobody had been seriously injured. He asked the magistrate to authorise the militia to fire and one of the magistrates did so.

The Clerk and the magistrates themselves were trying to physically to get the prisoners onto the train at the station. The Clerk was, of course, the son of the chairman of the magistrates. There is indeed no evidence that the prisoners were resisting being taken to gaol. They were equally in danger from the stones.

Kelly was a man with the common touch and was prepared to meet difficulties head on. I think he would first of all have tried and, probably, succeeded in influencing the decision on sentence. Five years later, he was able, when Conservative agent in the General Election, to address an open air meeting of miners in Wrexham Street on behalf of the Conservative candidate with no problems whatsoever. It was during the same election that all the windows of the Black Lion Hotel (the Conservative headquarters) were broken.

The fines that could have been imposed on Ishmael Jones and John Jones could have been higher than those imposed on their friends. He would have counselled caution before trying to move the prisoners at all and left them in the cells. He certainly would not have advised the magistrates to instruct the military to fire.

The Riot Act was not read at the scene but was read between 8 and 9 o'clock in the High Street by the Clerk on the instruction of his father, the Chairman of the magistrates. The damage was already done and to declare marshal law was foolhardy and futile as the riot was over. The conditions for reading the Act had not been met.

Thomas Thelwell Kelly and Alfred Thomas Keene were clearly very embarrassed by what had happened. They knew that it had been avoidable. The next event that occurred was the opening of the inquests into those shot dead. Both Kelly and Keene were present as observers. They had no evidence to give. Their presence showed their concern for the Practice and where blame could have been placed for what had happened.

The *Chronicle* of 12th June, 1869 reports in full the committal proceedings in respect of seven rioters one of whom is the husband of one killed. Sir Stephen Glynne chaired. Trevor Roper sat, as did his other son, the brother of George who sat as Clerk at the original hearing. Thomas Thelwell Kelly acted personally as clerk of the court and his influence was soon felt. Three of the men were represented by a Chester solicitor named Taylor.

Kelly charged each one of the defendants separately. Another of the defending solicitors submited that, there being no warrants, the men were wrongly before the court and the bench had no jurisdiction to go further with the case. Kelly is quoted:

> If they are charged with felony you can apprehend without a warrant. These men committed a felony and Mr Browne caused them to be apprehended for it but the magistrates take a lenient view of the offence and only propose to commit for a misdemeanour. So far from the prisoners having cause for complaint they should be satisfied.

Kelly's influence is written all over this lessening of the charge.

Kelly ascertained from one of the witnesses that it would not have been possible to read the Riot Act. At the time, concerning which the witness was being questioned, it was impossible. But, why not earlier? One volley of shots appears to have been fired and the crowd dispersed. An hour later, when the Riot Act was physically read, the crowd had dispersed. The police and the magistrates bungled and their mishandling was beyond belief. Their inability to accept their part of responsibility is historically the saddest part of what occurred. The miners were used to challenging authority.

We see the magistrates as being unable to accept any blame by writing to the Home Office through their Clerk on June 4th 1869 two days after the riot.

Mold
4th June 1869

Sir,

We have the honour to report that there was a most serious Riot here on Wednesday last in which we regret to say several lives were lost — circumstances under which it occurred are the following.

On the 24th a Warrant was issued on the Information of John Young the underground Manager of the Leeswood Cannel and Gas Coal Company Limited whose works are at Leeswood in this County against Ishmael Jones William Hughes Edwin Jones Robert Davies John Jones Richard Taylor Thomas Jones and John Hughes for a violent assault committed upon him whilst being forcibly removed out of the District.

On the same day one of the Defendants William Hughes was apprehended, and the following morning on his being conducted from the Mold Police Station to the Mold County Hall by four Police Constables, a mob of Colliers and others collected from the surrounding District and armed with sticks attacked the Police and rescued the Prisoner. Subsequently he surrendered and was admitted to bail to appear on the Wednesday week following the 2nd June.

On the 31st ult a special meeting of the Magistrates of the District was held, seven being present, to consider the steps that should be taken to preserve the Peace, and to secure the due administration of Justice at the adjourned hearing — the Chief Constable attended and stated that in consequence of information he had received he could not be responsible for the Peace of the County without Military aid and proof upon oath to this effect having been made a Requisition was forwarded to the Commanding Officer at Chester, for aid, who accordingly sent over a Company of the 4th Regiment of Foot.

On Wednesday the 2nd June the adjourned hearing took place, seven Magistrates being present — William Hughes appeared, and the seven other Defendants also surrendered, the whole were defended by Counsel — the complainant fully made out his case and two of the Defendants-Ishmael Jones and John Jones were each sentenced to be imprisoned and kept to hard labour for One Calendar Month — William Hughes and Edwin Jones each being fined 10/- and costs and the remaining 4 Defendants £1 each and costs. The hearing occupied about six hours, a large number of colliers and others came into the Town during the day and filled the Court, but their conduct on the whole was up to a certain point unobjectionable — Flint Gaol as you are aware is 6 miles from Mold and as it was not deemed prudent that the two prisoners committed to Gaol should be sent there by road, it was determined to send them by Railway through Chester.

About 7 o'clock in the evening of the 2nd the two prisoners were escorted from the County Hall by a force consisting of the Company of Soldiers and about 37 Police Constables. The distance to be traversed was only about 200 yards. Almost immediately after starting a considerable crowd which had remained about, no doubt waiting for the removal of the prisoners commenced to display hostilities. Sticks were used and stones were thrown both at the Soldiers and the Police from all directions. This continued down to the Railway Station, increasing in violence as the Station was approached — the window of the Telegraph Office and of the Railway Carriages were smashed the Soldiers and Constables were being most seriously wounded by a perfect shower of stones and the Commanding Officer Captain Blake having received a severe wound to the head- it was felt that unless strong measures were at once adopted many lives would be sacrificed.

Captain Blake appealed to the Magistrate who was near to him, Mr C. B. Clough and asked him whether he concurred in the mob being fired on — Mr Clough considered that this course was absolutely necessary for the protection of the lives both of the Soldiers and Constable and as the stones were flying so thick he felt it his duty to concur — the Soldiers fired — so far as can now be ascertained these lives were sacrificed namely — 1 — Edward Bellis a Blacksmith from Tryddyn an active participator in the Riot — 2 — Robert Hanaby a Collier from Brymbo in the County of Denbigh another active participator and — 3 — a young woman a looker-on named Margaret Younghusband — In addition Elizabeth Jones* the wife of Isaac Jones of Tryddyn was dangerously wounded — there is some reason to believe she participated in the Riot and Charles Kearn of Mold another looker on was also shot through he shoulder.

Of the Military the Captain, his Lieutenant and about 20 men were wounded — some of them seriously.

Of the Police the Chief Constable and 12 men were wounded, some of them also seriously — after the firing the mob quickly dispersed and there has been quietness in the Town since.

The Coroner's Inquiry was held today and a respectable Jury unanimously returned a Verdict of Justifiable Homicide in the cases of Bellis, Hanaby and Younghusband and the Foreman also expressed on behalf of the Jury a very strong opinion that the Soldiers had exhibited very great forebearance.

William Griffiths, a man who took a very active part in the Riot has since been arrested⁺ and he has been remanded until Monday morning next at 11 o'clock by which time it is hoped some other Ringleaders will also be arrested. The magistrates have deemed it advisable to retain a Company of Soldiers until after Monday.

Three Telegrams were sent to the Home Secretary yesterday reporting from time to time the state of affairs.

We have the honour to be
    Sir
        Your most Obedient Servants

Kelly Keene & Roper
Clerks to the Justices

Sir S. A. Glynne, Bart
Lord Lieutenant

*She is since dead. K.K. & R.
⁺3 others have since been arrested.

This incident has sullied Mold's history. It should not have happened and those who could have prevented it lamentably failed to do so.

Chapter 7
The Mold National Eisteddfod of 1873

It may come as a surprise to find a chapter dedicated to this subject. Alfred Keene was very English and Tom Kelly was clearly of Irish extraction. This, however, ignores the drive and involvement Tom Kelly had in Mold life since his arrival more than twenty years before.

There is no evidence that he ever learnt to speak Welsh but there is a suspicion his first wife did. At the time of the Eisteddfod he was a widower and his second wife Margaret clearly was to be Welsh speaking.

Tom Kelly was not afraid of getting involved, particularly if he felt he could contribute. This was a time before the introduction of the Welsh-only rule for the platform. So, when the town decided to invite the Eisteddfod it was inevitable he would be involved; his close friend William Theophilus Thomas was sure to be involved. For such an event, the provision of secretarial facilities was a first consideration. The Practice supported the joint appointment of two of its clerks as secretaries; Thomas (Gwilym Gwenffrwd) and Tom Ollive were appointed. He was later given an honorary bardic name of 'Orpheus'.

Initially, Tom Kelly, because of his business commitments, was an ordinary member of the committee but it soon became clear that he was needed in a larger capacity and Tom Kelly's organisational flair would be utilised by his appointment as one of two vice-chairmen. The chair was Llewellyn Falkner Lloyd of Nannerch who had been appointed sheriff in 1847 and J Williams Jones, at the time he was chairman of the Mold Local Board, was the other vice-chairman. They, I think, were, with the honorary secretaries, 'Estyn' (the Rev T. R. Lloyd) and 'Andreas o Fôn' (A. J. Brereton), had responsibility for the cultural aspects of a very varied programme. Kelly had no cultural responsibility.

The event was to take place in a field off King Street. Four days were allocated; Tuesday 19th August to Friday, 22nd August. The staging of such a prestigious festival as this was a very major event for Mold.

The *Liverpool Daily Post* in reporting the first day of the event sent an English reporter and, not for the last time, the paper was critical about Mold and the Welsh.

At an early hour yesterday morning Mold was all action and the stranger who happened to be within its boundaries could have seen for himself without much inquiry of others that something unusual was on the cards. In passing, surprise must be expressed at the decision to hold such a national gathering as opened yesterday in a place like Mold, even though it has claim to be a County Town. The place is small and the accommodation for strangers accordingly limited, whilst its railway communication with the Principality is most restricted. However, not withstanding all these disadvantages, the meeting has so far been a success and, should favourable weather prevail, no doubt it can be entertained that it will be pecuniarily many degrees removed from a failure and that even when the accounts come to be made up the balance will be on the right side. Perhaps on no previous occasion has Mold presented so animated an occasion as yesterday.

Bards young and old in green and blue cloaks marched in solemn procession hither and thither, no one but themselves knew whither.

Eisteddfod programme, 1873

This quotation shows both the challenge and apprehension over its success and where Kelly's influence was needed and was felt.

The *Observer* tells us of Kelly and the Eisteddfod:

In 1873, the celebrated Mold National Eisteddfod was held when Mr Kelly acted as one of the vice-chairmen and general advisor, two of the Clerks of the firm acting as secretaries and he entered with his whole heart into the duties and responsibilities of that position. We remember speaking with him on the evening of Wednesday in that week when he said he would have to be mulcted in his share of the deficiencies; when we took a more favourable view of the position saying that so far as it had gone the Eisteddfod had already paid its way and the probability was that the two following days would prove greater successes; and when we saw the crowds which came in on Thursday morning he came by the post where we stood and said 'I think you were right Mr —— the prospects have brightened' and when on the Saturday the Eisteddfod had proved itself the success it was he was all smiles and beaming with pleasure rejoicing as much as any Welshman in the success that had been attained.

The use of the word mulcted is of some interest here. Fine imposed for offence, punish by fine or deprive are the definitions in the Oxford dictionary.

Kelly was committed to help, to work and join in its ultimate success, but he was also prepared to accept blame and financial consequences.

No plans were so perfectly made and Thomas Cropper tells how a catastrophe became only a hiccup. The problem affected the printing of the programme.

> The programme ran to some sixteen pages and a cover, and Mr Morris's father-in-law, the late Mr Hugh Jones of New Street, was the printer.
>
> The Eisteddfod committee had bound Mr Jones down to deliver the completed programme not later than a certain date, and by the day preceding such date the type had all been set up, and everything was ready; nothing remained but the 'working off' on the machine. Then through some unforeseen cause, perhaps over anxiety, the accident happened — and these accidents do happen in the best regulated of offices — the mass fell in a jumbled-up heap of 'pie' to the floor. Here was a mess, and if these lines catch the eye of a printer he will shiver! What was to be done? The capacity of the little office in New Street was hopelessly inadequate to the situation, but not so Hugh Jones's resourcefulness. He dashed off with the copy MS. by first train to Denbigh, and there to his close friend, Thomas Gee, he explained the situation. Every man in Gee's office was there and then put on the job, and kept on it until the job was completed.
>
> The parcel of Eisteddfod programmes was duly delivered next day as per contract, with the imprint H. Jones Mold in its appointed position on each copy.

But we all know that events have to be prepared and do not just happen. Take the Eisteddfod choir for instance. The holding of rehearsals was always going to be a challenge but, because of the distances, the choristers would have to travel (probably walk) special rehearsals had to be held. The choristers would know well the pieces involved anyway.

So, for example, a rehearsal was held in March in public in the Assembly Rooms and is described in the *Wrexham Advertiser* as eminently successful. The choir was two hundred strong and were very crammed on the platform and the terrible heat of the room especially in the elevated position in which the tenors and basses were placed. It had been intended that the choir should enter half an hour before the proceedings were announced to commence but at that time the gate leading to the room was besieged by a large crowd and the arrangements for the evening were materially interrupted: great difficulty was experienced in distributing the copies. This was still more than five months before the event. It was also a formal occasion and an opportunity to tell the public what was going on so the Advertiser goes on to tell us:

The President of the evening, T. T. Kelly, Esq. (who was heartily cheered on taking the chair), in opening the proceedings said that the rehearsal was the first public recognition, or, in fact, the inauguration, of the forthcoming Mold National Eisteddfod: and judging from the energy and discretion displayed by the committee, and the strong feeling which had been aroused in its favour, not only in the immediate neighbourhood, but also throughout the Principality, there could be little doubt the Eisteddfod would be a great success — (applause) — and if they were honoured with the presence of their Royal Highnesses the Prince and Princess of Wales, it would certainly be a splendid success. (loud applause). He had hoped to be in a position to speak authoritatively that evening as to the certainty of the coming of the Prince and Princess, but so much time was necessarily consumed in procuring the signature to the memorial, that the committee regretted their inability yet to speak with certainty. But having regard to the number and character of the signatures already obtained — comprising Lord-Lieutenants of counties both in North and South Wales, High Sheriffs, peers of the realm, members of Parliament, Chairmen of Quarter Sessions, Justices to the Peace, Deputy-Lieutenants, Mayors of the towns and public officials — he thought it highly probably that his Royal Highness with his well known kindness of heart, and desire to meet as far as was possible the wishes of Her Majesty's Subjects, would accede to the urgent request made to him — (applause) — especially as the committee had prudently not restricted him to time. The president then proceeded shortly to combat the views entertained in some quarters, that an Eisteddfod not only did no good, but actually inflicted positive harm. He pointed out the absurdity of such views, and said that if for one moment he thought the Eisteddfod would have the effect of perpetuating the Welsh language to the exclusion of the English, he would not be in the position he occupied that evening. - (applause) — But he believed no such thing. (Hear, hear) The Welsh were naturally proud of their ancient language, and they were fully justified in using their best endeavours to preserve it. (Applause). At the same time every Welshman in these days knew the value of and advantages to be derived from knowledge of the English language. It not only gave him an opportunity of leaving — if he thought proper — his native country, and competing with Englishmen in every quarter of the globe, but also in his own country gave him a superior position and standing. (Hear, hear) It was simply absurd and unjust to attribute any such narrow- mindedness to the promoters of an Eisteddfod. (Applause) In conclusion, the president said the town of Mold was committed to the Eisteddfod, and it must be made to succeed. (Applause). He trusted that every inhabitant in the district, each in his respective sphere, would work harmoniously with the committee, so as to assure that the arrangements were commensurate with the occasion — (Applause) and in time to come the Mold National Eisteddfod would be remembered with pleasure and satisfaction. (Loud applause).

Daniel Owen after playing viola solo then joined the debate on the wisdom of inviting the Eisteddfod in the first place.

I believe that there is a great deal of truth in the old Welsh proverb *'Fod llawer scil I gael Will i'w wely.'* The great question is how to get the gwely and the skill will not be wanting to get Will there. Time and your patience will not permit me to go over the other attractions of the Eisteddfod, such as the choral competitions, the concerts, and particularly the praiseworthy intentions of applying the overplus funds towards erecting a free library at Mold, and establishing an Eisteddfod scholarship at the Welsh University. It is very evident, however, that such a gigantic concern as the Eisteddfod requires all our united energy and co-operation, and most perfect organisation; and if we fail not in these indispensables we may be certain of having a very successful 'what you call it' (loud applause).

This shows the presence in the town of the doubters and objectors to the invitation having been made but the commitment of Tom Kelly to his adopted town is completely unequivocal.

Llewellyn Falkner Lloyd of Nannerch was the chair of the Eisteddfod but he was taken seriously ill a little time before the Eisteddfod started and, indeed, died shortly after its conclusion. So more responsibility fell on Tom Kelly. The Prince of Wales (the future King Edward VII) accepted the post of patron but confusion existed over his possible attendance. It seems likely that he never actually agreed to come although the committee thought he had.

Tuesday 19th August, 1873, dawned and in the morning there was a two hour downpour and it rained on the Wednesday as well. But we know then it was an assured financial success, Thursday and Friday were fine. The site of the Pavilion was a field in King Street on the town side of the railway line.

The highlight of the Tuesday was to be an address by the Prime Minister Gladstone and it fell to Tom Kelly to deliver the address of welcome.

To the Right Honourable William Ewart Gladstone, M.P., Prime Minister of England.

SIR, — In consequence of the serious illness, which we all regret of Mr

Falkner Lloyd, the chairman of the committee of management, the duty devolves upon the vice-chairmen of tendering to you the sincere and heartfelt thanks of the promoters of this Eisteddfod for the distinguished honour you have conferred not only upon them, but also upon the entire Principality, by presiding upon this the day of inauguration. The claims of office must press heavily upon you and the committee felt extremely diffident in venturing to seek to increase your burdens and at a season, too when you have a right to expect some relaxation from your arduous duties; but knowing the deep and earnest interest you take in all movements having for their object the improvement and advancement of your fellow men and having regard to the high position you occupy both as a statesman and a scholar, and bearing in mind, too that you are not only a resident landowner in the Principality, but also closely allied with an ancient Welsh family, the committee could not resist the desire to ask you to preside for one day over this national gathering — a gathering which has excited considerable enthusiasm throughout the Principality, and from which substantial and lasting results are anticipated. The Eisteddfod is not infrequently adversely criticised on various grounds by those, we are compelled to say, who are not thoroughly acquainted with its scope and objects; but the committee venture to think that, apart from its national character and institution, which has for its aim the providing a public arena for those who are endowed in different degrees with literary scientific, and musical tastes to compete in a friendly and brotherly spirit must be productive of good, and is well worthy of public sympathy and support.

Again thanking you for your kindness and consideration in attending today at so much personal inconvenience, and trusting that you will return from Scotland with renewed vigour and strength, we have the honour to be Sir, your obedient servants,

J. W. Jones   ) Vice Chairmen of the
T. T. Kelly   ) Eisteddfod Committee

But securing his attendance was not easily achieved, The *Wrexham Advertiser* tells us:

Everything was prepared; the programmes were being printed and the large placards were being issued when the committee received an intimation that Mr Gladstone had to be in attendance on Her Majesty at Balmoral on the day upon which he was to preside at Mold. As might be expected this was a great discouragement, but determined not to leave a stone unturned, a letter was sent him by Mr Thomas, the secretary, representing the great disappointment his absence would cause to the Principality — especially as it followed the disappointment already experienced respecting the attendance of The Prince of Wales. Upon the heels of this appeared the announcement in the *Liverpool Daily Post*, and then persons who had shown a disposition all along to thwart the committee seemed to be in great glee, because the Eisteddfod was not likely to be as successful as expected. It is most difficult to account for this state of things, but that it existed there is no doubt, and persons who are the only ones to profit by the gathering did their best to circulate the bad news. On the other hand the committee thought they owed it to themselves and to Wales to make a last effort to secure the presence of Mr Gladstone. If it was a matter which affected themselves only perhaps they would not have moved further, but the Eisteddfod was a national one, its purposes were national, and any surplus accruing from it would be devoted in part to a national purpose, therefore it was thought desirable that a deputation should wait upon Mr Gladstone to represent the matter to him, and endeavour to prevail upon him to give his presence if it were at all possible. The gentlemen appointed were Messrs J. W. Jones (chairman), Henry Roberts, W. T. Thomas (secretary) and J. Morgan (corresponding secretary), and the name Mr B. Powell was added at the last moment. The deputation attended at Hawarden on Friday afternoon and were most kindly received by Mr Gladstone. Their business was stated by Mr J. W. Jones and although at first the right hon. gentleman was disinclined to comply, urging there were limits to every man's endurance, he at length yielded and consented to deliver the inaugural address, the deputation on the other hand undertaking to commence Tuesday mornings meeting half an hour earlier so as to accommodate him. As might be expected the good news brought home by the deputation was extremely welcomed, and new life was infused into all.

Gladstone did not waste his time by addressing his audience on international or British concerns but it was a Welsh address delivered to Welshmen and as a result very enthusiastically received.

The Eisteddfod itself was memorable and particularly the main choir competitions. Cropper again tells us:

After the choirs had sung, the adjudicators failed to agree as to whether the Rhos Choir or the Denbigh Choir should be awarded the first prize, and those choirs were requested to sing the test-piece again. Even then the adjudicators failed to agree, and the prize was equally divided between the choirs.

In spite of all the opposition to the event being held in Mold and those willing the town to fail the drive enthusiasm and above all UNITY of the committee meant it was a very great success culturally and financially with a very large profit.

It is now generally accepted that two great National Movements were the outcome of the 1873 Eisteddfod at Mold. It was here a meeting was convened by notice advertised in the Principality that resulted in the inauguration of the National Library of Wales at Aberystwyth and the revival of the Cymmrodorian Society in London.

Even after the competitions were finished on the Friday and all the crowds had gone home, Kelly was not yet finished with the Eisteddfod. In October 1873, the committee said thank you to the members of the choir by giving them a dinner at the Market Hall. The choir were volunteers and no part of the Eisteddfod funds were used. Instead, there was a whip round and forty-five pounds raised. Again the *Advertiser* tells us:

> With this sum it was first intended to have a trip for a day to some of the neighbouring towns, but owing to the lateness of the season this idea was given up and a public dinner was resolved upon. The committee met and completed the arrangements by which it was resolved to have a dinner at the Market Hall, on Wednesday evening last, and Mr J. Pryor undertook the catering. There was some difficulty, as is always the case, in arranging the programme, and some persons are offended because a prominence had been given to certain gentlemen whom they deemed unworthy. This feeling was carried so far that in one instance a remonstrance was sent, and that gentleman said he would not be able to patronise the choir with his presence as he had not been asked to take part in the proceedings. The committee of management were sorely troubled at this misfortune, it was a matter of great regret to them, but they could not alter their decision. At the same time it was felt they were not justified in retaining his subscription, so it was returned to him. The choir met between 2 and 3 o'clock on Wednesday at the Market Hall where the procession was formed, and before starting, one or two choruses were sung. The band of the Flintshire Militia also played one or two airs. The procession then marched to the Bailey Hill, when several photographs of them were taken by Mr Holden, Porthmadoc. Various games were indulged in for a couple of hours, and the procession was then reformed, and marched to the Cross, where a stand was made and two or three choruses sung. Everything being in readiness, the members marched into the large assembly room, Market Hall, to the dinner.

Predictably Kelly took the chair. It therefore fell to him to propose the toast to the Eisteddfod choir, and here we have Kelly at his most brilliant, reviewing the Eisteddfod and working on his audience with rapport, skill and humour.

> He said that the toast was placed early on the list because many members of the choir had a considerable distance to travel in order to get home, and some of them were of young and tender years. Before proceeding to propose the toast he could not avoid temptation of taking the opportunity to congratulate the town of Mold on the great success which attended their great national festival — the recent eisteddfod. (Applause) It

certainly was a great success, and he must say it was a very plucky effort on the part of a small town like Mold to incur liabilities — as the committee had — to the extent of something like £1,600. It was really a very serious matter, and he confessed that on the first and second day when the receipts were less than equal to expectation, some of them felt rather uncomfortable. However, the little town of Mold, which sometimes gets as much abused as most towns, had incurred this liability, and it was with much satisfaction that he was in a position to say that they not only recouped the £1,600, but has a balance to the good of at least £600. (long applause)

Perhaps it was a subject he was hardly justified in speaking upon, considering that the greatest amount of the labour with the Eisteddfod fell on others, but that was the first opportunity the Mold people had, had of publicly referring to the matter, and he must therefore, be excused if he congratulated the people of Mold, and he would add those of the district, and he might say the whole of Wales on the substantial success of their National Eisteddfod. (Applause) Notwithstanding the fact of its success, there was no doubt it was an institution which was capable of improvement. He was old enough to remember the time when the Welsh Eisteddfod was looked upon as a good joke, and the subject for sensational articles in the English — the London papers especially during the Parliamentary recess. The subject was also taken up in the comic papers, which made as much capital out of it as their wits were capable of. But now the Eisteddfod was looked upon from a totally different point of view, and it at last commanded the respect, if not the approval, of the majority of the press. It might be egotistical, but he ventured to think that their arrangements at Mold were very much superior to what they had been at other Eisteddfodau. He was told by a competent authority that the Eisteddfod in many other places had turned out a failure to a very great extent — at least from a financial point of view — and he was thankful they at Mold had kept clear of many difficulties of that nature made in other places. Perhaps they were not all aware of the fact that the Mold Eisteddfod was the first in history of Wales where the Prime Minister of England inaugurated the proceedings — (applause) — and the result was seen in the public press, particularly in the London press, in all of which there appeared articles on the Eisteddfod and mostly of favourable character. He considered that the attendance of the Prime Minister, and the speech that he made, had placed the Eisteddfod beyond the scoffs and the sneers of offensive and disagreeable people. It is now rested with those gentlemen who were responsible for the management of the Eisteddfod, to maintain and improve the high position attained by their national institution. In Mold the Eisteddfod had been a magnificent success, and if it failed elsewhere, it would be owing to the management on the part of those who are responsible for the getting up of the Eisteddfod. He hoped he would be excused for that digression, but as that was the first opportunity he had to refer to it he could not help doing so. He would, however, return to what was known as the toast of the evening. They knew better than he did that the Eisteddfod, to a great measure, was made up of literary and musical competitions. With regard to the literary, he took it that, that evening they had not so direct a connection as with the musical portion of the work. Although he did not claim any great proficiency of music himself, still he had heard ladies and gentlemen, who were competent to express an opinion, say that the Eisteddfod choir was a great success. (loud applause). He must certainly confess that he was very much astonished at the perfection they displayed, and he thought the least they could do would be to tender to them that evening their best and most sincere thanks for the exertions they must have made to acquire such perfection. (hear, hear) It must have been attained after a laborious exertion, and the whole of the services were rendered gratuitously; and they would be wanting in every feeling, and particularly of the feeling of gratitude, if they did not tender them their sincere thanks. (Applause) But, admitting they had a superior choir, the question was, ought that choir to be dispersed — disbanded? — (loud cries of 'no, no') — or whether they should devise some plan by which they could keep the choir together and render it still more efficient. (hear, hear) It was a choir, he thought, which ought to be kept together — (hear, hear) — and if they were lovers of music, it would be kept together. (Applause). It was a thoroughly non-sectarian choir, and he was happy to see in it church singers and chapel singers each being mixed together without distinction. Besides, it was a thoroughly Welsh choir — (hear) — and he would venture to suggest that an effort should be made for its preservation, a committee should be formed with that object in view, and if any funds were required, he was ready to offer his humble mite for such an object. (loud applause)' He might very probably be met by the inquiry — its all very well to have a good choir, but where are they to practise, and on occasions, where are they to sing? He was sorry to say that in that very energetic town of Mold, the only good room was that wretched, barn like building in which they were now assembled. (applause) He did not know the architect might be, and therefore he could not be saying anything personal but he did imagine that the architect must have been some spiteful and malicious Englishman. (Laughter and cheers) It was done he had no doubt with the object of preventing the Welsh people from singing in the manner they could do. But there was no use talking unless they could do something to have it altered, and have the room raised and the horrible executional-looking beams and rafters removed altogether, or at any rate placed where they could not be seen. He had attended on the secretary of the Market Hall Company that afternoon about the room, and with every possible respect to the shareholders some of whom were probably present, he would say that if they had a particle of pluck they ought to take some steps in order to make the room worthy of the little town of Mold. He therefore had suggested that the room should be raised and the wall dividing it from the small assembly room removed, and the building as a whole made so as to be worthy of the town of Mold. But the question was, how to obtain the means? That afternoon as he walked down to the town it occurred to him that as the eisteddfod choir was interested in obtaining a good room, and seeing that there was a large surplus in hand — the object of the eisteddfod was the cultivation of Welsh music, and also bearing in view that the literary and working men's societies had of late years not been flourishing as could be desired he suggested whether a moiety of the large balance which they had, could not be applied to supply the nucleus of a fund for the erection of a building which would answer the purpose of a concert hall and practising room. (hear, hear) He thought from what he knew of the views of the various landlords in the neighbourhood, that one of them might be prevailed upon to provide a site gratuitously, or, at any rate, on very reasonable terms, and if a sum of £800 or £1,000 could be raised, they could construct a building that would be adequate to the occasion. The choir was undoubtedly a good one, but it might be made better, and no better way of improving it could be imagined than for some singers of note to sing in their presence. No singer, who had the least regard for either his voice or reputation, would consent to sing in that barn. But, if they had a proper room, they could have the best artistes, and high class concerts which would be certain to act beneficially on the choir. These were the views which he entertained, and in entertaining them, he could not avoid expressing them. With the toast he would couple the name of the conductor — Mr Allen Jones (Loud applause). Mr Jones had good material to work upon, but all the armies in the world were of no value unless they had a good general, and so it was with a choir, unless they had a good conductor they were certain to fail. Mr Jones was present, therefore he could not say all that he would say, but he might say that Mr Brinley Richards was extremely satisfied and gratified at Mr Jones proficiency. (Loud applause)

The toast was then drunk with musical honours.

By the time the Eisteddfod next came to Mold he had been dead twenty-two years and it was his son, as Clerk to the Mold U.D.C., who was the conduit to succeed with the invitation and beat off other applications.

In 1919 the Mold Urban District Council of which Robin Kelly was the Clerk decided that they wanted the National Eisteddfod to return to Mold in 1923: this would be exactly fifty years since the previous event.

They set about enlisting support. Wrexham initially decided in October 1920 by the unanimous decision of a public meeting they wanted it as well. By the end of December of the same year the Wrexham Borough Council had thrown their hand in and agreed to support Mold. Rhyl in November 1920 were also bidding for it.

TO the Members of the Gorsedd and the National Eisteddfod Association.

MEMORIAL of the residents of Mold and District praying that the National Eisteddfod of Wales be held at Mold in the year 1923.

SHEWETH

1. THAT the Mold Urban District Council as long ago as September 2nd, 1919, unanimously resolved to invite the National Eisteddfod of 1923 to Mold. Further, at a meeting of the Council held September 21st, 1920, it was decided to convene a conference of representatives of the Public Bodies in Flintshire, and at that conference the following resolution was passed:—

"That this meeting, convened by the Mold Urban District Council, of representatives of Public Bodies in the County of Flint and others interested in Eisteddfodau, cordially invite the Welsh National Eisteddfod to Mold in the year 1923; and hereby unanimously pledge its support to the proposed application to be made on behalf of the Town of Mold at the Eisteddfod to be held at Carnarvon in 1921."

At a well attended and enthusiastic meeting of the residents of Mold and District held December 9th, 1920, the same resolution was passed unanimously.

2. THAT the invitation is supported by the following Public Bodies:—
The Flintshire County Council,
The Town Councils of Wrexham and Flint,
The Urban District Councils of Prestatyn, Buckley, and Holywell,
The Rural District Councils of St. Asaph, Holywell, and Hawarden,
The Parish Councils of Hope, Mold, Cilcain, St. Asaph, Whitford, and Halkyn,
The Holywell Board of Guardians.
The Mold Cosmopolitan Society,
The Cymrodorion Societies of Holywell and Wrexham, and
The Chester Welsh Society.

3. THAT the Town of Mold is convenient for every part of Wales, and within easy reach of the chief towns and the most populous industrial districts of England.

4. THAT no town in Wales can boast of a more honourable position than Mold in the history of literature, art, and music. It is the home of our national novelist,—the immortal DANIEL OWEN,—of ALUN, of ARWENOR LLOYD, and a host of others; here also RICHARD WILSON, the renowned landscape painter, dwelt for a number of years; here he died and lies buried in our Parish Churchyard. Adjacent to us on from Mold is situated Hawarden, a name universally familiar as the home of WILLIAM EWART GLADSTONE.

5. THAT Mold occupies also a prominent position in the history of Wales. The town and the County are of particular interest to the historian and the antiquarian. On one side of the town is situated Maes Garmon, the field of the "Alleluia Battle," on another side stands "The Tower," where Rhuinallt ap Cynfrid dwelt. The Parish Church of Mold is a fine specimen of Perpendicular Architecture, and a mine of information to the antiquarian; this nave of the Church is considered by some the finest in Wales. In this county also are Basingwerk Abbey, Moria Rhuddlan, and the Castles of Rhuddlan, Ewloe, Flint and Caergwrle.

6. THAT in bygone days Flintshire served as a bulwark against the invasions of the Saxons; so-day this county is a bulwark against alien influences of another nature, and we firmly believe that it would be an effective means of strengthening this bulwark to hold the National Eisteddfod in this town.

7. THAT four successful Eisteddfodau are held in Mold annually, and at least half a dozen Chair Eisteddfodau are being held in the neighbourhood this year.

8. THAT the successful Flintshire Eisteddfod of 1823 was held in Mold, at which the Chair was won by Alun with his awdl on "Maes Garmon." The National Eisteddfod was held here in 1873, at which the idea of a National Library of Wales was first mooted. The 1873 Eisteddfod was also a complete success, and to hold the National Eisteddfod in Mold in 1923 would be a fitting celebration of the Jubilee of the one and of the Centenary of the other.

9. THAT your memorialists undertake to abide by the authority of the Gorsedd, to make all the Eisteddfod arrangements in accordance with its regulations, to hand over half the net proceeds of the Eisteddfod to the National Eisteddfod Association, and to devote the other half to local and national objects.

10. THAT a sum of over £1000 has been promised as a guarantee fund.

11. THAT your memorialists pledge themselves, if their application be granted, to do all in their power to make the National Eisteddfod of Mold one of the most successful yet held in North Wales.

Signed,

T. G. WYNNE, *Chairman of the Mold Urban Council*
M. B. THOMPSON, *Ex-Chairman.*
R. STEWART KELLY, *Clerk.*

Memorial for the 1923 Eisteddfod[FRO D/DM/142/1]

The fateful meeting in Caernarfon was held in August 1921. Six speakers were lined up to present Mold's case as follows:

1. Introduction — T. G. Wynne, J.P. (Chairman of the Mold Urban District Council)
2. Unanimity of the County — Lieutenant Colonel T. H. Parry, D.S.O., M.P.
3. Finance — James Williams Esq., J.P. (Chairman of the Flintshire County Council)
4. Historical — The Rev D. Edwardes Davies (Vicar of Mold)
5. Literary — The Rev D. Egwys Jones (Pastor of the Welsh Wesleyan Church at Mold)
6. Eisteddfodic Spirit — Thos. Roberts Esq., J.P., Mold

The memorial submitted to the members of the Gorsedd and the National Eisteddfod Association makes very interesting reading. After the *Daily Post's* comments in 1873 about Mold, a very comprehensive attempt is made to overcome any conceivable objection. The invitation was well prepared and supported and was successful . Robin Kelly who had spent so much time in the preparation of the application must have been relieved by the decision. Once again, Mold proved how successfully it could support a National Eisteddfod.

In 1984, there was an echo of the Practice's involvement in eisteddfodau in that John Gregory chaired the Mold Fund Raising Committee for the visit of the Urdd National Eisteddfod to Mold. At that time John was under-sheriff for Denbighshire and thus three under-sheriffs from the Practice had had major involvement in organising three Eisteddfodau.

Chapter 8
Kelly, Keene & Roper

As we move towards the halcyon days of the Practice, we shall pause to see how the profession itself has developed. Lawyers are notorious for being resistant to change but tried and tested phrases that they and the courts understand are often safer than so called good English. This is particularly so for wills. It is a certain fact that lawyers make more money out of the wills that they have not made than from the wills that they have. I know of two entrepreneurs who were clients of the practice in my time who felt that they could save time and money and make their own. Both documents did not say what they intended and one even ended in the Palatine Court in Liverpool in a friendly action with five different groups of interested parties represented by counsel.

Kirk tells us 'there is the most ample evidence that by and large the fact of being an Attorney disqualified a man from decent society in the seventeenth and much of the eighteenth century'. This is probably why so little is known of the individuals involved in the Practice before the Wynnes.

A Society of Gentleman Practitioners had been formed in 1739 and they took the opportunity of renewal in 1749 to strengthen control on admissions and training under articles. It had been found that articles were being backdated so as to enable the candidate to be admitted without serving his term. By 1827, the need for a preliminary examination, attendance at lectures provided by the Law Society and a final examination were introduced. Arthur Troughton Roberts was one of the last trained under the old system. The Law Society was established in 1821 but priority had been given to the establishment of a law library.

Some predictability on salary occurred but so far as the employee was concerned it was still a buyer's market. A future Lord Chancellor said in 1840 that no solicitor ought to have a professional income of more then £500 a year.

In 1879, a young lady inquired of the Law Society if she could sit the examinations and was refused. In 1914, a Miss Bebb, who had had a brilliant academic career, applied to the Law Society to sit the examinations with a view to admission and was refused. It was 1922 before a woman was admitted as a solicitor. No publicity was given to this achievement and for many years women who qualified were listed under the heading 'Gentleman applying for Admission' in the *Law Society Gazette*. At the Annual Provincial Meeting in 1922, the President ventured the witticism that women would be better employed at home bringing up future generations of solicitors of the male sex.

The prospect of women being admitted prompted a question at the A.G.M. that what was to be done about cloakrooms if they were admitted. Is it any wonder women came very slowly into the profession? Even by the 1950s women entering articles had only risen to thirty a year. When I was doing my finals in 1960 there was only one woman in the class. Now something like fifty percent of all admissions are women.

Before 1949, Stamp Duty on articles was £80.

Things have moved a long way. The earliest attorneys had no offices at all. They carried their papers and such equipment as they needed or possessed in a bag. One of the problems of exercising any discipline over such a state of affairs was that, often, they had no fixed address where they could be found.

It is against this slow, laborious professional development that Thomas Thelwell Kelly and Alfred Thomas Keene started their partnership at the beginning of 1864.

Kelly had told Keene during the partnership negotiations that in any event there was plenty of railway conveyancing to be done. This was an understatement and under the Buckley Railways Acts of 1860 and 1863 Kelly was secretary to the company and the Practice were the solicitors. The Wrexham, Mold & Connah's Quay Railway had Acts in 1862, 1869 and 1873. These two railway companys operated in conjunction with each other and amalgamated in 1873. Kelly, Keene & Roper and Evan Morris of Wrexham were shown as solicitors to the Bill.

August 1864 brought the visit on circuit of the Lord Chief Justice to one of the Flintshire Assizes. Nowadays a judge, if he disagrees with a verdict of a jury, is discreet. This was one of Kelly's first experiences of organising an Assize. The judge was quoted in the *Wrexham Telegraph:*

> Decision in the rape case the previous day — Exhorting the County to endeavour to return men of more capacity for discharging the duties of juror than those who served on the first jury yesterday and returned one of acquittal. I do not remember in the course of my professional career to have met with a more signal instance of a complete failure of justice.

In 1865 Kelly appears for the owners of Leeswood Colliery at an inquest into two deaths. They are committed for trial on a charge of manslaughter but Kelly still maintains his unique relationship with the miners.

The post of Clerk of the Peace had a very wide range of responsibilities at the start of 1866 there was a major outbreak of cattle plague (foot and mouth disease) which lasted for about six months. The magistrates make regulations which have to be advertised and enforced. Movement of animals is restricted unless for slaughter and rules are introduced on hides and offal, *etc.* the details of the order are very full and we have no Ministry of Agriculture officials available to the Practice this is a challenge to be successfully met.

We had left Alfred going off to London on his honeymoon and one would have thought that Kelly would return to Mold to keep things ticking over. Kelly did not understand such a thought or expression and two days after the wedding he is in Mold addressing a public meeting concerning the formation of a building society for Mold. He gives a brilliant exposition of what is involved and his address is reported in the *Wrexham Advertiser*:

Mr Kelly on being called said that as he perhaps was the cause of calling the meeting together, it might be expected that he should state shortly why he had ventured to do so. Those present were well aware that all was not being done in this town as ought to be in order to keep in pace with its flourishing condition. Thanks to Mr France, the railway contractor, and to the enterprising spirit displayed in mining operations in every direction, the population was increasing very rapidly, work was abundant, and wages on the rise, but no corresponding effort was being made to provide adequate home accommodation, and this he believed would only be effectively done by means of a Building Society, which would be most beneficial to all working men — they were all working men some worked with their heads and others worked with hands. He would impress upon the meeting that it was both the duty and the interest of the people of Mold to use every effort in their power in inducing a large number of gentlemen who have recently invested money in the neighbourhood to come and reside in Mold, instead of being driven to Chester, but still could only be done be erecting for them suitable residences. Mr Kelly then went on reading rules of kindred societies established in other towns and also explaining the nature and benefits derived from Benefit Building Societies. He said that Building Societies generally are founded for the same object but carried out with various modifications. They were divided into two distinct classes — the one terminating, the other permanent. A terminating society is one which is intended to close at the end of a certain period when all the shares of the members have realized their full amount. In a permanent society, it is merely membership of a shareholder that terminates at the end of a fixed number of years, when he receives the full value of his shares the society itself continuing. In either case the object of the building society is still the same, namely to enable individuals to associate together and unite the subscriptions from time to time in one common fund, some for the simple purpose of placing a portion of their income in an advantageous investment, others with the view of borrowing money, by which they may purchase houses or other similar property. But in order that one man may borrow, there must be others to lend. To induce a person of limited means to lay by periodically a portion of his income, merely as an investment member, some strong incentive must be held out and the only one that has, up to this, been found successful is to offer him the use of his money. Mr Kelly accompanied his arguments with illustrations, with a view of showing the advantages derivable from these associations.

Mr Kelly said he preferred the permanent system rather the terminating one, and he hoped all present would take an interest in the society, and would induce their friends to take shares in it, he was of the opinion that a strong society might be established if all put their shoulders to the wheel.

Thus, the Mold District Permanent Benefit Building Society came into existence. We now only have the third annual report for the year ending 1st September 1868 showing a balance on the balance sheet of £2,614 13s. 9d. and we have Alfred's deposit book showing investments of one guinea every two months. The accounts show, of course, solicitors to the Society 'Kelly, Keene & Roper'. We do not know what happened to the Society but it was still trading in 1884 when the Practice was acting for it in the sale of a property which had been repossessed.

The Practice was going so well another partner was admitted in May 1866. This was on the basis of a 5/12, 4/12, 3/12 split. He was George Edward Trevor Roper who was born at Dramstadt, Germany in 1832. He was the second son of the squire of Plas Têg, Charles Blayney Trevor Roper. He remained as a partner in the Practice until July 1876 when he left to practice on his own account: it was his decision to leave. During his time with the practice he held no public appointments but would deputise for his partners. All appointments in those days were part-time and how Kelly & Keene dealt with the income they produced I do not know.

George Roper became Clerk of the Local Board on leaving the Practice and two years later in 1878 he became County Court Registrar for Mold and Flint for two or three years. If he had held these appointments whilst a partner, they could have taken no part in local litigation and there would have been potential conflicts with the Local Board. We have the Heads of Agreement in draft form on his departure from Kelly & Keene that were far from ungenerous towards him.

George Trevor Roper. This rather indistinct photograph is the only image that survives

THIRD ANNUAL REPORT

OF THE

Mold District Permanent Benefit Building Society.

How to provide healthful and comfortable dwelling-house accommodation for the industrial classes of the community has become one of the most pressing questions of the age.

"Benefit Building Societies have caused a great diminution of crime improved the habits of the working classes, fostered contentment, encouraged the practice of economy and sobriety, and have done, and are doing, an incalculable amount of good."—*Report of Committee of the House of Commons.*

The value and importance of Building Societies are now so generally admitted, that it is no longer necessary to dwell at any length upon the advantages which they offer for the investment of large or small sums of money, or to point out the facilities they afford for the purchase and improvement of land and home property upon easy terms.

Building Societies are, by law, prohibited from lending moneys upon any security other than the above property, and as all advances are repayable by periodical instalments, the security is constantly improving in value, and the risk reduced to an absolute minimum. All proposed securities are subjected to careful and independent survey, and the title deeds of all mortgaged properties are deposited with the Society.

The stability of properly managed Building Societies has been proved, by the fact that they have not suffered from the recent financial troubles, and they have thus escaped the discredit which has attached to most Joint-Stock Enterprises.

Experience has, however, shewn that the greatest amount of success has been attained by those societies which have been founded upon the permanent principle, and which have sought to represent particular classes or interests mainly.

THE GENERAL BALANCE SHEET

OF THIS SOCIETY, 1st SEPTEMBER, 1868.

DR.

		Balance now due from Members.
CLASS A. (Paid up Shares.)		
To Balance due to Members, Class A at 1st September, 1867	507 19 1	
" Amounts transferred from Class B to Class A	193 2 1	
" Subscriptions received, Class A	1060 0 0	
" Dividends allotted to Class A at 5 per cent.	37 16 8	
Total......	£1797 17 10	
CLASS B. (Subscribing Shares.)		
To Balance due to Members, Class B at 1st September, 1867	789 5 2	
" Subscriptions received, Class B	510 10 0	
" Dividends allotted to Class B ...	37 15 0	
Total......	£1337 10 2	
CLASS C. (Borrowed Shares.)		
To Subscriptions received, Class C.	215 9 9	
Redemption moneys, ditto	90 13 0	
Total......	£306 15 9	1067 14 3
To balance due from Bankers......		646 19 6
		£2614 13 9

CR.

		Balance now due to Members.
CLASS A. (Paid up Shares.)		
By Dividends paid by Cheque	16 9 11	
" repayments to Members of Class C during the year	31 4 2	
Total......	£47 14 1	1740 3
CLASS B. (Subscribing Shares.)		
By unpaid Entrance Fees, Fines, &c., debited against Class B shares	2 2 3	
" Amounts transferred from Class B to Class A	193 2 1	
" Repayments to Members, Class B	302 14 10	
Total......	£496 19 2	840 11 0
Class C. (Borrowed Shares.)		
By Balance Due from Members of Class C, at 1st September, 1867	1492 0 2	
" Advances made during the year.	744 6 1	
" Interest charged upon ditto ...	90 13 9	
" Unpaid Entrance Fees. Premium, Fines, &c.	6 11 0	
Total......	£2975 10 0	
By Balance due to Profit and Loss account		33 19 0
		£2614 13 9

Examined and found correct,

GEO. H. HALL, AUDITOR, CHESTER.

History has left us little knowledge of George Roper: it is known that he was a thespian and a founder of the Mold Operatic and Dramatic Society. We do have a picture of him as the presiding judge in an adaptation of Bardell *v* Pickwick from Dicken's *Pickwick Papers*. He formed the Mold Choral Society in 1869. He also had a fine voice and indeed when he and another joined the Parish Church choir in 1870, the *Chronicle* felt bound to report a marked improvement in the singing of the choir giving him the credit for this. In 1867 he married his cousin, Harriette Roper, who gave him eleven children, nine girls and only two boys. He died of throat cancer in 1893 at his home Richmond House, Chester Road, Pentre, Mold.

George Roper had started his legal career being admitted as a solicitor in 1858, practising for eight years in Chester at 5 Newgate Street. Kelly & Keene were not worried about the consequences of competition which only facilitated his departure. Why he became a partner in the first place is unclear. His father was one of the lords of Mold but the Practice acted for the lords before Roper became a partner and continued to do so well into the twentieth century. Other than family, no other partners were ever taken and the Practice continued to boom. It probably amounted to what seemed a good idea at the time that never somehow quite worked out. Roper was a gentleman of a quiet and affable disposition, a thorough sportsman whose chief delight was fishing and bee-keeping.

Perhaps we should now deal with the lords of Mold and who and what they were.

The lords of Mold were the holders of the mineral rights in large areas around Mold and will figure from time to time in this story. The lordships of the Manors of Mold, Hope and Hawarden were acquired in 1652 on the execution of James, Earl of Derby, for rebellion against Cromwell. Captain Andrew Ellis purchased the lordship of the manor of Mold under the Act of Forfeiture that necessarily followed, acting for himself, Sir John Trevor and Colonel Twistleton. Although the land was sold and partitioned, the mineral rights were retained in the three manors; effectively one share each for the three families. Thus the owners of the minerals rights became known colloquially as the lords of Mold.

In 1860 there remained to the three joint owners the excepted mines of coal and lead in the lordship. All three had to agree to a new lease. The one third share of Sir John Roper was held by his descendants, in the early part of the twentieth century, by Trevor Boscawen, the Misses Trevor Parker, Mr Darrell Charles Trevor Roper and Viscount Hampton. The third share of Capt Andrew Ellis passed by the will in 1710 of Andrew Lawley to his nephew Anthony Swymmer who, by his will in 1759, entailed it to his nephew Sir Thomas Champreys, Bt. and passed after sale to Lord Mostyn. Colonel Twistleton's share was held by the family of Lloyd, Hafod-un-Nos — now Howard of Wigfair, St Asaph.

Messrs. Kelly, Keene & Roper, Solicitors
To Wm. Dykins, Plumber

1869				
Jan 28	To Amount of a/c rendered	1	16	6
July 15	2 brass nipples for speaking trumpets			8

Copy invoice for office charges, Kelly, Keene & Roper, 1869
[FRO D/DM/716/4]

Adjoining the lordship of Mold there is the hundred of Iâl: this is an area of land adjoining old Flintshire but in the old county of Denbighshire in respect of which the minerals were granted in the seventeenth century to the Grosvenor family, now the Westminster estate. This grant still figures prominently in the need for an agreement for royalties for aggregates (limestone, sand and gravel).

The allocation seems to have been for Keene to do the work for the lords of Mold while Kelly did the work for the Westminster estate. The friendship that built up with the Duke of Westminster was surprising but the real chemistry of friendship existed. Kelly was not averse himself to getting involved in coal mining. Keene was always more interested in railways.

We know of the mining that took place on the Wrexham Road at Pen-y-Bont. Kelly and four others in June 1863 took the lease from the Davies-Cooke estate agreeing to pay a ground rent of £130 p.a. and royalty of 1/- a ton with 7d a ton on non-cannel coal. Again in 1872, Kelly confirms terms with his friend John Scott Bankes for a site at Sychdyn.

The volume of work was very heavy. Kelly was to speak at a dinner for the Local Board who moved the date to accommodate him and his professional commitments but he was still stuck in London on business on the adjourned date.

Keene in 1871 is using the telegraph widely and tries to obtain the support of the Local Board to protests that telegrams to Denbigh have to go through Chester and are taking over four hours. The office has been modernised in 1869 by work which includes new stoves, blinds and window sashes. Pigeon-holes and speaking tubes are installed.

The Practice had its parchment engrossments done in London and they used as accountants Cain, Butler & Eldridge who had offices in Liverpool and London and, after Roper's departure, the shares were 11/20 Kelly, 9/20 Keene. They also seem to use the London barristers.

Around this time W. T. Thomas as assistant clerk produces, in April 1876, an excellent and useful *Abstract of Licensing Acts 1872 to 1874*. No Innkeeper should be without one — price 3d.

Thomas Kelly served as a trustee of the Trustee Savings Bank and continued to give valuable counsel to them until his death. Acting for the Westminster estate did not only involve minerals. In October 1876, Kelly received a deputation from the Holywell Local Board concerning the leasing tolls for the market in Holywell.

As Clerk to the Peace, he confirms to his colleague in Caernarfon that their surgeon receives £60 per year including medicine.

Now the Mold gaol comes into the story. As Clerks to the Peace, the Practice was the direct servant of the magistrates who were responsible for the provision of prison accommodation. Local historians have been attracted by the story and Flint gaol did feature in the story of the Mold riots. The attempt has always been made to approach the matter as one of Mold bias by the magistrates and rivalry between the two towns. Alfred Keene anticipated that history might want to look at the matter in this way. He was Clerk to the magistrates and he has left us with a detailed treatise on the matter. I do not know if this has been published before so here it is in full.

Mold Prison
by A. T. Keene

Some most unfair statements are being made reflecting on the Flintshire Magistrates with regard to the erection of Mold Prison and it seems desirable that the real fact should be recorded. It is said there was no necessity for erecting it and that the Magistrates went out of their way to throw away the Ratepayers money. The facts are these:

The old prison at Flint was capable of receiving twenty nine prisoners only. At times there were fifty prisoners in and it therefore followed that no separate system could be adopted as several prisoners were necessarily confined in the same cell. The following extracts from the Visitors Book at the prison will give some idea of the state of things in the prison.

August 30th 1864 — Visited the Gaol which is sadly overcrowded; three available cells for females in one of which four slept last night, in another three and in the third two. One of the prisoners Mary Craig suffering from itch and vermin and ought to be kept separate. In the male side the prison fourteen slept on the ground last night.
Fredk Philips

Sept 9th 1864 — Visited the Gaol the number of prisoners for the last ten days has never been below forty-nine whereas there is sleeping accommodation for only twenty-nine many of the male prisoners have therefore to occupy the beds in turn and there are only three female cells occupied last week by eleven females and one child. The conduct of the prisoners with the exception for those for trial is reported to me as satisfactory.
J Scott Bankes

On the 5th August 1868 Lord Chief Justice Bovill was on the North Wales Circuit and he visited Flint Prison and in the visitors book he made the following entry.

I visited this jail and found everything clean and well attended to and as far as the accommodation of the gaol would permit the duties of the officers well discharged but I was dreadfully shocked to find that such a gaol with such arrangements only as the place would allow of being made was still in existence. The new Gaol I am glad to find will shortly be ready.

Wm. Bovill.
Lord Chief Justice of the Common Pleas

There were constant attempts to escape which rendered necessary the appointment of additional warders one man could not be kept in the gaol and by an order of the Secretary of State he had to be removed to Wakefield Prison.

There was also another serious question which the magistrates had to deal with and that was this — Messrs Muspratt's Alkali Works here erected close to the prison and many people contended they were a nuisance and that it was unfair that prisoners should be confined to a building close to a nuisance and be unable to get away from it and at last the question arose which was to remain — the gaol or the works — the stoppage of the latter meant involving the ratepayers in serious litigation and practically the destruction of Flint.

The prison being condemned by government officials and all in authority the Court of Quarter Sessions had to consider whether a considerable outlay should be made in Flint in erecting a new gaol or whether it was not more prudent to erect a new gaol away from Flint altogether and near the courthouse where the Azzises and Sessions are held, Flint being six miles away. The question was thoroughly thrashed out by both the committees and the court and in the end it was decided that a new gaol should be erected at Mold. This was done and the prisoners were transferred to the new gaol in 1870.

In 1871, Lord Chief Justice Bovill was on circuit again and on visiting the gaol he made the following entry in the book:

4th August 1871

I have visited the new gaol this day and have much pleasure in finding the building and all the arrangements in a most satisfactory condition a great contrast with the old gaol when I visited it on the 5th August 1868 and I beg to congratulate the Magistrates upon having successfully carried out so great and necessary improvement.

It was deemed by the criminal classes to be no punishment to be committed to Flint gaol where the prisoners were so huddled up together but the separate system in the new gaol soon told its tale and the average number confined ran down. The Court of Quarter Sessions then until the average increased utilized the vacant cells by taking in military prisoners in consideration of money payment making a profit thereby to the ratepayers.

In 1877 the new Prison Act passed whereby it was provided that all prisons in the country should vest in the Secretary of State and that the maintenance of such prisons and of the prisoners therein should be defrayed out of monies provided by Parliament the object of the measure being that all small prisons should be closed. Mold, having being so recently erected and being looked upon as a model gaol, it was never supposed that it would be closed but it so happened that Flintshire was grouped with Denbighshire and Merionethshire and the authorities in

London decided after lengthy consideration to close both Mold and Dolgellau gaols and make Ruthin (being in the centre) the gaol for the three counties although it was found that an additional outlay would be required for that gaol.

Under the provisions of the Prison Act the government sold Mold gaol to the Jesuits as a college and after deducting from the purchase money the several sums they were authorized by the Prison Act to deduct they handed over the balance to the county.

Such is the plain history of Mold gaol. The magistrates had a duty forced upon them which they performed. Parliament thought proper to take the gaol from the county and the magistrates were powerless. It is only fair to the government to say that by taking over the prisoners they relieved the county rate of about £1,200 a year. It is stated in some quarters that the magistrates had contributed a large sum towards Ruthin gaol. There is not one word of truth in this.

*

This, I would maintain is the very solid, well-argued truth of the position. Most of the building still stands. After it was closed it was used as a Jesuit College and for a homeless school. (You will learn how the Clarence School Band figured so prominently in the departure and return of the volunteers from South Africa.)

An interesting aside on the Mold gaol it has always been the task of the Clerk to the Magistrates to demonstrate that a child of tender years understood what it meant to give evidence on oath before allowing the child to take the oath. In one such case the Clerk asked a young girl what happened to little girls that told lies; after some hesitation she replied 'they get sent to Bryn Coch' (the area of Mold where the gaol was situated).

One of the interesting legal aspects that emerges from this period is the situation on the administration of oaths. When I qualified, I had to wait five years to become a commissioner for oaths. Later, it was decided that all admitted solicitors could do this as well as some County Court officials. But it was different in the nineteenth century. Keene had been admitted as a solicitor in 1853 but it was twenty years before he could administer oaths. Each court jealously protected its position.

So we have the certificates dated respectively 10th and 11th June 1853 saying he can act as an attorney in the Court of Queen's Bench and the Court of Chancery but it is 23rd March 1875 before he is authorised to administer oaths in both courts — for Chancery, anywhere and, for Queen's Bench, Flintshire, Denbighshire, Merioneth and the city and county of Chester.

Again, at this time, we see the only example of Tom Kelly over-stretching himself. Fresh from his involvement in the National Eisteddfod

I do hereby Certify, that a Commission, or Writ, of Dedimus Potestatem, under the Great Seal of the United Kingdom of Great Britain and Ireland, bearing date, at Westminster, the twenty fifth — day of February) last —— directed to ss Edwin William Philips Bryan George Davies Cooke and Charles James Trevor Roper Gentlemen empowering, them, or, two of them; to administer, the Declaration substituted for the Oath of Commissioner, to administer Oaths in Chancery, in England to Alfred Thomas Keene of Mold in the County of Flint ——

Gentleman, lately, admitted into the said Office of Commissioner to administer Oaths in Chancery, in England, is (with a Certificate thereon indorsed, under, the hands of ss Edwin Philips and W. G. Davies Cooke —— two of the said Commissioners certifying that the said Alfred Thomas Keene ——————— did on the sixteenth day of March instant —— duly make the said Declaration before them) returned into the Petty Bag Office, in Her Majesty's High Court of Chancery, and there remains filed amongst the records of the said Court

Dated the eighteenth — day of March — 1875

A. W. Holden

Entered 23ᵈ March 1875

J. W. Williamson
Deputy Registrar of Attys & Solrs

of 1873 he agrees to become the agent for Captain Rowley-Conway the Conservative candidate in the General Election. This would be just another challenge to a man like Tom Kelly. It is his only excursion into politics and was of course the first election on a secret ballot. Although there were two Liberal candidates, the Conservative still lost by four votes but the *Chronicle* tell us:

> On Wednesday evening a meeting of colliers was convened at Wrexham Street. It was said to be a private public meeting of colliers and was presided over by Mr T. T. Kelly Election Agent for Captain Rowley-Conway — We could not be present therefore we give the following in the words of our informant, 'I need not tell you that Mr Kelly acted as a gentleman all through'.

Clearly Kelly was enjoying himself but what about his legal work? Here we have the only case where we find him in difficulty. He wrote to John W. Hughes:

> I am concerned in a Parliamentary fight, in which sum £50,000 is at stake, both professionally and as a witness — the case was fixed to come on, on Friday last and there was I in attendance but to my extreme disgust the Chairman announced he would take us on Wednesday next. I applied for an adjournment until the following day. He explained himself willing to accommodate but regretted his inability to alter the appointment as that was the only day in the week he could attend. It is most unfortunate and were it not for the important interests involved, I would at once say I would keep my appointment with you but I need hardly remind you of the serious responsibilities under which our profession labours. I am however not beyond hope I can yet manage it, so anxious am I to do so.

If this was not enough, they were involved in the promotion of an Act of Parliament, the Halkyn District Mines Drainage Act, 1875 which is described as an 'Act to effect the drainage of certain mines and mineral lands in the county of Flint and for other purposes'.

The solicitors for the Bill which became the Act were Kelly, Keene & Roper of Mold and Walker, Smith & Way of Chester. This led to the promotion of the Halkyn District Mines Drainage Company. The clients of the Practice, the lords of Mold and the Duke of Westminster were very

Facing: Oaths authorities to allow Alfred Keene to act as an attorney in the Court of Queen's Bench and the Court of Chancery.

interested in the outcome. In November 1875, the company was soliciting funds to enable it to carry out the work required. Initial directors included the Duke of Westminster, Lord Robert Grosvenor and John Scott Bankes. The promoting solicitors were of course solicitors to the company. This work was to give an extended lease of life to the lead mines in the Mold and Halkyn area.

Chapter 9
Kelly, Keene & Son

In 1881, the mood of self-organisation amongst the legal fraternity reached Chester and north Wales with the formation of the Chester & North Wales Incorporated Law Society. It became the means of the local practitioners expressing a view on local important legal concerns and liasing with the Law Society in London. Coherence was gradually coming to the provision of legal services.

Membership was open to all solicitors practising in north Wales, the city of Chester and the county of Chester. It was inevitable that the only founder members from Mold were Alfred Thomas Keene and Thomas Thelwell Kelly: numbers 31 and 32 alphabetically. Initial membership for county members was 10/6d (a half guinea) a year. Alfred Thomas Keene joined the committee in 1882 and left after 1883. Members generally served two years and the committee was, and still is, representative of the geographical area of the Society. It seems very likely that Alfred Keene was involved in the drafting of the first Chester and North Wales Public Sales Conditions. The intention was to create a reasonably uniform approach to the written contracts for the sale and purchase of land. The detailed examination of the clauses, 'the dotting of the Is and the crossing of the Ts' would have seen Alfred at his very best. The Conditions of Sale were still in wide general use in 1955 when I started my articles but the demise came when less scrupulous members of the profession photostatted copies which had been printed and bought from the Society which received a royalty from each copy towards the Society's funds.

The practice was a strong supporter of the Society and, in 1888, Tom Kelly was elected vice-president and became president the following year. Alfred's service had paved the way for this: he never became president and would not have wanted to be. Kelly had not previously served on the committee.

Between about 1885 and 1897, the legal profession was involved in a feud with the governments of all colours over proposals for the introduction of land title registration. A compromise was eventually reached in 1897. Tom Kelly was a man who expressed himself freely in terms that were black and white. He did not know grey.

In his presidential year, on 18th March 1889, he moved a resolution in the General Committee of the Society in response to the latest government proposals for land registration 'that the principle of compulsory registration as propounded and proposed to be effected by the Land Transfer Bill 1889 is contrary to Public Policy' — and it was passed. The fuss that was made then is difficult to understand today because, now, all land transactions are subject to compulsory registration.

From the slackness of approach that existed before the creation of the Law Society in 1821, over the next one hundred years, the restrictive practice gained strength and influence and the local Society was the recipient of grievances as well as being the conduit of information for the national Law Society.

We have already met H. G. Roberts as the chair of the Kelly & Keene staff dinner to celebrate Kelly's marriage. After qualification he set up practice on his own in Mold and later joined the Chester Law Society. He was a great supporter of those restrictive practices. He complained to the committee when Tom Kelly used a policeman to serve a writ, but Tom Kelly had a completely satisfactory explanation. The person to be served worked away from home and only a policeman could be available on his odd visits home.

In 1887, when apologising for his absence from the A.G.M. he writes 'had I been present I should have drawn the attention of the members to a practice which seems to be growing of solicitors taking clerks from the offices of their neighbours and giving them Articles free or at a nominal premium. If ever I see down for ballot a member of the profession who has done this I shall spare no effort to attend and vote against him.' Was this Kelly repaying to another the kindness of A. T. Roberts to him? Another complaint the society received was that an under-sheriff was conducting prosecutions at Assizes and Quarter Sessions, but this did not appear to be Flintshire.

Keene is thanked on 29th August 1895 for a gift of volumes of the *Weekly Reporter* to the Society Library. Kelly's brother-in-law Charles Jones was Society President in 1903.

Keene becomes the first and only Clerk to the Mold Highway Board in 1879 at a salary of £40 a year and immediately creates a code of conduct for the members, in the course of time. It is established that all tramways need wayleaves where they cross a road. The Board receive a letter from Mr A. H. Williams of Glyn Arthur in reply to an application from The Board in which he stated that the road to Moel Arthur had nor been repaired and that in consequence he could not carry full loads on his traction engines and claimed £6 0s. 10d. as damages Keene was instructed to write and point out that he had exceeded the weight authorised to be carried by the traction engines and suggested a surveyor called on him to discuss the Boards claim.

KEENE, SON & KELLY,
SOLICITORS.

ALFRED T. KEENE.
THO? MANN KEENE.
R. STEWART KELLY.

TELEPHONE N? 7.

Mold,

Flintshire,

22nd September 190 4.

Letterhead, 1904

When the telephone was introduced the Practice telephone number was Mold 7. In 1955, when I joined the firm, it was Mold 356. Tom Kelly, in particular, before the introduction of the telephone, had learnt the benefit of the telegram. As Clerk of the Council, he used telegrams to make appointments and communicate simple messages. 'Text messages' are not new, only the means of communicating them!

The practice continued to be responsible for the administration of justice in the Magistrates Court. The witnesses who attended court to give evidence were as nervous then as so many are now. This is shown by a newspaper report of June 1904.

When is a man drunk is a proposition which ever appears to exercise the mind of those in authority and we fear the efforts of a Leeswood collier to provide yet another definition for inebriation will accomplish little beyond rendering more visible the figurative darkness in which the world is enshrouded on this particular point. He was called to give evidence for the defence in a licensing prosecution at the Mold Police Court this week and while the Court were convulsed with laughter at his unconscious humour his imperturbable gravity only added to the hilarity of those present.

The Collier was under examination when the following dialogue ensued:- Was the defendant drunk? — Witness (gravely): A man may have had a drink and yet be not drunk. I say he was morally sober and physically nervous (laughter). Advocate: Oh! you are going into ethics. Now you know very well he had had some drink — Witness: Oh yes but it had not affected his morals. (Laughter) Come now when he was told to stand up didn't he stagger — Well no he didn't exactly stagger. I shall say he vibrated (Great laughter)

I have been asked about the relationship between Tom Kelly and Daniel Owen. There is little or no evidence available of any relationship. Politically they were on different sides; whilst Kelly was not so conformist as Keene in religion, the question of language would have been a barrier. Daniel Owen's political activity was with the District Council and the Burial Board. Kelly's political administration was with the County Council. They must have known each other but not much more than that except in the organising of the Eisteddfod of 1873.

The late Victorian period saw the development of the divorce case and the publicity of the lurid details in the newspapers. There is no evidence of the practice being involved in any such proceedings and, indeed, I would envisaged that Alfred Keene would have fundamental objections to the Practice being involved in such work.

Tom Kelly held the position of under-sheriff throughout the partnership but time and time again when the Sheriff's Court sat to deal with a matter it is the deputy sheriff (Alfred Keene) who presided. It happened so frequently that it must be seen as an acknowledgment of Alfred's skills as a lawyer.

The conduct of elections was the responsibility of the practice. In 1895, it was reported in the paper under the heading — 'The conduct of the election' that

> The carrying out of the Flint County election by Kelly & Keene, the under-sheriffs, the bulk of the arduous duties connected with which were performed by Mr T. H. Ollive gave every satisfaction. There were thirty polling stations and in many instances the booths were miles away from a Railway Station. So perfect, all boxes delivered on Saturday and main result by 12 noon.

It might have been thought that the number of jobs held by the partners in the practice would have led to conflict of interest. It appears, however, that the Partners were well aware of the dangers.

After Tom Kelly was appointed County Council Clerk, he had to correspond with the Clerk to the Local Highway Board — Alfred Keene. In creating the County Council, Parliament in it wisdom, had allowed an overlap of responsibilities. So, for example, on 14th March 1889, the County Council Clerk, Tom Kelly, wrote to the Clerk to the Local Highway Board, Alfred Keene:

> The Main Roads Committee of the County Council have had under their consideration the various clauses of the Local Government Act relating to the main roads in the County and the maintenance thereof from the 1st April next and referring to Sub Section 4 of Section 11 of the Act I am instructed by the Main Roads Committee to enquire upon what terms your board will undertake to maintain for the year from the 1st April next the Main Roads within your District within the meaning of the Highways and Locomotive Amendment Act 1878 in such a state of repair as will enable the County Surveyor to certify that they have been maintained to his satisfaction during the year. The roads over and out of the ends of every bridge carrying main roads whether repairable by you Authority or the County must be included on the list.

Those readers who are town or community councillors will recognise this proposal to be the forerunner of matched funding. This is a process whereby the County Council will only perform its obligations if some other authority contributes to the cost. The letter was delivered across the office landing to Alfred who took it to his board.

There was no problem of conflict for Alfred who wrote to the Clerk of the Council with his Board's answer. It is a judicially written 'get lost' and was delivered across the landing to Tom Kelly.

In the Mold community, at that time, was Andrew James Brereton who was very well known throughout the Principality of Wales by the bardic name of 'Andreas o Fôn'. He died in December 1885. He was a native of Anglesey who started in business in Liverpool, but moved to Mold for the last thirty-eight years of his life, joining the brewers Jones, Lloyd & Co. and rose to managing partner before his retirement. He was recognised as one of the driving forces for the invitation to the National Eisteddfod of 1873. He was one of the two honorary secretaries to the committee. I do not know the difference between a secretary (W. T. Thomas and Tom Ollive) and honorary secretaries (Andrew Brereton and Rev T. R. Lloyd).

In 1878, the town chose to honour Andrew Brereton by a dinner in his honour at the Black Lion where was to be presented with a testimonial in acknowledgement of his long service in aid of the National Eisteddfod and of Welsh literature generally. Two hundred and sixty citizens of the town had contributed £320 to a fund for the establishment of a scholarship at Aberystwyth University to be known as the 'Brereton Scholarship'. A silver tankard (which had cost twelve guineas) was given to him with the inscription 'Presented to Andrew Jones Brereton — Andreas o Fôn — together with a scholarship at University College, Aberystwyth, value £300, in an acknowledgement of his services in connection with the National Eisteddfod Mold: 28th January 1878.' The *Flintshire Observer* reported this dinner and the subsequent cheque presentation to the honorary secretary of the college in April of the same year. The money was invested in 3% consols and the college passed a resolution,

> that the congratulations of the Council be offered to Mr Brereton on his occupying so high a place in respect and esteem of his fellow towns men as testified by their funding a scholarship in this College in honour of him and the Council would also assure him of their gratification at his having suggested that the tribute should take a form which evidenced his own affection of the College and at the same time constituted benefit to young Welshmen.

At the dinner at the Black Lion, Tom Kelly was invited to chair such an important occasion with over 120 guests. His duty was to propose the toast of the evening and he spoke in very high terms of the services rendered to Wales by Mr Brereton. This was clearly a very Welsh occasion but only Tom Kelly was thought appropriate to make the speech.

Tom Kelly served most of the major families in Flintshire during his time as under-sheriff but there was a peculiar affinity between the Kelly's and the Gladstones. We will learn later of Robin Kelly attending an execution with C. A. Gladstone but the close relationship existed in Tom's time.

The family treasure an original letter from W. H. Gladstone written on second November 1889:

> When I was in Chester the other day I tried to find something which would serve as a memento of our relations together as High Sheriff and Under Sheriff respectively and also be a testimony of the sincere regard and esteem in which I have now for many years held you — I hear it has just been sent to you and I trust you will like it. I am sorry to say my own health is scarcely sufficient to warrant me resuming my public duties as yet — but I am far better than I was. May I ask you to return me the Official Seal.

Yours Very Faithfully,
W. H. Gladstone.

The gift was a leather cigar case which the family still have.

We will learn that it was another Gladstone, William Ewart, his father, no less, who opened the Jubilee Bridge in 1897. W. H., the eldest son of W. E. Gladstone, suffered in his health as did Kelly and who died in 1891 leaving a son aged only six who was killed in action during the First World War.

Tom Kelly had to wait until 1888 to become Clerk of the Peace for Flintshire, although, in real terms, he had done the job for the previous twenty-five years as Acting Deputy Clerk. Arthur Troughton Roberts went to Menton in the south of France for his health in 1893, and died there from a stroke in April. It fell upon the practice to make the arrangements for the return of his body to Rhydymwyn where it was interred in the family vault in the churchyard. The original documents in French were preserved by Alfred Thomas Keene and are now held in the Flintshire Archives.

Tom Kelly was at the peak of his popularity and was feted. In December 1880 he was given a silver salver by a grateful client, Mrs Peters of Frondeg; it is a gift the family still treasure. They still also have a silver cup presented by the Marquis of Anglesey for the officer commanding the Liverpool Brigade, Royal Naval Artillery Volunteers, for the best company drill for the Caernarvon Battery, December 1887, but this I suspect was awarded to Margaret Kelly's side of the family.

The lawyers respect for legal precedent makes them natural historians. Alfred Keene and Tom Kelly became notable for their local historical

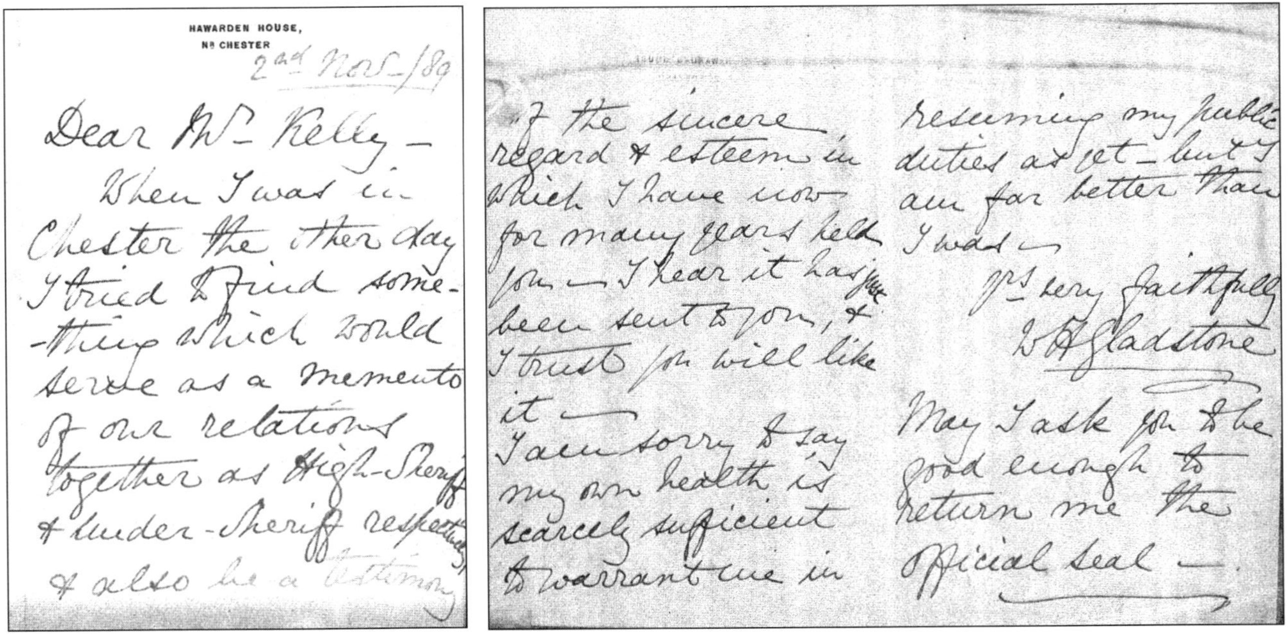

HAWARDEN HOUSE,
Nr CHESTER
2nd Nov. /89

Dear Mr. Kelly –
When I was in Chester the other day I tried to find some-thing which would serve as a memento of our relations together as High-Sheriff & under-Sheriff respectively, & also be a testimony of the sincere regard & esteem in which I have now for many years held you – I hear it has now been sent to you, & I trust you will like it –

I am sorry to say my own health is scarcely sufficient to warrant me in resuming my public duties as yet – but I am far better than I was –

Yrs very faithfully
W H Gladstone

May I ask you to be good enough to return me the official seal –

W. H. Gladstone's letter to T. T. Kelly, 2 November 1889

knowledge and they would respond to requests for assistance. There are, in the National Library at Aberystwyth, letters that they have written to major researchers, in Kelly's case, about the Wynne families of Mold and, in Keene's case, about Richard Wilson and his ancestry.

Alfred Keene was a great student of history and as vestry clerk he has access to much information. He contributed to periodicals such as the *Cheshire Sheaf* with articles, as in 1891, on 'Briefs and collections made in Mold Church in 1661'. He has published a book *Historic Notes on Mold* but I have not been able to secure a copy.

1881 saw both Alfred and Mary Keene and Tom Kelly involved in the opening of the Cambria Cocoa Rooms, the purpose of which was to provide small meeting places that were off licensed premises and whilst the men were involved in raising funds for the project Mary Keene became secretary of the ladies committee.

The press records from time to time the success or not of local property auctions and almost monotonously Kelly & Keene were vendor's solicitors as in 1883 when seventeen lots of out-lying parts of the Davies-Cooke estate were sold.

In January 1893, the three brothers were out early on the Bryn Coch Hall land where they found people trespassing in pursuit of game. When it came to court, with two prospective solicitors and one doctor to give evidence for the prosecutors, the defendants inevitably pleaded guilty!

There were two Miss Howards that lived at Sychdyn House. They died in 1892 when they were the owners of property on the Cross in Mold which was not properly maintained. The Local Board and, then, the Urban District Council were always complaining about their condition. The Practice was able eventually when winding up the estates to resolve the problems.

As Clerk to the Lieutenancy, Kelly issued a circular inviting the residents in the county to co-operate in the promotion of a gift for George, Prince of Wales, and Princess Mary of Teck (later King George V and Queen Mary) on their marriage from the people of Flintshire.

They were administrators supreme. The District Auditor went out of his way to complement Alfred Keene on the keeping of his accounts as Clerk to the Highway Board.

In 1900 mortgagees of the Leeswood Estate attempted to sell as Mortgagees in Possession but were prevented from doing so by Keene, the case went to court and the then heir was then able to show the unreasonableness of such an action.

Chapter 10
Clerk to the County Council

In 1887, Parliament passed the County Council Act settling the structure for Local Government for the next eighty years. The boundaries of the counties had been clearly established for many years and were the administrative units already used by the lords lieutenant and high sheriffs to name but two. The Act required the Clerk of the Peace to plot out the county into electoral divisions. There was no structure to build on, so the work was undertaken from scratch. In Flintshire, this challenge fell upon Tom Kelly who prepared the structure that, subject to minor amendments, still exists today.

Before the introduction of county and district councils it is interesting to see how the county was administered. We have a copy of the accounts of the Clerk of the Peace for 1843. This was of course before the introduction of the Local Highway Board. The first thing to notice is the cost of maintenance of the bridges and road together with the gaol and house of correction. The rest is the cost of administering justice. Hugh Roberts as Clerk of the Peace is responsible for the county administration overall. Yet the prison chaplin is paid £51 2s. 0d. in the year by way of salary whilst Hugh Roberts only receives £22 2s. 0d. showing that the lawyer has never been overpaid! Over £12 was spent on stones and their cartage for hard labour prisoners. There is recognition of the extra work the Clerk of the Peace has to do under the Reform Act and generally as well — clearly just reward for very hard work.

Publication of the accounts then attracts the need for explanation from the Clerk to the ratepayer. In July 1843 Hugh Roberts is replying to Richard Thompson of Stansty Hall (in Denbighshire), a known vexatious litigant, about Flintshire expenditure on repairs to Bangor Bridge, a shared responsibility with Denbighshire. The amount spent was £22 6s. 3d. and Richard Thompson appears to have been satisfied.

The novelty of the situation was that the election was to be county-wide and with a very wide franchise (women excepted), electing representatives for each community. But, it is the contrast with today which is so dramatic. Looking through the list of successful candidates the calibre was very high. The first chairman for quite a few years was Sir Herbert Lewis (one of the county's two Liberal M.P.s) who represented Caerwys. There were two clear political groupings, Liberal and Conservative and the candidates had stood

1843.

COUNTY OF FLINT.

THE

TREASURER'S ACCOUNT OF RECEIPTS & DISBURSEMENTS,

From Epiphany Quarter to Michaelmas Quarter, 1843,

(BOTH INCLUSIVE),

ALLOWED AT THE GENERAL QUARTER SESSIONS, HELD AT MOLD,

On the 11th day of April, 1844.

THOMAS WYNNE EYTON, TREASURER.

RECEIPTS.

	£. s. d.	£. s. d.
Arrears of High Constable, charged last Account,..		104 3 0
RATE, { Epiphany Quarter, ... 800 0 0		
Easter ditto, ... 800 0 0	3200 0 0	
Trinity ditto,.................. 800 0 0		
Michaelmas ditto,............. 800 0 0		
Amount received from Treasury,................	804 8 6	
Fines received,	39 7 6	
Balance in Hundred Rate Account,	8 0 9	
Balance due to the Treasurer,	594 7 0	
		£.4840 6 9

DISBURSEMENTS.

	£. s. d.	£. s. d.
Balance due to the Treasurer last year, ...		640 2 0
SALARIES.—		
Clerk of the Peace, ...	22 2 0	
Treasurer,...	61 2 0	
County Surveyor,...................................	101 2 0	
Crier of Court at Quarter Sessions,................	2 2 0	
Trumpeter,..	2 2 0—	188 10 0
BRIDGES AND ROADS.—		
Robert Blackwell, bridges near Northop and Flint,..	22 2 0	
William Wilson and George Davies, ditto in Maelor,	16 0 0	
Repairs & bridges in Maelor, Northop and Rhuddlan,	71 9 10	
Griffith Williams ditto, near Mold, ...	37 11 0	
Robert and John Jones ditto, near St. Asaph,	53 4 0	
James Woodcock ditto, near Hawarden, ...	26 2 0	
George Davies ditto, near Hope, ...	23 2 0	
Repairs at Bangor,...................................	22 6 3—	273 17 1
GAOL.—		
Chaplain's Salary, ...	51 2 0	
Gaoler's ditto, ...	151 2 0	
Surgeon's ditto,.....................................	31 2 0	
Maintenance, Clothing & Sundries for use of Prisoners,	296 13 1	
Repairs and alterations, ...	134 6 3	
Conveyance of Convicts for Transportation,.......	33 8 0	
Ditto of Prisoners for Trial, ...	4 16 0	
Stones and Cartage for Hard Labour, ...	12 18 8	
Reservoir Keeper's Salary, ...	2 2 0—	714 10 0
HOUSES OF CORRECTION.—		
Keeper of Overton's Salary, ...	16 2 0	
Maintenance of Prisoners and Repairs, ...	15 12 0	
Ditto at Mold and Repairs,..........................	16 9 6	
Rent of Holywell Lock-up,...........................	1 5 0	
Erecting new Lock-up at Bangor, ...	197 14 0—	247 2 6
COUNTY HALL.—		
Hall Keeper's Salary, one year,.....................	9 0 0	
Rates, Taxes, Insurance, and Sundries,............	20 16 11	
Mr. Williams and Mr. Thomas reporting state of the working of a Colliery, whereby the safety of the building was endangered, ...	15 4 0—	45 1 11
WEIGHTS AND MEASURES.—		
One year's Salary of four Inspectors,..............	59 8 0	
Expenses of adjusting and comparing Weights, ...	9 8 0—	68 16 0
Prosecutions at Assizes, ...	760 19 0	
Ditto at Sessions,....................................	648 3 9—	1409 2 9
Clerk of Assizes, Marshall, and Crier, ...		34 18 8
Printing Register of County Voters, Binding Acts, Statutes, and Term Reports, &c. &c.,		143 9 3
Coroner, and Constables, and Witnesses attending him,........		201 10 5
Clerk of the Peace for general business, and for business under Reform Act, ...		276 14 11
Bailiffs attending Insolvent Debtor's Court,		1 10 0
Constables apprehending and conveying Prisoners, and Prosecuting Vagrants,		104 2 4
Bank Interest and Commission, and charge for light Gold, ...		63 11 8
Judge's Lodgings, half year, ...		10 5 6
County Surveyor's expenses at Sessions, ...		2 2 0
Burial of dead Bodies cast on Shore, ...		4 8 2
Magistrates Clerks, ...		11 7 6
Surgeon attending Coroner in a case of murder, ..		2 2 0
Ditto attending Magistrates in a case of violence to the person,..		1 1 0
Undersheriff publishing Queen's Proclamation,		7 12 11
Queen's Prison subscription, ...		2 0 0
Arrears of High Constables, ...		386 8 2
		£.4840 6 9

Examined,—LLOYD KENYON, *Chairman.*
C. B. CLOUGH.
FRED. C. PHILIPS.
E. PEMBERTON.

THE TREASURER'S ACCOUNT FOR THE HUNDRED RATE.

	£. s. d.	£. s. d.
By Arrears of High Constables received, ...		192 8 2
Balance due to Treasurer last year, ...	184 7 5	
Balance due to the County, accounted for in General Account, ...	8 0 9—	192 8 2

N.B.—The Amount of £.7 9 6 was paid in 1841, to James Maurice, on this Account.

Examined,—LLOYD KENYON, *Chairman.*
C. B. CLOUGH.
FRED. C. PHILIPS.
E. PEMBERTON.

Mold, 4th May, 1844.

T. PRICE, PRINTER, HIGH-STREET, MOLD.

under a party label. This first democratically elected council pursued a course putting the well-being of the county first. There was a real attempt to arrive at a consensus on all the issues. The debates were held in public — even the appointment of the Clerk and the fixing of his salary.

Tom Kelly was appointed Clerk by a unanimous vote in 1888, but his pay level seems to have been left in the balance. The Flintshire Joint Standard Committee dealt with this in July 1890. The *Wrexham Advertiser* reported the meeting held in public very extensively.

> The Chairman said the meeting was an adjournment from the meeting held on that day fortnight, the principle business being the application of the Clerk of the Peace for an increase of salary, and in considering it he hoped they would not permit themselves to be swayed by any personal consideration, but only what was right and fair as between Mr Kelly and the ratepayers. Let them consider not whether they were directly the representatives of the ratepayers, nor whether they were the elected of the magistrates, but what they honestly believed would be for the good of the County. He was enabled to say on behalf of the magistrates that they were disposed to agree to what was fair and reasonable. He trusted sincerely that he would not be called upon to give a casting vote, and if he might suggest he would that any proposition that was made should come from the elected councillors, seeing they would then be more likely to arrive at a unanimous agreement, and therefore one that would most likely commend itself to the approval of the public generally (hear, hear). He asked the Clerk whether he had any statement to make in addition to what he had sent to them each, individually.
>
> Mr Kelly said it had come to his ears that at the last committee when they had deliberated in private, that he was in receipt of a salary of £1,000 from the County. There was no foundation whatever for the statement. The facts were these. The salary of the Clerk of the Peace had been fixed in 1852, 38 years ago £450 a year, to which he had in addition a salary of £30 as Clerk of the Police Committee, making a total of £480. But the fees were returned to the County and last year they amounted to £47, but he received a sum of £40 on account of registration. Out of that salary he kept two clerks constantly at work, and sometimes under pressure, no less than six or seven were at work, so that he received no more than £200 a year net for all the work he did for the County. His firm were also Clerks to the Justices for the divisions of Mold, Northop Hawarden and Hope, for which they received £480 a year, and for that department of the business two clerks were constantly engaged, one at a salary of £2 a week and one at a salary of £1 per week. But all the fees were returned to the County. Formerly they averaged £400 a year, but lately owing to the diminution of crime they only averaged about £300 a year.

Facing: Quarter Sessions Accounts, 1843 [FRO DD/HB/357]

Mr Wheldon: Is the £300 returned to the County? Mr Kelly replied that it was and that it had been said he acted as Under Sheriff. Well he had been appointed Under Sheriff on many occasions and hoped to be appointed again, but there was no more reason for asking him what he received in that capacity than for asking him what he received in any case he might act for any gentleman around the table (hear, hear). He only asked them to do what was fair and reasonable in the matter, and he wanted no more.

The Chairman asked whether the Committee would like Mr Kelly to retire.

Mr A. Lloyd said that speaking for himself he preferred Mr Kelly staying in the room, and this appearing to be the general feeling, Mr Kelly remained at his seat.

After a pause, Mr Herbert Lewis rose and said that having received the return from their Clerk of the sums which were given in other Welsh counties, he had gone into the question, and found that in some counties no applications had been as yet received for increase. But in those where such applications had been made he found that the result had been as follows:- In Brecon, which had a population of 57,000 and a rateable value of £262,000 the increase made was from £330 to £500, so is £480 to £727. In Meirionethshire, where the population was 52,000 and the valuation was £246,000, the increase was from £250 to £420, so would £480 be to £809. Carmarthen with a population of 124,000 and a valuation of £438,000 from £500 to £750 and a proportionate increase in the case of Flint would make the salary £720. In the case of Denbighshire no addition was granted, and averaging the increase on the basis of the four counties, it would amount, in the case of Flintshire, to £682 but if a proportionate increase had been made in Denbighshire the average would have been £720. In the case of small counties, the duties would not be proportionately smaller than in the larger ones for there would be the same number of meetings and committees to attend to, while on the other hand they had a strong Clerk and he questioned whether there was a stronger in the whole of Wales (hear, hear).

Mr A. Lloyd said he was much obliged to Mr Lewis for his views, and if the Chairman of the Finance Committee would give the Committee his, it would help them much in arriving at a conclusion.

Mr G. A. Parry said that in the case where increases had been given perhaps the previous salaries were positively too low.

Mr Herbert Lewis said that in Wales as a rule the salaries of public officials was fixed by the magistrates, were not generally too low (a laugh)

The Chairman said the Committee were much obliged to Mr Lewis for the trouble he had taken, and for the lucid statement he had given them.

Mr Pennant sincerely trusted they would arrive at a unanimous decision on the point, for if it was so the clerk would be more likely to be satisfied, and to work with a heartier good will in the future. They agreed that he had performed his duties most satisfactorily and he had within himself arrived at two sums one of which he considered a fair sum and the other a liberal sum, which should be paid their clerk. It was for them to say whether he received a fair or a liberal increase.

Mr P. A. Lloyd suggested that two gentlemen on either side should go into the other room and arrive at an agreement what increase should be, returning to the Committee to have it confirmed. This suggestion was taken up warmly, but eventually abandoned, Mr Lewis being firm in declining to accept the responsibility involved.

Mr Bate trusted the Committee would take a liberal view of the question, for they might depend upon it the office was no sinecure and the county had a population of 80,000 and a valuation of £421,000.

After some further conversation, Mr Pennant proposed that the room be cleared, but Mr A. Lloyd strongly objected, saying if the reporters went out he would go out also.

Mr Wm. Davies said that in order to bring the question to a crisis, he would propose that the salary of the Clerk be increased to £650 to include all charges, which was seconded by Mr G. A. Parry.

Mr A. Lloyd said that the figure read by Mr Lewis pointed to £700 as a fair and equitable sum, and he proposed this with a view of accruing unanimity.

Mr Herbert Lewis seconded the proposition, which he thought to be a perfectly fair one. Before he had come into contact with Mr Kelly, he had entertained very exaggerated notions as to the sums which he received from the County, but the explanations which Mr Kelly had given him had quite disillusioned him.

Mr Pennant supported the proposal it being what had commended itself to his own mind as a very fair on.

Mr Davies then said he would be happy to withdraw his proposal in favour of that of Mr A. Lloyd.

The Chairman was about to put the proposition when Mr Kelly asked whether it included the fee for registration, which he contended should be extra.

The Chairman strongly advised Mr Kelly to accept it, and if he found it too small, he could make a further appeal to the Court after an enlarged experience. The proposition was then put, and fourteen hands were held up, on the contrary being put, two hands were put up and instantly put down again, the increase being practically unanimous.

On the question whether the resolution should have a retrospective effect, Mr Wynne moved that the increase should date from the first of April 1889 which Mr Weldon seconded, saying it was right to increase the salary, it was right to date if from the time of increased duties. The motion was put and agreed unanimously.

Mr Kelly then thanked the committee for the kind things which had been said of him, and for the increase which had been granted him.

Kelly had no doubts of the merit of his case. What public servant now would have no wage increase for thirty-eight years? But what open government! The councillors would have to defend meanness or over-generosity as would Kelly.

One of the startling examples of openness is the willingness of the councillors to acknowledge in public when they have not taken the advice of their clerk. In 1894, the County Council was sued for an unpaid tithe on a road. They decided to defend the case against the advice of their clerk and this was fully reported in the *Chester Chronicle*. When the reserved judgement was given against the County Council the Conservatives sought to blame the Liberals because they, as non-conformists, had an inborn objection to tithe.

The County Council was a statutory body which was interested in what other public bodies did: so, when the London & North Western Railway published a bill to extend their powers, the County Council were bound to have a view on it and object. So Kelly & Keene, well experienced in the procedure of parliamentary bills, were cast in the role of objecting.

In 1897, an application from Lancashire County Council was also the subject of objection. The Clerk certainly had presence. In June 1897, he rebuked a member of the County Council for speaking against a resolution he had not read.

But the issue that dominated much of the first twelve years of the Flintshire County Council was the proposal to build a bridge over the Dee at Queensferry — that which became known as the 'Jubilee Bridge'. Looking back now, it is difficult to imagine that whilst there was a railway bridge, all other traffic wishing to cross the river had to use the ferry. As ferries go, it was not all that wonderful. The chairman of the Local Highway Board complained that in 1882 he had crossed the river by the ferry with his horse and gig and that, immediately afterwards, the ferry sank.

The commercial interests of Deeside persuaded the County Council that they should promote a bill to construct the bridge at Queensferry to replace the ferry. So was passed an act in 1895:

> To authorise the Construction of a Bridge over the River Dee at Queensferry in the County of Flint and the discontinuance of the existing Ferry at that place to make provision with respect to the Maintenance and Repair of Roads now repairable by the Dee Land Company in the Counties of Flint and Chester and the City of Chester and for other purposes' known as 'The Queensferry Bridge and Sealand Roads Act.

The solicitors to the bill were Kelly & Keene, Mold. Needless to say, the

*Design competition advert for the
Jubilee Bridge, Queensferry
[FRO]*

published bill attracted objectors including the Dee Conservancy. Where his health permitted, the work fell upon Kelly himself but the ever-willing Keene was always there when needed to support or replace him at a meeting. The telegram came into its own as a means of communication.

The project started in 1891 and the bridge opened in 1897. 1895 was the year of activity and negotiations. An early letter to Walker, Smith & Way in April 1894 read:

We are very much obliged for yours of yesterday and Mr Kelly is leaving for London on Monday evening. He goes to the Hotel Victoria and if you have anything to communi-

£100 PREMIUM FOR SELECTED DESIGN.

MOVABLE ROAD BRIDGE OVER THE RIVER DEE AT QUEEN'S FERRY, IN THE COUNTY OF FLINT.

The Flintshire County Council invite COMPETITIVE PLANS and SECTIONS for the above Bridge, together with Estimates of the Cost of Construction.

Copies of the Conditions of Competition and Instructions to Competitors may be obtained from the undersigned, upon payment of a deposit of £1 1s., which will be returned on receipt of a *bonâ-fide* Design, Set of Plans, and Estimates complying with the conditions above referred to.

The Engineer of the selected Design will receive a Premium of £100, and in the event of the work being proceeded with and his being employed to superintend the execution of the Works the Premium will be deducted from the Commission to be paid to him. The selected Design, Plans, and Sections shall be the property of the Council.

The Council will be assisted by a competent professional Assessor, but they reserve to themselves the right of ultimate decision.

The Council do not bind themselves to accept any of the Designs.

The Designs, with Estimates, without signature, but with a motto or device and a letter sealed and containing a corresponding motto or device and the Engineer's name and address, must be sent to me here on or before but not later than the 1st day of December next, endorsed "Designs of Queen's Ferry Bridge."

By Order, THOS. T. KELLY,
Clerk of the County Council.
Mold, 25th September, 1893.

cate to him he will be glad if you write to him there. He will let you know from London when he is returning. As time now is so great an object cannot your Council dispose of the matter definitely on Wednesday.

Kelly ran out of energy and Keene became directly involved. On the 17th June 1895, a telegram was received by Walker, Smith & Way as solicitors to Dee Conservancy.

Mr Keene proposes calling upon you tomorrow Monday morning immediately on the arrival of the 9.08 train from here on an important point with reference to the above bill and he trusts you can see him then.

But the challenge that promoting such a bill presented is admirably shown in the four letters extracted below. The problems that the project presented for Kelly's health and the problem of satisfying everyone is well nigh impossible, but they did.

Mold
5th April, 1894

Dear Sir
Queen's Ferry Bridge

Our committee have considered the Clause you drafted after the meeting on Monday last in lieu of the two Clauses proposed by the Board of Trade and they do not object to the principles of it but they are alarmed at its 'width' and consider there ought to be a sane limit to which their liability should extend. They would agree to 150 yards above and below the bridge 300 yards in all, this, we fancy, would be approved by your committee.

Next they consider there ought to be some summary mode of settling any differences which may arise under the Clause, a future Conservancy Board in years to come may not be so reasonable a Board as the present one and we therefore propose that the Clause should go on to provide that failing to agree any difference shall be settled by an Engineer to be appointed by the Board of Trade — this provision may assist the Board of Trade in consenting to waive their Clauses.

We were astonished to find this morning that the Great Western Railway Company have presented a Petition against — you have had to deal with this Company several times on Petitions against your Bills kindly tell us who is the best man belonging to them to go to.

We shall be glad to receive your Clauses as soon as possible we are being closely pressed for time now.

We are pressing Mr Gee to come to terms if possible both with your Council and also with the Wirral Highway Board at once — if you fail to agree all we can do is to insert Clauses in the Bill enabling you to agree and giving power to release the Charge on the land as part of the terms of the Agreement — can you suggest anything beyond this?
Yours faithfully,
Kelly & Keene
Samuel Smith, Esq. , Clerk to the Dee Conservancy Board

Mold
30th June, 1894

Dear Sirs,
Queen's Ferry Bridge & Sealand Road Bill

Mr Gee writes us that he has arranged a meeting with you at your office on Tuesday next at 2.30. We have now asked Mr Reginald Potts to meet us there. Mr Kelly will not be sufficiently recovered to attend but Mr Keene will attend for him.

Mr Gee proposes to strike out the words 'as and to the extent aforesaid' out of line 30 on page 28 of the Bill. There can be no objection to this the words appear to have been left in by mistake.

He also proposes that in lieu of the words 'from all liability in respect thereof' on line 10 page 29 the following words be inserted 'from the charge thereby created and from all powers and remedies for enforcing the same'. On behalf of our County Council we see no objection to these alterations and we don't think you and Mr Potts will object.

Yours faithfully
    Kelly & Keene

Messrs Walker, Smith & Way
Solicitors
Chester

Mold
4th July, 1894

Dear Sirs
Queen's Ferry Bridge and Sealand Roads Bill
    Referring to our meeting yesterday we have now fully considered the position.

We are placed on the horns of a dilemma; if we satisfy Mr Gee, the client of Mr Smith and of Messrs Potts, Potts & Gardner will petition against us, If we satisfy Mr Smith and Messrs Potts & Co, Mr Gee will petition against us. It is obvious therefore, if the Bill is to be saved, some middle course must be adopted. With regard to the proposal the Flintshire County Council should take over the whole of the Roads in Flintshire, metalled or not, that is entirely out of question, as they have specially resolved not to do so, and no cash payment would induce them to depart from this Resolution.

The suggestion thrown out yesterday that a portion of the charge only should remain to cover the non-metalled roads, we think is a fair and equitable one and affords a basis upon which an arrangement ought to be worked out. Taking the metalled roads, roughly, as representing three fourths of the whole roads, we would suggest that a sufficient portion of the lands now charged representing in value one fourth of the amount charged by the Act of 1889 should remain charged to cover the non-metalled roads. We shall be very glad if you can let us hear from you by this evening's post what you think of this proposal. We have summoned a special meeting of our Committee to consider what should be done as the expenses of the Bill are running on and far exceeding our estimate. We should regret extremely that all the expense and labour which has been bestowed on the Bill should be thrown away by our being compelled to withdraw the whole or a portion of the Bill.

Yours faithfully
Kelly & Keene

Messrs Walker, Smith & Way
Solicitors
Chester

6 Plastirion Terrace, Rhyl
July 11th, 1894

Dear Smith

Many thanks for yours of Monday — my Doctor has ordered me down here for a short time to recruit. I am thankful to say that I am pulling round again but I have had a bad month of it —

Martin prepared a clause and I had it down yesterday but I didn't like it so I sent it back asking him to prepare a fresh one and send it to you in tonight's post — he had prepared it on the lines of the old clause restricting the payment to so much a year but I have told him the land edged red are to be charged, without reference either to the fee simple in annual value, for the maintenance of the roads not taken over and that any landowner who may be affected by the roads not being maintained is to have a remedy against the land so as to secure maintenance. This I gather was your idea.

The cyclists are a nice lot to adopt such an underhand move of proceedings. We have not had one single word of complaint from an outsider, it would have course have been dealt with — personally. .

I should like to make the 6d into £1 but that is out of the question — 6d is a maximum toll — I can hardly credit the summons we have had so many obstacles conjured up with regard to the Bill that I am getting rather hardened.

I don't quite know the effect of blocking a private Bill seeing that any one complaining have a right to petition but I wrote to Martin last night to enquire. Can you tell me who the prime mover is?

Yours faithfully
    Thos T. Kelly

The loyalty of Alfred Keene to his partner and his own personal skills shine through in this period together with Tom Ollive's contribution to the general running of the council.

We have the minutes of a meeting with Cheshire County Council on 29th May 1894 when Tom Kelly successfully negotiated away their objections to the Bill and they would still contribute financially.

This was probably one of the first major schemes undertaken by a new Welsh county council and Kelly and Keene fulfilled their task admirably obtained the authority of Parliament to proceed. But they were not engineers and the county went to outside consultants for advice on speci-fications and how the quotations received matched the specification. In March 1895, Sir Francis Fox of London assured Kelly that he had examined the detail plans and reports prepared

The designs conform in all respects with the general conditions as to span head-way, width of roadway and gradients as laid down in the notice served by the Bridge Committee in connection with the competition notably on the strength and stability of structure. I consider that the various proportions of the design are sufficient and that the vertical and lateral stability of the structure are properly provided for. The piers are designed to effect the least possible obstruction to the tide.

It was a bridge intended to open to allow ships to go up river and it passed in all respects.

What would now be described as 'consumer research' was faulty. The traffic that used the Bridge was heavier and more numerous than expected. The bridge had three spans with the middle one constructed to open. The original estimate of £13,000 was to be split £6,000 for Flintshire £3,000 for Cheshire

---

AN

A C T

(*As amended in Committee*)

To authorise the Construction of a Bridge over the River Dee at Queen's Ferry in the County of Flint and the discontinuance of the existing Ferry at that place to make provision with respect to the Maintenance and Repair of Roads now repairable by the Dee Land Company in the Counties of Flint and Chester and the City of Chester and for other purposes.

---

57 & 58 VICT.—SESSION 1894.

KELLY & KEENE,
Mold,

Solicitors for the Bill.

MARTIN & LESLIE,
27, Abingdon Street, Westminster, S.W.,
Parliamentary Agents.

Geo. Kelly & Co., 11 & 13, King-st., Westminster, S.W., Printers.

Act of Parliament authorising the construction of the Jubilee Bridge at Queensferry
[FRO D/DM/223/23]

The Jubilee Bridge at Queensferry
[FRO PH/51/9]

W. E. Gladstone at the opening of the Jubilee Bridge, Queensferry, June 1897.
The imposing figure on Gladstone's left is Thomas Thelwall Kelly, Clerk to the County
Council [FRO 51/8]

and £4,000 for the Dee Conservancy. Costs spiralled to £23,000 with Flintshire having to find the extra money. Tolls were payable. By 1914, only seventeen years after it was built, the bridge was worn out and it limped through the First World War to be replaced in 1926 by the Blue Bridge still in use today. The old buttresses can still be seen alongside it. But let us return to the preparations for its building.

Kelly wrote to the Dee Conservancy on 28th May 1895, and it is as almost as though he has foresight of the problems to come.

> Personally I shall never fail to regret that the County Council had anything to do with the bridge or ferry. It is a constant source or irritation and trouble to one and I suppose it will continue to be so to the end. All sorts of difficulties and claims are cropping up and we get very little assistance from quarters we have a right to expect.

The concept of a bridge was a good idea but even then the active support of central government financially should have been a prerequisite.

The Victoria Jubilee Bridge as it was to be called was opened at the beginning of June 1897 and who else could open it but W. E. Gladstone, then aged 88 and only a year before his death. We are told that his arm was in a sling from a slight accident and many others from his family were with him.

The speech fully reported in the *Chester Chronicle* was an amazing effort. A few cordial words, a press of a button or cutting of a tape would be the format now. But not for this amazing man. He speaks at great length comparing developments during his lifetime. The improvement in transport from the stagecoach to Cooks Tour

> In my youth you know that there were, here and there, a certain Mr Bretherton in Liverpool who was a coach proprietor and those wagons that I spoke of no doubt they had a proprietors somewhere or other — but the owners of the vehicles employed for carrying on communication were comparatively an insignificant class. But with improved means of communication all that has changed and at the moment when I speak it is probable that not less than a twelfth or a tenth part of the whole property of the County is represented by the railways that carry our goods backwards and forwards from one part of the County to another. That shows the enormous convenience of this sort of change. Well of course railways are very grand things and a bridge like this in comparison is a comparatively humble thing but a bridge like this is a feeder and it is by means of these feeders that railways are sustained. When the Railway Bridge a little lower down the stream was constructed people might have supposed that that would be a great blow and a great damage to the road and but for the Railway Bridge it might have been long before we had this bridge built.

This little river is rather a formidable river of course as those who have had to do with it — engineers — know very well: the mouth of the Dee is a portion of a district beset with dangers and quicksands making the construction difficult: we get over all these difficulties now and we shall be able practically to go forward. [This is only a short extract]

He was not able to stay for the official luncheon at the Hawarden Castle Hotel. He pressed the button to replace the central span and crossed the bridge.

At the lunch, there were several toasts drunk including one to Tom Kelly. Dr Easterby, ex-council chairman for Flintshire, said he did not think 'there was a County Council in the kingdom that had a Clerk to equal him. His abilities in directing the business of the Council in interpreting the law, and in his knowledge of the law were exceptional and ought to be highly appreciated.' We have to remember Dr Easterby was a great supporter of Kelly. On another occasion when supporting a nomination for the chair he says 'Mr Kelly was the pivot around which everything in the Council turns'. The Chairman added 'He was the best Clerk in Wales'.

He had delivered the Bill as was the lawyer's brief. Had the engineers done their part? Had the contractors built the bridge under adequate supervision?

At the end of June 1897 Cheshire County Council received a letter from John Thompson:

Netherleigh House
Chester
28th June, 1897

Smith, Esq.,

Dear Sir,

I went with the Committee to inspect the Queensferry Bridge this morning and I am sorry that I am obliged to attend the works committee of the Weaver tomorrow, where important matters in reference to the New Bridges are to be discussed and decided upon.

It is quite obvious that the new Bridge is not built square across the river: it appears to have followed the direction of the Roads in the two sides of the river.

The effect of this is to contract the span of the bridge, so that the opening available for ships coming up and going down is appreciably less than that stipulated for in the Act of Parliament.

I do not see how this is to be remedied except by removing and altering the line of the piles in that the faces of the piles shall be in parallel to the outer line of the river.

This will be an expensive job and will mean the stoppage of the working of the Bridge for some time.

The only other thing that I can suggest is for the Flintshire County Council to give their guarantee that if the experience of working the Bridge in its present state be found to be dangerous to shipping using the River alongside the loading stages on the south side of the river above the bridge, they shall hold themselves liable for all damage done to the shipping and do whatever the Conservancy Board may think necessary to remedy the obstruction.

Yours faithfully
John Thompson

What was achieved was the permanent road link to Merseyside that we regard as being so normal today.

In March 1899, Kelly is called upon to give evidence to the Parliamentary Committee appointed to consider how it had been done. Kelly told them of the circumstances under which the roads of Sealand were taken over by the County Council authorities, the difficulties which have been met with an erection of a bridge and the inability of the Local Government Board to grant the County Council power to raise the further capital required.

September 1889 sees the opening of the new county headquarters at Hall-fields.

The new county council had many challenges to meet. One of these affected the drainage of what was known as the Llanarmon District Mines. We have already learnt about the Halkyn Drainage Scheme for which an Act of Parliament was required. The prosperity of the area would be safeguarded if this problem could be solved.

The solution was to create a system of tunnels to link into the Halkyn scheme. The area affected had the Mold to Ruthin Road on one side and the Mold to Wrexham Road on another. It stretched to Leeswood and into Denbighshire at Llanarmon and Llanferres. Three new tunnels were proposed being respectively 2,721, 3,034 and 1,710 yards long. They would cover all the area including Nerquis and Gwernymynydd. One started 22 yards from the Rainbow Inn, deep underground.

An Act of Parliament was required and the bill for their works was published on 12th November, 1891. The solicitors for the Bill were Kelly & Keene, assisted, as with the Halkyn Bill, by Walker, Smith & Way. Amongst the consultees were over 500 owners and occupiers of the surface land affected. All these are set out in great detail inside the Book of Reference which had to be prepared. This was a major engineering project but it could only take place once the lawyers had delivered the bill into an act and gained the drainage company the authorisation required.

The bill was passed during the 1892 session of Parliament and the work was completed. The combination of Tom Kelly and Alfred Keene had once more delivered for Flintshire and the County Council.

This chapter clearly demonstrates that the original Flintshire County Council was very fortunate in its choice of Tom Kelly as its first Clerk as, indeed, it was in Haydn Rees as its last.

Chapter 11
The Clerks

Nothing can be achieved without the right staff and both partners were well aware of this. The only assistance available to them were the penny post and the expanding railway system and later the telegraph. Over the years, Tom Kelly and Alfred Keene employed an amazing collection of men. These are some of them:

Tom Kelly himself had come to Mold in 1852 as a managing clerk. He qualified nine years later after encouragement and probably free articles from Arthur Troughton Roberts. Charles Dickens has portrayed the Victorian law clerks as down trodden ineffective people but for the Practice Trollope's 'Three Clerks' are a much better comparison. I suspect that staff selection and encouragement was a joint enterprise but as you will see it was very successful. Their lives were committed to the town as a whole and not just the Practice. They played their full part in the community.

Mold had early established a Clerks' Association which had annual dinners. This association did not restrict its membership to Kelly, Keene and Roper but they clearly had a major influence. A major local figure was invited to be guest of honour and to propose the toast to the Association. In 1870, William Theophilus Thomas replied 'after an apt allusion to the Suez Canal, the Atlantic Cable and the network of cables that had knit nations together' he further went on 'A substantial dinner was a most beneficial thing to a strong constitution and also that legitimate worth was equally beneficial to a delicate constitution. They had the authority of the Hebrew Sage that a merry laugh did good like medicine and a hearty laugh far better but much cheaper than medicine.'

These clerks were clearly very intelligent men. Tom Ollive replied at the dinner in 1872 and John Mould in 1875.

William Theophilus Thomas
He arrived at the Practice about the same time as Thomas Thelwell Kelly. He was born in 1824 in Holywell and went to Manchester when a young man. Whilst there became a member of the Welsh Congregational church at Gartside and assisted other Welsh chapels in the area as a lay preacher. In 1851 he moved to Anglesey, was ordained and he became the minister at Cana, Llanddainel, but his health failed after some time and he had to give up the full time ministry.

He came to Mold in about 1853 and entered into the offices as a clerk for Arthur Troughton Roberts where he remained until his retirement in 1895 as Deputy Clerk to the Magistrates. He died in 1899.

When he came to Mold he was part-time Congregational minister to two chapels (Soar at Pantybuarth and Jerusalem, Rhosesmor) until 1874. A presentation was raised for him by his congregations that attracted a large attendance. The report in the *Wrexham Advertiser* was ninety-two lines long and concludes, 'We are sorry that the space at our command compels us to abridge out report of what we would have wished to give at greater length.' A purse was given to him and immediately returned to them to be used for new communion vessels.

He was a keen supporter of all the Welsh societies, a regular contributor to Welsh newspapers and periodicals and an author whose work was published locally and was of all types. In 1857 he published a volume of poetry in Welsh. The dedication reads 'These Poetical effusions are respectfully dedicated to Mr Thomas Thelwell Kelly the esteemed friend of the author.'

His work in English and Welsh was widely published. In 1863 he wrote in Welsh a guide for the preparation and proving of wills — *Y Trefruedydd Cyfreithiel* and in 1883 an essay in Welsh on the soul — *Sylwadau ar Fedelaeth Exaia*. He became a member of the Gorsedd of Bards under the name 'Gwilym Gwenffrwd'. Any concert in Mold in the second half of the nineteenth century was not complete without a recitation from him. He was involved in the formation of a debating society.

The National Eisteddfod came to Mold in 1873 and this was a very major cultural event. This was before the all Welsh rule and Keene & Kelly were fully involved. They provided the joint secretaries William Theophilus Thomas and Tom Ollive, of whom we will hear more later. William Thomas's son, Richard Hughes Thomas, maintained the legal tradition as Chief Clerk at the County Court.

Thomas Holt Ollive

He joined Keene & Kelly in about 1870 and was used as an administrative clerk by Thomas Thelwell Kelly so successfully that, on Kelly's death in 1901, Ollive was appointed the Acting Clerk to Flintshire County Council.

He was joint secretary to the 1873 Eisteddfod and for his services a bardic name 'Alpheus' was conferred upon him.

In his early days he took a lively interest in outdoor sports, especially cricket, the tradition continued by the Keene family. He was also an elocutionist of more than average ability and took an active interest in the 'Penny Readings' which were very much in vogue in those times in Mold and in amateur theatricals. In February 1885 such a production was raising funds for the cricket club.

For some years prior to his retirement, in about 1918 he was head of the financial department of the County Council. He acted as Deputy Returning Officer (the key job at elections) for many years. He was clerk to the County Governing Body whose educational functions were taken over eventually by the County Council.

Ollive was a man described as well liked by everyone although somewhat reserved and taciturn. He was an active churchman serving as a church warden several times. In 1911, he is on record as opposing a tax on the vicar's Easter offering. He is described as most approachable and always helpful. He was for many years an active member of the Sir Watkin Masonic Lodge. He originally came from Upton near Birkenhead but his acceptance by the community was clearly complete.

John Mould
Another clerk was John Mould who died in 1899 at the age of 81. He was the mainstay of the Clerk of the Peace operations. He joined Arthur Troughton Roberts in 1860 and was at work as late as August 1899. In his youth he had rowed in the Chester VIII and maintained an interest in the sport till his death. Originally he was an Anglican but converted to be a Congregationalist.

William Bayne
He is one of the constant supporting people who feature in the life of Mold. He served on the cricket club committee with Colonel Keene and was fully involved in the life of Mold Parish Church, attending vestries, *etc*, in active participation.

David Lloyd Gylp Pugh
Keene & Kelly attracted him from his position as Chief Clerk at the St Asaph Probate Registry in 1875 and he remained with the firm until his death in 1900. He had also been Chief Clerk to the Mold and Flint County Court. He was a Freemason and a Liberal of the old school. His son became the organist of the English Congregational church.

Joseph Thelwall Roberts
He came to Keene & Kelly from Potts & Roberts, Chester. A native of St Asaph, he was the first organist of St John's Welsh church.

Robert William (Bob) Roberts
Here was another clerk who went on to higher things. He was Clerk of the Mold Urban District Council from 1938 when he succeeded Robin Kelly as Clerk having been Financial Officer and Deputy Clerk from 1928. He was

Bob (R.W.) Roberts in the office

Clerk for thirty years. To most people in Mold during his term of office he represented and was the face of the Urban District Council.

He joined Keene & Kelly before the First World War as a boy and remained with them until his appointment as full-time Council Clerk. He was well versed in all the work of the unqualified legal clerk.

On the outbreak of the First World War he volunteered and, despite his being a humble clerk, Colonel Keene, was able to use his influence to enable him to join the Artists' Rifles. This was a unique Territorial Army regiment in that almost all its members were deemed suitable for commissions (and many were commissioned into other regiments) but acquired considerable kudos by just serving in the ranks.

After the war, Bob Roberts returned to Mold and worked again with Robin Kelly. As my research progressed I became convinced that there was almost a uniform amongst the clerks. Firstly there was the hand-tied bow tie. With this there was a flower in the button-hole according to the season.

His daughter told me a secret about her father's bow tie. There was a period of six weeks when the bow tie was replaced by an ordinary tie. What we did not know was that it was his wife who tied the tie standing behind him. However, she broke her arm and was in plaster for six weeks so Bob had to wear an ordinary tie for that period.

He was very patient in waiting for the vacancy as Clerk. Robin Kelly was always going to retire 'next year'.

I knew him from 1955 and he always had time to talk to me because he was well organized and was not in conflict with his council. I suppose this was because he was trained in the old school. He died in 1968.

David Rutter Thomas

Much of this section dealing with David Rutter Thomas substantially appeared in the Christmas 2002 edition of Ystrad Alun, *the Journal of the Mold Civic Society.*

David Rutter Thomas was continuously employed by the firm for seventy-two years. He was retired when I knew him but would come in to see Hugh Gough (a later partner in the firm). He would by then have been in his late

80s and would announce himself as 'Mr Thomas Hemington' (the house where he lived in Pwll Glas) He would be wearing the 'uniform' which marked out Kelly & Keene's clerks of a bow tie and a seasonal flower in the button-hole. He was essentially a very gentle and unassuming man but he had had a very full life.

In 1879, on 3rd October (the same date as I started with the Practice in 1955), Rutter Thomas started work with Keene & Kelly. He remained with them for seventy-two years. Coming from a home where books were obviously important, he had considered teaching but was drawn to the law.

He had a delicious sense of humour. On his retirement from practice the *Chester Chronicle* invited him to write four articles on his memories and they are very illuminating. He described William Theophilus Thomas his predecessor as 'Assistant Clerk to the Justices (with a side line of a Congregational Minister)'.

He was in his ninety-first year when he died in August 1957. The family home was at Oak Villa and his father was employed as a booksellers assistant and printer. David Rutter never married nor did his three sisters who became elementary school teachers. He bought Hemington (behind the Bailey Hill) with his sisters in the 1920s and lived there until his death.

He was a very devout high churchman and was associated with Mold Parish Church all his life. He was the oldest member of the church choir having been a member since boyhood. After receiving communion he would remain standing alone to say quietly to himself verses 1–14 of the gospel of St John. He first appears in the parish records after baptism in 1874. He won first prize as best reader in English of a portion of scripture for under-nine age group. He was about six and it was clear that first prizes were withheld if they were not up to standard.

He told the story of when, as a boy chorister, the services of the Mold church choir were secured to sing at services at Hope church to commemorate the re-opening of the organ. Excitement was high when all the surplices where packed into a huge wooden box and they all went to Hope by train. The first service passed by uneventfully in the afternoon and the choir boys were given tea in Abermorddu School. The boys retired to a hill nearly covered in blackberries. They were engrossed in picking and eating these when they heard the ding dong of the church bell recalling them. There was a stampeded and they arrived back at the church breathless with no time to spare and no time to discriminate in the selection of vestments. As a result, some of the bigger boys were garbed in short surplices while the smaller boys had them trailing.

He recalled that when disestablishment took place he became the first secretary of the and remembered the completion of the Richard Wilson window.

He assisted the Practice in all aspects of its work. He succeeded William Theophilus Thomas as Deputy Clerk to the Magistrates, remaining in that post until his own retirement in 1951 when the *Chester Chronicle* wrote that his knowledge of Mold was extensive 'like his knowledge of *Stones Justice Manual'*. He was also Clerk to the Mold Rural Parish Council from 1894–1940 and became the first Senior Worshipful Master of the Sir Watkin Lodge in 1908.

In the early 1900s when Colonel Keene was Chairman of the Cricket Club who was Treasurer — yes 'R. T.'.

His organizational skills were used for the triumphant return of the R.W.F. Volunteers in 1901 and in the 1890s he was fund-raising for Mold Red Star F.C.

His sense of fun meant that he was a keen political observer. He would have been seven or eight at the time of the 1874 election when Thomas Thelwall Kelly was the Conservative political agent. He could recall every window in the Black Lion (the Conservative Headquarters) being broken and two close friends severing their friendship because they could not agree on how the empire should be run.

He told of Joseph Eaton in the 1890s and his politics:

Sixty years ago Mr Joseph Eaton, the doyen of the Eaton family, was one of the town's local celebrities. (Of the family it was freely stated, 'Whatever you discovered in the Eaton family you would never find a fool'). Latterly the old gentlemen and his aged wife occupied a shop in Wrexham Street, wherein no business was transacted and in the window was displayed a card inscribed, 'Mind your own business'! Joseph Eaton was a person of strong mentality, an uncompromising radical and nonconformist, dour and almost vitriolic in speech and pen.

Mr Gladstone had presented this devoted disciple with a discarded top hat which was greatly prized by the recipient. On the occasion of a Conservative meeting at the Market Hall, the audience consisted largely of devotees from the opposition camp, Mr Eaton was wont to cross the entire front of the Hall wearing the Gladstone headwear. This was promptly and enthusiastically recognized by the audience with results which can readily be imagined … And now for the reverse side of the picture. Accompanied by two school-fellows I attended a Liberal meeting in the same building. We were perched on the back of a form at the rear of the Assembly room. Half a dozen fellows (known to me) were present, bent on making trouble.

The first 'turn' was a diminutive tailor who was greeted by the obstructionists first 'bombshell' — 'give him a pint he's nervous'! Thereafter every succeeding speaker was subjected to interruption and endeavouring in vain to gain a hearing. The position became intolerable and then ensued a scene I shall never forget, infuriated, the audience turned and made en masse for the interrupters whom they bundled bodily down the steps of the Halls rear entrance and into the street. To resume with the original programme was out of the question and for the remainder of the evening Mr John Morgan, the Liberal Agent ('Rambler' of the *'Wrexham Advertiser'*) gave a blackboard demonstration on 'How to fill your ballot paper'.

Rutter Thomas was also a teller and presiding officer for elections and tells us

Despite the extension of the franchise (the vastly increased size of the lists of voters tells its own story) the role of the Returning Officer is in some respects no more exacting than that of his predecessors, thanks to the arrival of the telephone and the motor car. I recall the time when the voting compartments were delivered by road and the ballot boxes conveyed to the presiding officers by rail, when a special train was chartered to bring the Maelor boxes to Flint for the counting of the votes. In those days the votes were counted on the evening of the poll and after the declaration, the Mold counters were wont to seek well-earned relaxation. On the last of such occasions I well remember the participants were Thomas Holt Ollive, Alfred Herbert Parry, Wilfred Trubshaw, Will Evans (chemist) and myself. Those were the days! A long experience of the polling stations served to convince me that the temperament of the individual is materially affected by occupation and environment. By way of illustration I found the average miner voter dour and unresponsive, while his surface-working brother — the brickmaker for instance — was a more animated proposition.

His sense of humour again gets the better of him when he describes acting as an elections teller.

Years ago I was presiding at an important Buckley Polling Station. One cheery voter carrying a euphonium and obviously en route to band practice having recorded his vote said 'Shall I give yer a chune, mister?' I politely, but firmly declined the offer, whereupon he left the station, but compromised by playing 'The Last Rose of Summer' on the mat outside.

Again, he refers to a town that raised a fund to buy a hearse. The dance that contributed to the fund was named the dance of death. He also recalls the Whit Monday celebrations

In the days of my youth the county town donned festival garb on Whit Monday. High street was crowded from end to end with an alluring array of booths and stalls containing ginger bread to 'Jack-in-the-box' and shooting galleries. The Friendly Societies celebrated their anniversaries. They were the Foresters with headquarters at the Black Lion Hotel, the Star Club, the Royal Oak, and the Oddfellows (Lower Vaults) Headed by a brass band the members walked in procession to the Parish Church for service and afterwards repaired to their respective headquarters for dinner.

In the evening, dancing took place on the Bailey Hill, music being supplied by a band conducted by Mr Luther Jones, a noted cornetist. My aesthetic soul revolted against the rough wooden boards which constituted the band stand and that the musicians were regaled with beer! The only musician I remember at the moment apart from the conductor was 'Sam the Mangle'! Owing to drastic legislation the Friendly Societies were dissolved, the survivor for a brief period being the Royal Oak Club. The members continued their anniversary, including church service and dinner but excluding the band.

David Rutter Thomas had a pride in the Mold Cosmopolitan Society:

I am obsessed with a desire not to conclude my causerie without including a reference to the Mold Cosmopolitan Society of which I was privileged to be one of the original members. It was founded in 1891 and our hopes that it would attain its jubilee were not destined to be realized. Its founder was Mr E. P. Edwards, M.R.C.V.S., a native of Mold who fresh from college experiences in Edinburgh, framed its constitution which included meetings in camera, the exclusion of the eternal feminine and the Press and voting for membership by ballot. But Mold was not the Scottish capital and in course of time these restrictions were cancelled. During its long and not unchequered career the society was regarded as an important factor in the cultural life of the district. I have only space to refer to one memorable incident which serves to lend truth to the adage 'times change and we change with them.'

At a weekly meeting held 25 years ago (about 1926) an address was given by a member of the Liverpool Fabian Society who in unmeasured terms indicted the Royal Family and monarchial system.

In the discussion which followed Mr W. B. Rowdon, a resident much respected for his intellectual attainments stated he was grieved and shocked to hear the views expressed by the speaker especially with regard to the Royal Family. Mr Lecturer in no way abashed, rejoined that he was glad to hear Mr Rowdon was grieved and shocked as that was what he had come to Mold for Later the Society passed a vote of censure on the committee for having included a Fabian lecture in the syllabus.

A staunch friend and supported of the Society was Mr Peter E. Roberts of Bromfield Hall who for some time occupied the dual position of President and chairman of committee in presenting to his native town the handsome municipal buildings in Earl Road the donor stipulated that one room known as the 'lecture room' should be reserved for the exclusive use of the Cosmopolitan Society.

Described as the Mold Cosmopolitan Society Literary, Scientific and

SYLLABUS OF SESSION, 1909—10.

Date.	Subject.	Name.
1909.		
Oct. 5	Business Meeting	
,, 19	Robert Owen : Dreamer and Reformer	T. Artemus Jones, (Barrister-at-Law)
,, 26	Social Evening.	
Nov. 2	Dramatic Recital	Miss Daisy Halling (Manchester)
,, 9	Dramatic Recital:—"An hour with Shakespeare "	D. E. Oliver (Chester)
,, 16	The Moon (illustrated)	Geo. A. Parry, C.C.
,, 23	Emerson...	J. Watson
,, 30	An Englishman in New Zealand,— with notes on a journey round the World	F. G. Skempton (Chester)
Dec. 7	Debate—"Married v. Single " ...	Miss M. Thomas Miss E. M. West
,, 14	Is Unemployment Remediable? ...	John Edwards (Liverpool Fabian Society)
,, 21	What we can do with our leisure time	Mrs. Yates, Cilcen Hall
,, 27	Boxing Night Social.	
1910.		
Jan. 4	Paper	T. Alyn Jones
,, 11	Inter-Debate with Buckley Cosmopolitan Society—"Does State Legislation Promote Temperance?" ...	Aff.: Mold Society Neg.: Buckley.
,, 18	Scenery, and the causes to which it is due (illustrated)	J. E. Parry, B.A.
,, 25	Some Dreams in Literature	W. J. Roberts, B.A.
Feb. 1	Address	T. Dudley Morgan
,, 8	Debate—"Ought the State to provide Religious Education ?"	Oscar Jones W. Ll. Thomas
,, 15	Motor training, or Education through activity	Percy Wood
(Tu.) 24	Inter-Debate with Denbigh Literary Society—" Conscription "	For—Denbigh Society Against—Mold Society
Mar. 1	Jesters—Ancient and Modern... ...	J. R. Ll. Hughes
(Tu.) 10	The Wales of the English Poets ...	T. Gwynn Jones, Carnarvon
,, 15	Debate—" Is municipal trading to the advantage of the community?" ...	Aff.: Frank Davies Neg.: Fred A. Roberts
,, 22	Social.	
,, 29	Business Meeting.	

Mold Cosmopolitan Society programme, 1909–10 [FRO D/DM/122/1

Social — 'A Society formed for the discussion of Literary, Scientific and Social Subjects upon a common platform of human brotherhood' it was established in 1891. There were clearly defined rules and over 160 members there were in 1906. Speakers and subjects were very wide ranging and designed to stimulate.

They had a Fabian whose topic was 'Is unemployment remediable?' This caused a furore among the Tory members but another Fabian came six years later. Other subjects included:

'The Petty Annoyances and Worries of Life'
'Marriage customs'
'The petty annoyances and worries of life'
'National Awareness in Europe during the 19th Century'
'Borderland of Insanity'
'Jesters ancient and modern'
'Is municipal trading to the advantage of the community'
'Robert Owen Dreamer and Reformer'
'Scenery and the causes to which it is due gases.'
'Nature and Properties of a Gas Flame'
'British Government Funds'
'Vaccination'

The society met once a week on a Tuesday from October to March, with a committee of seven men and four women. It is easy to understand how David Rutter Thomas found such an intellectual stimulus from this. The advent of radio and the moving pictures (which came to Mold in 1913) did not sound its death knell, but the Second World War did.

His court memories recall another such as munition manufacture for the First World War and W. E. Gladstone. He tells us ...

William Ewart Gladstone was at the zenith of his fame when to the surprise of Bench, Police and officials he entered the Court House at Hawarden while business was in progress. The call of the eminent visitor was explained by the fact that the list of business included a case where a farmer on the Hawarden Estate had been assaulted by gypsies.

He occupied a seat in my vicinity and I observed his penetrating dark eyes, a feature I had not noticed in any pictorial representation of the great statesman.

During the period of the Irish Home Rule troubles Hawarden Castle was guarded night and day by Police officers. Subsequently the cost incurred by this protection was the subject of protest by the Police Authority, which was humorously referred to by *Punch* as 'the Skinflintshire Constabulary'!

In preparation for the National Eisteddfod in Mold in 1873 the Executive Committee decided to appeal to Mr Gladstone to preside at one of their meetings. A deputation was appointed to attend a Hawarden Castle to present a personal appeal. Mr Gladstone agreed on condition that he was enabled to reach the House of Commons the same day in time for an important Home Rule debate. It is interesting to see in the final accounts for the Eisteddfod which show a profit of over seven hundred pounds an item of expenditure for Mr Gladstone's train of Ten pounds. The deputation gave the required assurance and a special train was chartered. During this period Hawarden was the 'Mecca' of Gladstone 'fans' — especially from Lancashire.

On one occasion a huge train-load of visitors had arrived and were assembled outside the Glynne Arms Hotel, opposite the main entrance to the Castle grounds. The veteran statesman appeared through the door and an indiscreet admirer — seeking notoriety among his fellow excursionists — approached the G.O.M. [Grand Old Man] with extended hand and a cordial 'How are you Mr Gladstone?' 'I don't know you, sir,' responded Mr Gladstone, eyeing the stranger with disfavour. An incident which served to show that if the great man did not resent the role of national idol he had no room for presumption.

Mr and Mrs Gladstone were frequent visitors to Mold, traveling in an old-time and comfortable 'Victoria'. They visited the residence in Gladstone-street occupied by P.C. and Mrs Pearson, the latter having been a valued member of the Hawarden Castle ménage. A collateral attraction was tea including 'Mitcham House' light cakes, a delicacy much enjoyed by the distinguished guests.

Farewell dinner for Rutter Thomas. John Cwyfan Hughes has his back to the mirror and in front of him, to his right, are Cyril Jones (Wrexham) and Kerfoot Roberts (Holywell) and, to his left, Rutter Thomas.

But we shall not think of Rutter Thomas as on organizer only. He was more. This man of small stature in the 1909 production by the Mold Amateur Operatic and Dramatic Society of *HMS Pinafore* played the part with his baritone voice of Sir Joseph Porter. He sang the immortal lines of W. S. Gilbert:

> When I was a lad I served a term
> As office boy to an Attorneys firm
> I cleaned the windows and I swept the floor
> And I polished the handle of the big front door
> I polished of the handle so carefully
> That now I am the ruler of the Queen's Navy.
>
> As office boy I made such a mark
> That they gave me the post of a junior clerk
> I served the writs with a smile so bland
> And I copied all the letters in a big round hand
> I copied all the letters in a hand so free
> That now I am the ruler of the Queen's Navy.

Perhaps the last line of each verse should be changed to be his epitaph — 'That I was indispensable to my community'.

The *Chester Chronicle* reported his retirement and, after seventy of his seventy-two years service, Cwyfan Hughes, (the Keene & Kelly senior partner) decided that David Rutter Thomas was so special he would organize a dinner for him at the Dolphin Hotel.

All the real great and the good of the Chester and north Wales legal profession were there and Edward Jones, later a judge, was the guest speaker. He was a Welsh speaking teetotaler who could get high on a pint of orange squash ('Jungle Juice' as he called it).

The official photograph of the dinner shows them all clustered around and in the middle a little man completely bewildered by the event. Alongside him are Kerfoot Roberts and Cyril Jones the criminal advocacy giants of the time. Hugh Gough is almost obscured on the right of the back row.

When he died in his ninety-first year, the vicar of Mold, Canon John Davies, the father of the present Bishop, drove back 250 miles from Scotland where he was on holiday. An area meeting of bell ringers rang a muffled peal and two former curates assisted with an 11a.m. requiem service and another at 2p.m. Anybody who was anybody joined the High Sheriff, the Chief Constable and civic leaders at the church. So Mold said farewell to a most remarkable man.

But where did all this happen? For the last fifty years the Practice has been at The Limes (called after the trees) located at the top of the High Street

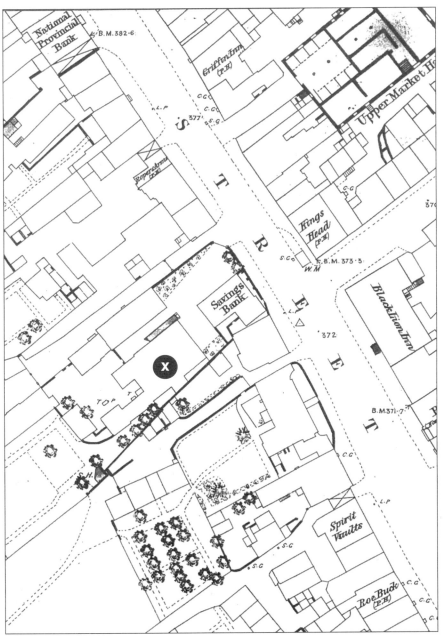

Ordnance Survey map of Mold, 1871. The Mansion House
premises are shown with an 'X'
[FRO 13/8]

Above: Exterior view of the office, front and side
Below: Exterior view of the office rear

(a former dame school). Before then, for approximately ten years, it was at Dyffryn House in Wrexham Street. But before that it was for about one 150 years located in the same building, originally a mansion house located off the High Street. Earl Road did not exist in any form until the twentieth century.

This was a very desirable property built around the end of the eighteenth century. There was a turning space for carriages in front and after a piece of land was sold to build the Savings Bank, there was still a major drive coming in off High Street. A separate block of stable buildings was located to the right of the mansion house as you look from the High Street in the middle of what is now Earl Road.

Originally the Practice occupied only a small part, but in the hey-day of Alfred Thomas Keene and Thomas Thelwell Kelly, it occupied the whole building. The *Chester Chronicle* obituary of Kelly tells us that in the 1870s, he and Keene were working at 'high pressure' and their clerks hardly knew what it was to get off until the small hours of the morning.

If you go into Earl Road you can see the first and second floor as they were. The ground floor was converted into shops in the 1960s and destroyed the Georgian façade. It is a listed building with a Georgian classical staircase between the first and second floors and what heavenly sash windows. It is off course the side of the building that fronts Earl Road.

The layout of the first floor is particularly interesting as it shows an early office layout. Entry was from the yard where the butcher's shop is now and was upstairs direct to the first floor.

Bob Roberts' daughter told me of visiting the office in 1934. On the first floor were the solicitors' offices — one with R. S. Kelly on the door and the other had Colonel Keene still on the door (even though he had been dead for thirteen years). There were files on the floor all over the place but 'Rutter Thomas knew where everything was'. This was the building whose occupants dominated the town for so many years.

Chapter 12
Keene — the Next Generation

All parents like to consider they have made a major contribution to the development of their children and I leave you, the reader, to decide for yourselves with the Keene family. They are undoubtedly multi-talented as history has shown. Henry commends Alfred for his extra commitment to his children.

Let us start with Alfred and Mary's eldest child, Benedicta Jane Keene. She had the benefit of a full education as has been shown. She completed her working life as some form of matron in a school for clergymen's daughters in Bristol. She was very round and jolly as the memories of her are recalled by the next generation. In the archives in Hawarden there is a photographs of a ladies cricket team at Mold during the period 1888–94. Alfred's grand-daughter believes that she is third from the right on the back row with her sister Frances on her left. From Alfred through to the grandchildren, this was a family absorbed by cricket as will be seen. The photograph is from the Rhual collection and the Keenes and the Phillips were known to be two very friendly families. Benedicta, born in April 1866, died in May 1929.

Mold Ladies Cricket Team, 1888–94

George Apthorpe Keene was the eldest son, born in April 1867, while the family was at Llanerch, Mold. The Apthorpe name, as we have seen, came from Alfred's mother's side. He went to King William's College on the Isle of Man with his brother, entering the school in April 1879. He was in Davidson House and left King William's College at Christmas 1883.

He then went to a recognised school of engineering to obtain what were paper qualifications and was then apprenticed to Sandycroft Engineering for three years. This firm operated Sandycroft Foundry and the proprietors were two brothers called Taylor. The apprentice received three shillings per week in the first year, four shillings in the second and five

Four Keene sons: (L–R) Bill (William), George, Horace and Tony

shillings in the third. A premium of £150 was paid. We have a delightful insight to George and Alfred from a letter that Alfred wrote to Taylor on 31st December, 1885.

I certainly was under the impression that you were prepared to take my son for three years on account of his having already trained for two years at a recognised School of Engineering but that, otherwise, the terms were to be the same as Acton.

However, as you think otherwise, I must be prepared to pay the premium you name £150.00 for the three years. But no ready money is now very available. I should like to pay the £50 paying £100 on signing if this is agreed. I would endeavour to arrange his lodgings and go at once on trial.

My doubt is as to his health. He feels the cold and I am a little afraid of the sudden changes from the works to the outside area. However, one can but try — I suppose he will only be doing what others do.

I remain yours
A. T. Keene

George was to follow the trade or business of mechanical engineer and manufacturer of engineering and machinery. In spite of Alfred's anxiety, he completed his apprenticeship and served all over the world, but some of George's postings according to H. G. Keene (the Younger) could not have been in worse parts of the world for climate. In 1900 he was an Assistant

Mining Engineer in Krugersdorp in the Transvaal.

He married Violet Evelyn Elkington, the daughter of Howard Elkington tenant of Leeswood Hall for a time. They had a son, Richard, and a daughter, Joan. He served in India (inevitable for a Keene) and Italy as well as South Africa before returning to Mold to live in retirement at Dolfechlas Isaf, Rhydymwyn (the only one of the sons to return), where he died in 1931. He was probably the most like his father, coming through as a very nice gentleman.

Tony never really left Mold and his story is told in chapter 14.

Charles William Keene was a real contrast. He went to school in Berkhampstead but appears to have clashed with his father. I suspect it was the impetuousness of youth but, at 17, he ran away from home to join the Sherwood Foresters. There was a partial reconciliation with his father and a commission was purchased the Royal Welsh Fusiliers by a combination of father's money and a legacy of £50 received by Willie Keene. This was in 1892; the dress uniform alone cost £64 5s. 3d.

He found his way to India and was stationed in the North West Frontier region. I always knew that bridge was a more dangerous game than chess — during a game, Willie Keene was 'dummy' and went out for some fresh air and was shot by a renegade sepoy sniper. The bullet went very close to the heart and he only just survived. He could no longer serve in that climate and returned home to Britain, continuing his army service at a desk.

He caused a real surprise on 20th September 1916 by marrying Winifred Turnbull of Penarth whose father was a shipowner. Charles was aged 45 and she was 18, and working as a nurse. There were three children of this union — a son, Charles Michael Keene, who responded to the lure of India so often seen in his family by spending his working life in post-Independence India managing tea, coffee and rubber plantations, and two daughters, Mary and Cynthia. Winifred Keene was a Catholic and how Alfred would have responded I do not know.

Cynthia was one of only a few Keene women to marry — but Charles's son Michael had four daughters who all married.

Michael's widow and Cynthia (whose talents are as an artist), have been particularly helpful in my research for this book but I could trace no more. Charles William Keene died in Torquay in 1950, described as a retired Lieutenant Colonel.

Frances Keene was clearly a character and was the last of the children to die, in 1962. We know very little about her. To Willie's children she was very affectionately known as 'Auntie Froggy'. She never married.

Alfred Horace Keene was clearly the most flamboyant of the brothers, but we know less about him than we would like. He was born in 1876 and after school followed his brother George to Sandycroft Foundry in 1893. He was to have a fifty-three hour week and the same premium of £150 was to be paid.

Taylor tells Alfred:

> I have omitted to say that I feel sure two years in our works would be a valuable preparation for him before entering exclusively upon electrical engineering as our work though confined entirely to mining machinery is of a very varied character.

He went out to the diamond mines of Kimberly in South Africa and made his fortune. We see him next visiting Willie and his family when he had a smart car and a chauffeur who played cricket with Willie's children. He has clearly married earlier than usual for the male Keene's as his son Ralph was born in 1902.

Horace is doing well and his son, Ralph Horace Percy Keene, followed his grandfather to Marlborough, entering in September 1916. During his time there, his home address was his grandmother's home in Mold as his father was clearly working overseas. He left in July 1920. He demonstrates the diversity of this multi-talented family. He went into film production and is credited with being the first to photograph a flower opening. He married twice, having a daughter by his first marriage and a son by his second: the latter is believed to have gone into television production.

Ralph was a close friend of Laurie Lee and was killed in a shooting accident near Ipswich in 1960.

Leticia Rose Apthorne Keene was born in 1881 and was the youngest child. She eventually went to British Columbia, Canada, to be near other members of the family and died there unmarried. In years gone by, it was believed her estate should have returned to Britain but it did not and the possibility of inheritance has probably been abandoned.

Nephews and nieces are not, strictly speaking, descendants, but Alfred had both that are of a little more than passing interest. His brother is dealt with extensively elsewhere. He married twice having seventeen children of whom fourteen survived to maturity. All were born in India and their careers, so far as the boys were concerned, kept them there.

Henry George Harris Keene was the apple of his father's eye, joining the Government of India Financial Department in 1874 — a lawyer recognising it is the accountants that make money. He rose to be Assistant Controller-General, Burma. His brother, Alfred was an action man when compared with his uncle. He served in the Afghan War and was on the march to Kandahar and in the Burma Expedition. He was mentioned in dispatches twice and also got the D.S.O. He married twice in India.

Marie who, after marriage in India to a retired colonel, was accidentally drowned at Aberdyfi at the early age of twenty-six, leaving three children.

Dorothea, also married, was killed by a fall from a bicycle at the age of thirty-four.

The most interesting is Helen Alicia Des Valles Keene born in 1870. She is described in one of her father's letters to his brother Alfred as 'our musical member' who returns home after a long visit to Manchester. She is known as Alice and does appear both gifted and adventurous: it appears she remained single and pursued a career as a musical performer. She finds herself in St Petersburg during the Russian Revolution in what would have been a very daunting prospect for any other single lady. From a letter sent home it is to her an adventure and not an anxiety as she writes:

> I tried at several places but was always turned back. At last my driver said it would be best to get across on foot and he seemed very frightened. I got rid of him and got another one who said it would be quite safe much further down and there I found it quite deserted and got home safely, but to find the people putting up a barricade right across our street. They, soon after, put out all the street lamps and they very coolly and methodically without the least excitement or noise removed our gates which are of iron and all other gates in the street, wooden and iron and the whole length of the street is barricaded being about one hundred yards from the other, but so far all is perfectly safe and there are two or three men at each barricade on watch. One hears constant firing in the distance. We have no newspapers so one only has rumour to rely upon as to what is going on and the only papers to be had are Petersburg ones but they are a day old. They say the Governor made the soldiers all renew oath of allegiance and any that showed reluctance to do so were not pressed but calmly set aside and kept in barracks so that they knew those who were ordered to shoot would do so. Every shop is shut of course. This morning they were opened the food ones at least, for a few hours, so we are not starving. You cannot imagine how wonderfully and quiet and well conducted these crowds are and no drunkenness or disorderly behaviour, in fact, were it not for the firing to be heard every now and then, I couldn't believe this afternoon that a revolution was going on. There would be no bloodshed either, if the soldiers did not fire, and there certainly will be no pillaging or burning on the part of the Revolutionaries.
>
> Will write soon again.

Your ever loving daughter
    Alice.

Our final character is not strictly a Keene at all. She is Alfred's niece Violet Bradburne, the daughter of Mary Keene's brother William. She had all the resource and drive we have come to expect from the Bradburnes. Whether she was Alfred's god-daughter, I do not know, but he could not do enough for her. Her father was in banking and either he lost some of his money or Violet needed a challenge to earn her own living and, of course, who else would she turn to for legal advice but dear Uncle Alfred? She was determined to support herself.

Her first venture was to run a coffee shop in Church Stretton, perhaps appropriate for someone in her position, but that clearly was dull and unrewarding to the Bradburne spirit. So she sets up the Shropshire Ham and Bacon Company and we have their brochure: 'Their pigs reared at a Country Farm twelve miles from the nearest town and fed on vegetable food only including Milk Potatoes and Corn — and other pigs according to

Violet Bradburne's publicity leaflet [FRO]

Better than . .
. . the Best.

From the Farm
to the Table.

TRADE MARK.

TRADE MARK.

THE alarming increase in the number of cases of Cancer is attributed by some medical men to the large consumption of unwholesome pork, ham, and bacon, obtained from improperly fed pigs. These animals are generally reared near large towns, upon offal, dead horses, &c., their flesh, under such circumstances, often proving actually poisonous.

To insure the PUREST and HIGHEST-CLASS of human food from the pig is the object of

. The Shropshire .

Ham and Bacon Company,

who direct attention to their brands of

Ham, Bacon, Fresh Pork, Brawn, Sausages, . . and Lard. . .

Their Pigs, reared at a COUNTRY FARM, twelve miles from the nearest Town, are fed on Vegetable Food ONLY, including MILK, POTATOES, and CORN.

some medical man if fed near large towns upon offal, dead horses etc often prove actually poisonous with an alarming increase in the number of cases of cancer.' Her products are:

Better than the Best
From the Farm to the Table

We are told of her 100 year old recipes for Watling ham and Watling bacon, entirely different to the ordinary chemically cured trade ham. 'The secret of the recipe is their number and combination and its success their daily and careful application'
She was not bashful at all in her publicity.

N.B. The Company do not sell their Hams and Bacon through grocers etc as exposure to dust, gas fumes and the heat of oily shops would utterly spoil their subtle flavour. The expense of middle men being thus avoided the Company are enabled to send direct from their Farm to the consumer high class Ham and Bacon. Carriage Paid to any railway station in England.

The Company decline to sell the heavy newly cured 'green' bacon usually offered so cheaply but which in reality is most wasteful for the buyer.

The Watling Bacon Recipe far excels the usual salt soaked Bacon sold to the public. On effect of this superior curing is to make the lean of the Hams and Bacon particularly digestible.

Alfred fortunately was not asked to advise on the claims made on the form of the brochure, but to prepare an agreement for her use to tie farmers to sell her all their production. She could not believe how little Alfred charged for what would have been unique documents, but we can! She at the beginning of 1899 is already having difficulty fulfilling orders. The picture that we have of Vi Bradburne is confirmed by her Keene cousins: she was something special.

Chapter 13
In Retrospect

I recognise that hindsight is both an advantage and a disadvantage for the biographer. From an event or a series of events, or from a contemporary comment, he will draw conclusions and advance detailed and positive views. He will feel that his research places him on intimate terms with his subjects. Conscious of all those dangers I still feel that some attempt should be made to evaluate these two men, Thomas Thelwell Kelly and Alfred Thomas Keene — two who were so very different but are seen as synonymous with each other.

Tom Kelly was certainly a giant of a man within the community. As I learnt more I could not understand why he had never been knighted. His record of public service is second to none. He moved comfortably in the most influential circles. He was a known Conservative who were in power at Westminster for most of the 1890s. Then as I got to know him more and more, the overwhelming quality he possessed was the common touch. This put him into direct communication with everyone in the community. He would not have been easy as Sir Thomas. He knew he would be unhappy with this. Sometimes knighthoods are conferred to gratify the wife. Margaret Kelly would have been completely content with Tom's decision whatever it was. She had her family and perhaps her upbringing where English honours were not encouraged. I do not know that any offer was ever made, but I am sure it would have been refused.

The contrast in the men is shown by the friends they made in Mold. Tom Kelly was great-friends with John Scott Bankes, going back to the days when they were both privates in the Volunteers. Alfred Keene never seems to be anywhere around when Bankes was present: Bankes is on record, when appointed sheriff in 1870 with Tom Kelly as his under-sheriff, as saying he did not believe in compulsory education. That would not have been acceptable at all to Mary and Alfred Keene. The relationship with the Duke of Westminster shows Kelly's magnetic personality. Time and again Kelly crosses the boundary between church and chapel, Conservative and Liberal, English and Welsh speakers.

The Keene's were close friends, on the other hand, with the Phillips of Rhual whose profile in the community was much lower. This relationship clearly started when the Keene's were living at Llanerch or Bellan within the Phillips sphere of influence. Alfred became a governor of Gwernaffield school. The day book tells us Mary Keene was taken round the school by Captain Phillips on 14th March 1873, and in October 1877 Mary Keene and Benedicta were present at the Sunday School treat held in the schoolroom. More significantly Mary Keene in April 1873 is a performer in a concert to raise funds for the school. She sings two songs 'The Foresaken' and 'Esmerelda'.

There were daughters of the same age which would have cemented the relationship. They were not out in society very often but it was their choice. Their social life revolved around the parish church. There is a record of their attending a ball at Llwynegrin given the Postmaster-General, Henry Raikes, M.P. But they were clearly chaperoning their daughter Frances.

When it was proposed that a reredos be installed in the church in memory of Mrs Phillips. Tom Kelly was, with Alfred Keene, to support the project.

Alfred Keene's particular friend was Henry Lloyd Jones who was a ladies outfitter whose shop was on the Cross. He, incidentally, on his death, left twice as much as Alfred. On the day of his death, Alfred had signed a letter of condolence to Mrs Jones and was about to go to his funeral.

The contrast in their investments is most marked: Alfred went for railway shares — then a safe investment — whilst mining, with its risks, attracted Tom Kelly.

Alfred Keene, though a Conservative, had a very low political profile. Tom Kelly was the parliamentary agent in the 1874 General Election and served local candidates as well but was, essentially, a public servant.

Tom Kelly was under-sheriff for most of the period from 1863 until his death, but when there was a need for the Sheriffs' Court to sit to assess damages for breach of promise or other shrieval functions it was Alfred Keene who sat as a deputy more often than not, an example of this occurred in October 1895. It was a claim for damages for slander (the spoken word). A man who had courted a Leeswood girl — they fell out and he called her for everything under the sun. The jury assessed the damages at £50 after directions from Keene. The Practice clearly regarded him as more judicial.

Public appointments abounded. They each had responsibility for two Petty Sessional Divisions as Justices Clerk. Kelly succeeded Arthur Troughton Roberts as Clerk to the Income Tax Commissioners and held the post for a little while. He was Secretary of the Trustees Savings and legal advisor for many years after he ceased to be secretary.

He was under-sheriff for over forty years, but this was an appointment directly under the control of the incoming sheriff. As Deputy Clerk of the Peace, he administered the carrying out of justice but there were prior to 1889 additional civil responsibilities. He was clerk to the lord lieutenant, whose powers were more active than purely advisory at that time. He became clerk of the peace and clerk to the newly erected County Council for the last twelve years of his life.

Keene occupied three additional posts Vestry Clerk, Clerk to the Parish Council and Clerk to the Highway Board. They both served at various times on local school managers and other authorities. They created a reputation for integrity and honesty and did so much to restore the jaded reputation of the Victorian solicitor.

The personality of Tom Kelly radiated out of him. He could talk to anyone and was universally popular. This is illustrated by the obituary in the *Chronicle*.

> Mr Kelly must have realized himself that there existed something like a bond of affection between him and his colleagues in public life for at a public dinner a year or so ago when his health was proposed by one of the members of the County Council he rose to respond but so intense was the emotions that came over him that he burst into tears and was unable to proceed with his speech.

I have scoured the local papers for a report of this dinner in the three years before his death without success. I therefore conclude that this incident was well known to the press but such was their affection and respect for him they would not publish the story in his lifetime and embarrass him. Can you imagine today's press acting in this way?

But publication after his death, they recognised, increased his credibility and standing. Tom Kelly's 'courtesy, tact and impartiality were also conspicuous characteristics of his public life and won him universal respect'. He had a host of friends by whom he was held in the highest esteem for his geniality kindliness of heart and ready disposition to do anyone a good turn.

The *North Wales Guardian* says that Kelly's death 'removed from the scene of his labours one of the most prominent figures in the history of the last three decades of the county of Flint. An astute lawyer of infinite tact and a born organiser he was withal of a sympathetic and tender-hearted nature and he leaves behind him a reputation beyond reproach'.

The *Chester Chronicle* says 'His courtesy, tact and impartiality were also conspicuous characteristics of his public life and won him universal respect'. The city edition says,

> Few of those best acquainted with the deceased gentleman would claim that he was endowed with ability or intellectual gifts to an extraordinary degree, rather was he the possessor of infinite and it was undoubtedly this feature added to a capacity for taking pains and business probity and uprightness of the highest order that combined to raise him to the exalted positions which he adorned.

The word 'tact' as used 100 years ago has not the same meaning now. To say someone is tactful today is often saying they are indecisive. We have seen that Kelly was the opposite and grasped the nettle where appropriate — the Bailey Hill and the National Eisteddfod are examples of this. It signifies his skill at inter-personal relations — hence my comments on the Mold riots.

The city edition again says,

It is easily conceived that a man so thoroughly engrossed in business affairs as was Mr Kelly would be afforded few opportunities of participating in the pleasures of social life but when able temporarily to cast aside the official and professional shackles of the daily round he was ever a welcome and entertaining guest. He was of Hibernian Origin and to this fact may probably be traced two of the most charming traits of his character with a keen sense of humour and a highly sympathetic nature. Of the former characteristic it may be said that as a smoke room raconteur or in the role of after dinner speaker he was found in his happiest vein. The outcome of the second trait we have indicated an unbounded liberality, a tale of sorrow always affected him deeply, and his apparently stern and impassive exterior was not infrequently unmasked by emotion at a recital of the misfortunes of others or the loss by death of a beloved friend.

The *County Herald* tells us:

a merrier man never breathed. He had a happy and jovial manner even in the midst of the most formal business and it was always a pleasure to observe his great good humour and buoyancy of spirits which he was in the Prime of life. He had the rare gift of reading the dispositions and characters of those with which he came in contact and what was more he was not often wrong in his surmises and estimations concerning others.

Was ever regarded as a man who was broad in his views and who was not captured with the fleeting fashions and opinions of the hour.

He was very much a self-made man but he had admittance to most of the leading county houses.

The provision of articles to enable him to qualify as a solicitor was a great kindness from Arthur Troughton Roberts but he took payment by holding onto the office of Clerk to the Peace until 1888.

The *Wrexham Advertiser* tells us:

The Justices of the County in the meantime did all their power to force Mr Roberts to retire from the position but he was too discreet to be disturbed and we remember that in 1870 and 1871 the Justices appointed a committee to report as to how the several official performed their duty. We were present when Colonel Davies-Cooke read the report which stated that the duties of the Clerk to the Peace were done — though most efficiently by the deputy. It was in vain though to spread the net in the sight of the bird.

It was not till the year 1888 that Mr Roberts resigned the office of the Clerk of the Peace and then it was that Mr Kelly was formally appointed to perform duties which he had already performed for a quarter of a century or so.

He had started his Mold career in lodgings in Wrexham Street and spent over thirty-five years at Bryn Coch Hall.

The attack of typhoid in April 1885 left its mark and the ebullient leader of the community ceased to exist. It is not surprising to learn that, by going out too soon after his attack, he became ill and undermining his constitution further. But he did adapt to the new situation as we have seen from his performance as Clerk of the Council.

The city edition of the *Chronicle* tells us that, after the return home from London on 15th April 1885,

> … business knew him no more until late in the following autumn when he re-appeared in his accustomed walks of life a changed personality and aged almost beyond recognition. The interval had been followed by visits during tardy convalescence to Capel Curig, Rhyl and Buxton. From that period Mr Kelly never regained his former vigour and as time advanced friends and relatives watched with anxious forebodings what was unmistakably a very gradual breaking up of the constitution.

But that does not allow for his indomitable spirit. He achieved much in the last sixteen years of his life and this was due to the complete support freely given of Alfred Keene who did the Parliamentary Work for the County Council and Tom Ollive the administrative work. Alfred Keene understood loyalty.

Thomas Thelwell Kelly was last in the office about two weeks after the 1900 General Election and died at his home on Saturday the 26th January, 1901 at 1.45p.m. This was within hours of Alfred Keene as deputy sheriff appearing on the balcony of the Assembly Hall with the high sheriff to proclaim the new King Edward VII. When his death was imminent, H. G. Roberts, who had been articled to him and then practised on his own, paid tribute to him at a meeting of the Savings Bank directors and again in court,

> Mr Kelly had been a most able public official and had on all occasions placed to the full extent his meritorious talents at the service of the Council and of the respective public bodies with which he had been connected. The members of his profession in particular felt that they had lost their local leader. He left a noble example of one who was industrious when in health and patient when in sickness. That example they should always endeavour to follow.

The funeral was a very memorable occasion. The weather was terrible.

Tom Kelly's funeral

Early on the day snow started to fall and continued to do so until noon. After stopping for an hour or two the conditions became wintry and in the afternoon there was a much heavier snowfall. This did not deter many from attending.

The procession left Bryn Coch at 2 o'clock after a short service with the hearse escorted by a body of the Flintshire Constabulary. Eight police officers acted as bearers. At Penyffordd (which is where Hendy Road and Bryn Coch Lane meet Ruthin Road) the full procession formed with the vehicular procession from Bryn Coch being joined by county councillors, justices, county officials, Kelly & Keene's clerks and representatives of other public bodies and the general public. The procession came down New Street and then up High Street. Blinds on all private houses and business's were drawn the *County Herald* and the *Chronicle* tell us that 'the streets were lined with spectators hats doffed and many visibly affected.'

After the full choral service the procession resumed down High Street and Wrexham Street to the cemetery and the *Flintshire Observer* tells us 'all the business establishments and private houses en route displayed signs of mourning.'

Tom Kelly was buried with his son Arthur in a double grave close to the cemetery car park where he was later joined by his son Cecil and his wife Margaret. There are many very imposing monuments in Mold cemetery but not for Tom Kelly. A stone cross lies on his grave, slightly elevated at the head, with a very simple epitaph, as he would have wanted.

With Christ which is far better

But where would Tom Kelly have been without Alfred Keene? We have already learnt how a sick man was able to be such a dominating clerk to the county council for twelve years.

Alfred Keene did not have the person-to-person qualities of Tom Kelly but was almost shy and diffident. When the *Chester Chronicle* described him 'as one of the most systematic and methodical solicitors, extant, punctual to his business and in whatever was entrusted to him he gained the respect of all with whom he came in contact, ' we know what they mean. He was an erudite scholar especially in historical and antiquarian lore and further was looked upon as a sound conveyancer. In private life, the contrast with Kelly becomes apparent.

The *Wrexham Advertiser* tells us:

> Though the duties of his several offices were punctiliously performed it was as a Chamber practitioner that that Mr Keene excelled and he invariably won high tributes as a sound conveyancer. Methodical to a degree his sole pleasure outside the pursuit of his profession was bibliophilism and his collection of ancient volumes and engravings must by this time be of considerable value.

The *Chester Courant* said of him

> As a public official Mr Keene was most punctilious in the discharge of his duties but it was as a private practitioner that he was seen to the greatest advantage and he was held in high repute as a conveyancer of rare acumen.
>
> In private life he was unaffected unostentatious and methodical to a degree.
>
> A life of devotion to duty and high principles and one forming a noble example to those who follow. He died as he had lived with pen in hand.

The contrast with Kelly continues to be so evident. He had the qualities Kelly did not. Keene was the lawyer and Kelly the businessman. They were so different but came together like bread and butter.

Keene's relationship with the church was stronger and he clearly was of the 'high church' persuasion. He was always working for the church as vestry clerk, warden or committee member but, as Keene became available, Kelly shed responsibilities. It was the same vicar, the Rev Poole Hughes, who commented on the loss of Kelly on the Sunday from the pulpit who said of Keene on his death in 1904.

> This day week, both at matins and evensong one of the leaders of this congregation was worshipping here with us. His day's work was a long one, and he worked to the end. Now that he is gone, there are many points of view in which we can admire his life. Work was a prominent feature in

his career. His ability in his profession was well known. In his hands the honour of his profession was in safe keeping: his uprightness and probity gave a tone to his calling. As a member of this congregation, what more can I say than repeat his own words to me on a similar occasion to this, 'It is in church we shall miss him most.' I can add nothing to this, it is so absolutely true and complete in itself. No one worked harder or more consistently in his secular vocation, but its claims were not allowed to interfere with his duties as a Christian man. His work raised up no barrier between him and his duty to God.

As an educationist he was a strong advocate of efficiency and secular instruction, but not to the exclusion of religious teaching, and he took a deep and sustained interest in the trend of recent education legislation. I cannot refrain from a brief allusion to his hobby. It was a good and sound one. He was a lover of books; his hours of recreation were largely spent among the goodly folios which stacked his shelves. The old English classics were among his most intimate friends, Boswell and Johnson, Addison and *The Spectator*, Oliver Goldsmith and all that goodly company were a joy to him. In him we part with another of the old school.

As one of the 'Old School' one of the virtues Alfred Keene valued most was loyalty. He was always before Kelly's illness apparently prepared to play second fiddle but as time goes by his influence behind Kelly becomes clear. After his illness he takes upon himself all the extra work and responsibility that was needed — he could not have done this without the strength of their clerks and became more involved in parliamentary work as the county council progresses.

Throughout the whole period of their partnership the word integrity is never far away. There are not any attempts to suggest sharp practice or dubious ways of tackling a problem. A Flint solicitor, T. W. Hughes, said of him 'he had always received great kindness from him and courtesy. He was a man of marked ability whose advice was so sound'.

When the *Wrexham Advertiser* says of Kelly

> When the firm was at the acme of its prosperity its legal successes were not so marked. If he could avoid it Mr Kelly would not go into litigation. He preferred to rely on his management of men and we think he was right especially from his client's point of view, and he thought if an end could be obtained without embarking into great cost it was better to secure it peacefully and if his client was in the wrong it would be cheaper to get out of the difficulty by acknowledging a little wrong than by fighting it out in the law court.

This attitude would be a firm policy of the Practice and so different from the macho approach encouraged by some solicitors nowadays.

But if court action was required Tom Kelly would conduct the case — a matter of presentation but when a Sheriff's Court sat a lawyer was needed and Keene as deputy sat as the tribunal more often than not.

There is plenty of evidence of Alfred Keene's legal skills but he was also a shrewd diplomat. He was the only clerk there ever was to the Mold Highway Board, being appointed at its inception and still being in the post when its responsibilities were transferred to the Holywell R.D.C.

There was an incident in January 1880 when some members were very aggrieved at the decisions taken at the previous monthly meeting and the information that had been given by the chairman to achieve those decisions and using the standing orders relative to their deliberations, they called for a special meeting for the purpose of discussing these. The clerk, on receiving the notice, arranged for the special meeting to be in the morning and the monthly meeting in the afternoon. There was naturally a large attendance. Following the last meeting, the members had received a communication from the Clerk of the Peace, Tom Kelly, that was at variance with the Chairman's (Colonel Davies-Cooke) statement. It said:

> To comprise the several townships in parishes from time to time forming the several highway districts namely 'The Mold Highway District', 'The Holywell Highway District', 'The St Asaph Highway District' and 'The Hawarden and Hope Highway District', and to declare that no separate way-wardens shall in future be elected for such townships, and that the several parishes in which the said townships are comprised shall be subject to the same liabilities in respect of all the highways within them which have hitherto been maintained by such townships separately as is all their several liabilities had attached to the whole of such parishes respectively, and further that a prescribed number of way-wardens shall be elected for each of such parishes as a whole but excluding from the operation of such proposal any portion of any such parishes as do not in compliance with the provisions of The Highway Acts form part of the said highway district.

On receipt of the requisition, Mr Keene said that he had communicated it to the chairman, from whom he had received the following letter:

> I am in receipt of your letter about a special meeting of Highway Board wished for by Mr Elwood and others. I object strongly to any such meeting on the following grounds.
> 1. That it is not imperative on you to call it, the words of the Act being may and not shall; it is therefore optional.
> 2. That the matter for which the special meeting is requested to be called was fully discussed and explained by myself as Chairman at our November meeting, and a resolution was passed approving of the alteration of district, and the consolidation of townships into parishes.

3. That two out of the three members of the Board who have signed the requisition were present and had every opportunity of stating their views.

4. That no Board could carry on their business if under the circumstances above stated any three members could call a special meeting, and try to upset a decision previously arrived at.

5. That the proposal before the Quarter Sessions is one that commends itself to the common sense of all; it will simplify the accounts, largely conduce to economy and efficiency, and there is not the slightest chance of the magistrates at Quarter Sessions taking any other view on the matter, and that therefore the time of the Board would be uselessly wasted, and the proposed meeting would be a great inconvenience to many.

The *Wrexham Advertiser* reported:

Mr Keene on receipt of that letter from the Chairman wrote to Mr Ellwood advising him not to insist on having the meeting called, but the requisitionists insisted and hence the meeting: Mr Ellwood then said:

That although he had seconded the Chairman's proposition at the November meeting, he did not understand its tendency, and when he read the circular of the Clerk of the Peace, he found that he had been misled. He consulted some of his fellow wardens, and they thought it most important that the Court of Quarter Sessions should not be under the impression that they approved the proposal. Therefore they thought the question should be reconsidered, so that the deliberate opinion of the way-wardens might be expressing the Board's approval of the proposal be rescinded.

This was seconded by Mr Hughes, who argued that the 'may' referred to was optional to the way-wardens only, but imperative on the Clerk. The words were these 'An extraordinary meeting may be called at any time on the requisition of three members of the Board, addressed to the Clerk of the Board'. Mr Thompson moved, and Mr Buddicom seconded, the confirmation of the minutes in question. There was a long and warm discussion, which ended in Mr Bowdage proposing, and Mr Darbyshire seconding, that the parishes be the units, and that the rates should be levied on the parishes, but that the number of representatives be the same as the number of townships. On a division this was lost by a great majority, and the resolution of Mr Ellwood carried. The ordinary business was transacted in the afternoon meeting.

The meeting, described as 'stormy', arrived at decisions consistent with established procedure with no resignations and a new policy — a triumph of diplomacy. Once again the ability of Kelly & Keene to avoid conflict of interest is clearly demonstrated in spite of the very wide range of public appointments they held.

In the early 1870s. the *Chronicle* tells us that Tom Kelly and Alfred Keene 'were working at high pressure to get off until the early hours of the morning.'

Kelly, 'along with others, took a foremost part when the living of Mold became vacant in approaching the Lord Bishop of the diocese to allow parishioners a choice in the selection of a Vicar'. They were both real democrats and behind this quotation is the legal knowledge of Keene of how to do it.

With clients like the lords of Mold, the Duke of Westminster and most local landed estates they were recognised as experts on mining law.

Their humanity shone out as the *Advertiser* says of Kelly which was equally true of Keene,

> he never insisted on his pound of flesh and for many years to come his memory will be revered by all whose good fortune it has been to come in contact with him.
>
> With his dependants he was specially indulgent and if possible he never changed a servant or an employee. In short we shall seldom if ever see the like of him again.

This was a Liberal newspaper writing about a known Conservative.

On 26th April 1904, Mary Keene was away in London visiting her daughter. Alfred the punctual man left his home at The Cottage in Hendy Road to walk to the office as had been his usual practice. He arrived at the office in his funeral suit as he was due to go to the funeral of his close friend Henry Lloyd Jones who had died a few days earlier. He signed a letter of condolence to the widow and conferred with his chief clerk, William Bayne. He was then conferring with his partners Tony Keene and Robin Kelly when he changed colour and fell back in his chair and was dead by the time Dr Trubshaw arrived. He was almost 76. The suddenness of his death stunned the town and for the next thirty years, whenever the press referred to him, they reminded the readers of the manner of his death. In 1932, his son George died and the report referred to his father in these terms.

The flag on the Parish Church was immediately lowered to half mast. At these times the Funeral was an Act of remembrance for the men in procession and if the Widow attended she was 'within' ie waiting for the cortege almost to arrive. Not so of Mary Keene because we learn from the *County Herald* specifically 'Mrs Keene and her three daughters attended the funeral service at the Church'.

Alfred had been for Mary everything she hoped. He shared her concern for education and the poor. He had encouraged and was a proud of her participation in the affairs of the town in her own right and she saw the affection in which he was held. The words that the public find difficult to accept together 'an honest lawyer' were so applicable to Alfred Keene.

The interests of the whole town were represented. Besides the Vicar and his curates they were joined by Calvinistic Methodist, Welsh Congregational, Baptist, English Congregational and Methodist Ministers. Magistrates and Members of the County Council, Urban District Council and Mold Parish Council would have been expected together with Police Representatives. There was a profusion of solicitors practicing in the general area. Then there were large representations of educationalists and theologians including C. H. Dodd. Then there was a large representation from the Commercial Sector.

The *County Herald* was prompted to say 'a feature of the funeral that was noticeable was the unusual number of wreaths brought to the graveside personally by various friends of the deceased gentleman.'

It should be stated that the funeral was acknowledged to be one of the most touching and solemn in its character ever seen in Mold and many who assembled to witness the last ceremony were much affected.

I am sure it was the passion and commitment of Alfred and Mary Keene to education that caused such a remarkable non-conformist turnout at the funeral of a High Churchman.

Business in the town was suspended during the procession and service. Alfred was laid to rest in a simple grave just under the wall of the extension of Mold Churchyard. It already contained two sons who had died in infancy and he was later to be joined there by Mary and his son Tony. There is a red marble surround with a cross lying on its back and the inscription is simple 'R. I. P.' There is no extravagant memorial stone. At the memorial service the following Sunday, the Vicar said of Keene's support for 'education' his attendance 'at those meetings was as regular and punctual as it was in this building'.

Alfred Keene had reached the hearts of so many people in the area and this would have surprised such an essentially modest man. I will close by quoting a letter from Tony Keene to his mother enclosing a letter he had received for her. This letter is also set out in full and it is impossible to add to it.

The Office
Saturday

Dear Old Mater

I enclose a letter which was handed by the Chairman of the Parish Council yesterday at the graveside to Rutter Thomas.

It is from one of the Councillors, a working collier, and I think one of the most touching tributes of the universal respect felt for father.

Apl 28/04
Queen St
Leeswood

Dear Friend

I much regret that I cannot possibly attend the funeral of our late highly esteemed friend. We shall sadly miss him, as he was always so courteous and forbearing and he seemed to me to be one of natures gentlemen and were there more of his like the gap that separates and classifies would soon be bridged over. My sympathy is with the family who I am sure will feel a terrible loss.

Yours truly
Thos. Jones

Chapter 14
Colonel Keene, Mold's Forgotten Hero

When Bob Roberts' daughter exchanged words with Robin Kelly on a visit to the office in 1934, she also saw the door to the other partner's room in the office. On the door was clearly painted 'Colonel Keene' although he had been dead since 1921. Why had it been left?

'Colonel Keene' was the second son of Alfred Thomas Keene and his wife Mary and was known in the family as Tony. He was born at Mold on 28th April, 1868. They chose for him and his elder brother George to attend King William's College, Castleton, in the Isle of Man and they started there in April 1879. The choice may seem to be unusual and there is no evidence of any family connection or interest. But a train to Liverpool via Hope Junction would take them to the quayside where in all probability they would be met by a school representative.

He was at King William's until midsummer 1884 when he left at the age of 16. By January 1885 he has passed his preliminary law examination and qualified as a solicitor in 1890 at a young age and was admitted as a solicitor in 1891. He had been articled to his father and stayed with the Practice all his working life. He undoubtedly had a charm that enabled him to handle his father and get whatever he wanted. When you see a letter from London to his father when he was studying for his finals prefaced 'PATER' you know it is a request for money.

The major change in his life took place when he and Robin Kelly joined the Volunteers and were gazetted second lieutenants in 1892. He had a love affair with the Volunteers for almost the next thirty years and treated his involvement not merely as a hobby but as a vocation and was continually seeking experience and more qualifications. He attended camps all over the U.K.

In June 1893, he went to Chelsea to undergo a course of instructions with the Coldstream and Grenadier Guards. In 1896, Alfred complains to his brother about his son's absence from the practice and he has not heard from him. We then learn that Captain Keene (yes, he had promotion), who had undergone two months training course at Hythe, has passed his examinations (musketry) and also obtained extra marks and was placed 16th out of 81. He was also in possession of the following certificates: tactics, organisation and equipment; military law and fortification — Robin Kelly was never more than a 2nd lieutenant for most of his career.

He had also been appointed one of the range officers at Bisley. The *Chester Courant* tells us 'apart from his interest in the Volunteers, and consequently the Territorials, he took a keen interest in Engineering in which he was a skilful mechanic'. He was therefore the third engineer in the family.

The town of Mold was imperial and on the outbreak of the Boer War was very supportive of the position of the Conservative government. When, therefore, it was decided to supplement the regular soldiers who were in South Africa to fight the war, it was natural enough for Keene to volunteer to serve. He was a very highly qualified volunteer and the War Office was delighted to accept his offer.

A company was assembled of officers and men drawn from the 1st, 2nd and 3rd Volunteer Battalions, Royal Welsh Fusiliers as the 1st Volunteer Active Service Company. There were two lieutenants, Bamford and Jones Parry, and the command was given to Captain Thomas Mann Keene. They sailed for South Africa on 11th February 1900 on the *Douane Castle*. The send-off from Mold was memorable and the bands played the usual patriotic songs.

The company was raised from north Wales and Mold wanted to contribute. A fund was raised which resulted in the presentation for a pair of field glasses and a revolver to Captain Keene. His brother officers presented him with a telescope to assist 'in making an inspection of the triumphant entry to Pretoria: that he would have a closer inspection within the walls of that interesting city'. A highly successful smoking concert was held which lasted over four hours to raise funds. Each of the Mold volunteers was given a purse containing a sovereign, tobacco, handkerchiefs, socks, *etc*. Shopkeepers gave them underclothing. After two days further training at Wrexham Barracks, they were ready for South Africa. When they left Mold for Wrexham on the 10.36 train, they were seen off by the local Volunteers Band and the Clarence Band. Tunes included 'Say Au Revoir', 'The absent minded beggar', 'Men of Harlech' and 'The girl I left behind'. Tony's sisters saw him off. Of the116 who left, only 80 returned with him, although some had been invalided home earlier and some remained in South Africa.

Although this was a war of aggression and Britain was attacking a very small nation, support for the war was considerable. Mary Keene (Captain Keene's mother) served on the committee established to look after the dependants of those volunteers.

There were war correspondents serving in the Boer War. Winston Churchill was one. The quickest method of getting news home however was from the men themselves. It was long before the Official Secrets Act and the ease of communication with South Africa itself was not anticipated by the War Office. So when the men wrote home they could send a completely uncensored account of what they were doing. Captain Keene was able to write home and request his letters be given to the local press and there were several papers circulating at the time.

The original period of the posting became extended and the worries about the Volunteers home employment developed Tony Keene becomes very worried, particularly about his teacher from Llangollen.

On the 21st January 1901. Captain Keene writes to the press in the following terms.

Britstown
South Africa
21st January, 1901

It is twelve months today since we were enrolled at Wrexham, the war is still dragging on with no immediate prospect of its ending.

When we volunteered no one thought that it was likely to be such a protracted struggle, and the impression was that Volunteers at any rate would be able to return within nine months at the very outside.

Employers accordingly engaged to give the men under them who left for service out here leave of absence, with a promise to keep their places open for them, or find others equally good, when they returned. This of course meant great inconvenience to the employers in many cases, but for a period it could be borne, and it was never thought that their patriotism would be put to such severe test.

But employers are now beginning to find that they cannot continue to keep places open any longer as it may mean serious loss to them, and one after another men are losing their billets, and will find when they return that they are out of work.

My colour-sergeant, for instance, who was a schoolmaster, and who received permission from his Board to come out here, with a promise that his place should be kept for him, has received a notification that he has been dismissed, owing to the impossibility, and he was told, of carrying on the school with temporary masters, as the grant was being lost for that reason. The result is that when he returns home he will have to spend some time finding fresh work, to say nothing of the anxiety and disappointment he has been put to out here.

This is only one instance, but I need not take up your space by quoting others. What I want to do now is to appeal to employers and others of men who are serving out here to do all they can to still keep the men's places open for them, or at any rate give them work of as remunerative nature when they return.

It would be a disgrace to the British nation — and I feel sure that employers of labour in Wales would be the last to wish to see it — that men who have done so well, and gone through what these have for their country, should be allowed to beg for work. Those who from sickness or other causes have already gone home have found, and rightly too, their billets still waiting for them. They, through no fault of their own, have not gone through the hardships that those who are still out here have undergone, and it would be hard that those who have borne the burden and heat of the day should have to suffer still more with it.

I hope therefore, that those to whom, I appeal will give this their careful consideration. I can assure them that they will not regret it, as men who have served as well as these have, and stuck to it so long are men who will be worth their salt in any walk of life — Your, &c

T. M. KEENE, Captain
Officer Commanding
Volunteer Company Royal Welsh Fusiliers

But the ranks could write home too. A private soldier wrote home after Keene had returned.

By the time you get this Capt. Keene and the boys will no doubt have arrived home, and they will have some startling news to tell you- much more than we shall, I am afraid, as regards fighting.

We haven't seen a Boer hardly, except a few prisoners at De Aar. Capt Keene has done some wonderful work out here, and has proved himself not only a good soldier but a most capable administrator as well, and he was the only commandant who did his work without fault. Mold has need to be proud of her captain. Most likely our chaps will be giving Captain Keene a bad name because he was strict. It is all nonsense. He was obliged to balance his authority between Dutch and our fellows, and of course any leniency on his part when there was a breach of discipline would be a mistake.

Captain Keene led his men at the siege and battle of Frederickstad and sends home a detailed account on 26th October, 1900. Let him describe it in his own words

A mounted patrol with a wagon that had gone to a farm about four miles out to get forage were caught in a trap and five or six were killed and several taken as prisoners. The next morning part of the regiment and some of the T.L.H. [Transvaal Light Horse] went out to destroy some bridges and a mill a few miles out, and while away news suddenly came into camp that De Wet was on the other side of the hills with at least 800 men. Our force was immediately recalled, but by this time they had come into contact with the enemy. They, of course, proceeded to retire in accordance with instructions, and as always happens with brother Boer when he thinks he has driven us off, they immediately began to follow up and press hard; and then on top of it about 200 men of De Wet's were sent across to join in the action, things became distinctly critical and unpleasant, especially when the company which was doing rearguard ran out of ammunition. The Boers came on in clouds closer and closer, and if they had had any real enterprise might have done a lot of harm. However the force at last managed to reach camp in safety with, comparatively speaking, only a few casualties. For the rest of the afternoon the Boers contented themselves with hanging about some distance off, and our advanced companies with loosing off long range volleys at them. It was evident, however, that it would be impossible for us to hold the ground we were encamped on, as it was right down in a hollow, and we had not a large enough force to occupy all the high ground surrounding it, so the order was given to retire to a ridge about two miles further back, one end of which rested on the river. We managed to do this without any loss, although two companies, A and mine, might easily have had some, as A was escort to the guns, and we had to cover the retirement of the advanced companies, which necessitated out lying down on ground as devoid of cover as a tennis lawn, while the enemy blazed away with rifles and pom-poms at the guns which were just behind us, and some horses which were just on our right. One lot of 'pom-pom' shells fell just behind us, and one man had a bullet between his legs which, fortunately for him, were spread out at the time, or it must have hit him. We got into our new position late that night, and then next morning the fun began. I have often wondered what it must be like to be besieged, and now I know. For five blessed days we have been stuck up here, with bullets and pom-pom shell shrieking overhead from morning to night and I can now sympathise with the poor folks who were shut up in Ladysmith and Mafeking all those weary months. Of course we were not short of food like they were, but, on the other hand, we had much less room to move about in with impunity. In fact it is perfectly true to say that as far as my company is concerned we had not a hundred yards of ground along which we could walk without the possibility of a bullet whistling past us. We were not, of course, really besieged, as we could with a certain amount of difficulty have cut our way out, but we were very short of big gun ammunition, and it also suited the General's purpose to sit tight here, so it came to the same thing in the end surrounded by 1800 Boers who sniped at us from every direction, wondering (because at the time no one except the General knew the position of affairs- that a convoy with ammunition and supplies was coming in) why we didn't clear out, knowing that we were short of ammunition and had only six days' supplies of food. It was just as anxious a time for us as if we were actually besieged, because we didn't know whether — in fact we thought at the time we couldn't get out. De-Wet, with two or three commandos, had got right round us, and apparently there was an un broken chain of the enemy on every side. Then day after day we heard rumours of the Scots Fusiliers, who were in the far end about two miles away, being heavily pressed and having losses, that the camp was to be rushed and then that De Wet had got hold of the telegraph line and was playing 'hoodman' with the telegrams and sending false messages through to Pretoria and to us about being relieved, and when day after day no one came even the most optimistic began to wonder if anything was up. But De Wet, with all his cunning, had had his eye wiped this time. The wires which he had cut and destroyed everywhere were not the ones we used, as only lately a new line had been laid underground, and he, of course knowing nothing of this, had sat down quite contented, thinking that we could not get any message through. Poor Man! Here Captain Keene gives a ground plan of his position and description, and continues 'Each man had to set to work and build himself what is called out her a 'sangar', or small stone wall, behind which he could lie, and so dodge the bullets and shells. We christened the cattle shed 'Pom-pom Villa, ' because our pom-pom used to stand at the corner and their pom pom used to play at it, and their shells came cracking all round us. Our one form of entertainment was to watch the animals coming to water across our open bit and the water carts. They used to form beautiful targets, at which the Boers plugged for all they were worth, and we used to sit and watch how many would be hit. Fortunately, no one was hit only an old mule or two. They also used to amuse themselves plugging at us game. The enemy had the range to a nicety, so it was a good thing it was done. During the whole time of course we never took any of our clothing or now and then, when we had to go to the other end of the line, as we sometimes had to, and also we crossed from the 'villa' (behind which by-the-bye, we three officers and the pom pom officer used to stop) to the kraal: but the first night that we were there I had a wall built across, which 'spoofed' their little boots, very rarely washed and never shaved; had our grub as best we could get it, and had to get up every morning at three, so as to have the greatcoats and blankets packed and the cart sent away before it got light enough for the enemy to shoot at it. So you can imagine the sights we all looked at the end of the five days. The first day we used to snipe back at the brutes, but an order was issued that we were not to fire unless we could actually see anybody, in order to economise the ammunition, so that for the next four days there was only very desultory shooting on our side — an odd shot or so from some enthusiast, who used to watch the whole day for an opportunity and an occasional 'pom-poming', when firing from the other side used to get unusually aggressive. One morning the long looked for convoy arrived, and it was decided to go out and attack one of their positions, where they had worked dangerously close, and then for the comparative quiet of the usual dropping rifle fire a perfect pandemonium broke out. Two guns just behind us opened fire with a roar, the 'pom-pom' started its door-knocker hammer, my company and another opened fire for all they were worth, the Maxim joined in like a big coffee grinder, then to our left two other guns and another 'pom-pom' started, the big 4.7 joined in like an earth quake, and in the distance we could just hear the Scots' guns and pom-poms. The Boers replied with heavy rifle fires, and while the bullets and shells shrieked and whistled overhead the three companies went out to the attack.

After remarking upon the opportune arrival of the convoy, as the Boers had decided to 'rush' the camp that very night, Captain Keene describes the attack as follows:

About a mile out we came on their position. No one knew then how many were in this particular place, as far as could be judged only about 14 or 15. Imagine our surprise when it was found that there were 150 or more. They had got into a donga along the railway line, into which they had crawled from a village in the distance, through the intervening ravine. It was only by the merest accident that it was discovered. Some of our mules had been sent down in that direction to water, when one of their men fired at and killed the boy who was driving them. This game gave the show away. Until our men got within 500 yards of the enemy they never fired a shot; then they let drive, and in twenty minutes out of four officers and three companies two officers and 45 men were hit. But the advance never stopped for an instant. It was simply magnificent; the men went on as steadily as rocks through a perfect hail of bullets, and when the Boers saw it was all up they chucked down their rifles and, clearing out of the dongs, bolted in every direction. Then there was Tommy's chance: with a yell he went for them like a maniac, shooting them down in every direction, and out of the 150 and odd men there we accounted for over 50 killed and wounded, and prisoners.

All over the place, as far as you could see, were men flying — some old, some young, one not more than about 14, some dressed in frock coats, some in khaki, others in rough clothes all tattered and torn, and most of them without boots on (they had taken them off to steal into the camp more quietly that night) — shrapnel shells bursting over them and bullets peppering round them. Men dropping by the score, they ran until they could run no more, then walked, and finally crawled away on all fours, utterly done up, and vanished in twos and threes to goodness knows where. Apparently the ground swallowed them up. So ended the siege and battle of Frederickstad, probably the severest blow De Wet ever had. All in a few hours it happened, like a thunderstorm from a blue sky. Just as he was anticipating a great coup and an easy victory perhaps he found his whole scheme smashed up, his best men scattered and utterly broken, and most of them placed beyond annoying us again for ever. It was a fine thing magnificently carried out, and as the General told the regiment after it was all over, 'Of all the gallant deeds done by this fine old regiment, nothing has ever more finely done than this.' The men of the regiment are simply splendid, they will go anywhere and do anything. Three of the prisoners who were taken were tried by field general court martial for treachery and shot in the morning. They held up their hands and surrendered just as our men were closing up their trenches, and then picked up and then picked up their rifles and shot three of them. After the battles we spent the afternoon burning every farm and house in the valley, and taking away all the forage and food stuff. One of the houses, the best in the place was used as a sort of fort by the enemy, from which they kept up a continuous sniping, and yet they had the face to hoist the white flag on it! Needless to say we took no notice of it, and shelled the place vigorously, and eventually burnt it.

Again we have a report from Britstown, January 7th, 1901:

This is a life of changes. Here I am now commandant of the Britstown district, a county about as big as Flintshire an absolute autocrat with powers of life and death almost. The place is under martial law, and I can do pretty well what I like, Close the pubs, make the inhabitants be in their homes by 9 and put their light out by 9.30,

Major Tony Keene, a photograph taken during the Great War.

make them bring their guns and any spare horses, and generally ride though shod over everybody if I felt so disposed. We have to be careful though, not to put people's backs up if possible. At the beginning of the war nearly every farmer in the place was pro-Boer, and rebel at heart and ready to assist the Boers in every way, but owing to recent events they have very much changed their minds. Last Sunday week, or just a week before I arrived, a Boer commando invaded this district and town, and as they went through took all the farmers' horses and forage, and killed what sheep they wanted. This so annoyed their pals, that they are now ready to do anything against the Boers; they come to me and give information about them and do all they can to assist us; nothing could have been better from our point of view, than this invasion, as instead of people crowding in from all parts to join them they are all cold shouldered everywhere, and if the feeling lasts it will do much more towards stopping the war than any amount of fighting and chasing them about. When they came in here they took all they could carry, stuffed the magistrate in gaol, took his pair of horses, put the bank manager under arrest, and pretty well cleared the town out. They cut the wires between here and a place called Howwater for miles, and broke down 100 telegraph poles which are all made of cast iron in these parts. I have sent a repairing party to mend them, so far they have been at it for four days and haven't finished yet. The enemy seem to have cleared pretty well out of this district for the present, but there is no knowing when they will not break back again from the Orange River Colony. I came here in charge of a convoy consisting of 70 wagons, with an escort of 100 infantry and 80 mounted men. The column was about 2 miles long and if the Boers had chosen to attack, they could have cleared half of eat, with the greatest ease. I was in command of the show, and I was jolly glad when it arrived safely; you never saw such a circus in your life, mule wagons, and donkey wagons, all straggling along at their own pace, the mule wagons in front shoving along at about three miles an hour, and the donkey wagons bringing up the rear at about two miles an hour, the consequence was it used to take about two and a half hours and longer up at each halt, as they used to come straggling in at all hours. The original intention was that were to go straight along to Thorneycroft and take the convoy on to him, but by the time we got here he had pushed on beyond our reach, so we were stopped there, much to everyone's relief, for it was very trying work for the men marching along with a convoy in this weather.

The heat is terrific in the middle of the day, about 100 in the shade, and it simply kills the men and animals having to march through it. I think now we shall remain here as a garrison, as I have strongly recommended that one should be kept here. I am collecting all the stray horses in the district, Boer and military, and as soon as fit I send the on to De Aar. I have got 166 already, but they are nearly all of them run down, but some of them will pick up in a week or so, when I expect to get some serviceable crocks of some part. I have already sent 28 to De Aar, and by the time I have sent the next crowd in they ought to have something to go on with. This is rather a pretty little town, with a good church, I am getting some photos of it which I will send along. I am also getting my own mug snatched by the local photographer, the result will probably be ghastly, but that is a detail. We are right in the middle of the Karoo desert not a tree to be seen in miles, but there is something very fascinating about this kind of country. It is very flat, with low scrub and patches of grass, and you can gallop for miles without a hill. I went yesterday to a farm about horses, 10 miles out, and drove back in the moonlight; it was a ripping drive and the air was lovely and cool. — CAPTAIN T. M. KEENE — Britstown is 25 miles west of De Aar Junction.

It was always intended that the posting of the Volunteers to South Africa would be a short term posting but this company did not return until May 1901. They had remembered the folks at home at Christmas 1900: a telegram was received in Mold sent at 1.35 on Christmas Day 1900 from Capetown.

Volunteer Company of Royal Welsh Fusiliers all flourishing and send heartiest wishes for Merry Christmas to all our friends and relations at home — Please send to all North Wales Papers. KEENE.

Keene recognised that as well as leading Volunteers in Africa the public relations job for those back home in north Wales was also important.

I have quoted extensively from Keene's letters as they show the open nature of the information that arrived home. They show that the Volunteers were used as real fighting men and not as reserve guards. They also show the real quality of leadership given by Keene in the war situation. It is reminiscent of his grandfather's conduct at Seringapatam.

He would have used his field-glasses and also the telescope he was given by his brother officers before his departure. One of the artefacts in the Royal Welsh Fusiliers Museum at Caernarfon Castle is a White Ensign brought back by Keene from South Africa. It is full of bullet holes and it is obviously a keep-sake from one of the sieges. It could be from Frederickstadt, but Keene's company was involved in a visit to Mafeking and in the relief of Ladysmith and that seems, therefore, more likely.

The time came for the company to return to north Wales after completing their tour of duty. They sailed home on the S.S. *Formosa* arriving in north Wales in May 1901. It had been a difficult time for the Practice with the last illness of Tom Kelly (died January 1901) and Tony Keene being away and Alfred Keene had had shouldered the responsibility with Robin Kelly.

The town had notice of the return of the Volunteers in good time and could make preparations for their reception. The news of their exploits had of course been publicized on a regular basis for fifteen months. The people were very proud of their achievements and all the circulating papers very well reported their return. So a committee was formed and what a reception the men received. They returned to Mold by train from Wrexham, coming on the through route via Coed Talon and Brymbo, arriving at Mold Station at 5.47p.m. The streets of the town had been decorated and as recognition of the mix of Welsh and English speakers the banners erected were in Welsh and English. One report said that:

... never had the town presented so gorgeous as appearance as on the occasion under notice and the enthusiasm, displayed by the townspeople encouraged in no small degree the reception committee and officials who spared neither time nor labour with a view to success of the undertaking.

The *Chronicle* tells us 'the train was due at Mold at a quarter to six but long before this country visitors came pouring into the town in all sorts of vehicles and as time approached there was a great surging mass of people right to the railway station the estimate being 7,000 to 10,000'. The *North Wales Guardian* agrees with estimate whilst *Flintshire Observer* says 9,000.

Approaching the railway station an arch had been erected upon the top of which was the Prince of Wales' feathers. Artistic work was done in the blending of the colours. The mottoes that were worked out in ivy leaves were *CROESAW CARTREF* (Welcome Home) *GWNAETHOST YN DDA* (Thou hast done well). From here to the Cross, tradesmen had flags and streamers across the street. At the Cross, another handsome arch had been erected. On the top was a well-designed crown. The mottoes were 'Well done Keene & Co.', 'Welcome Home'. It was a Saturday and the sun shone brilliantly. The front of the Town Hall (the old assembly hall) was transformed from a sombre appearance to one of gaiety whilst right to the top of the town the shopkeepers vied with one another in decorations.

Captainl Keene was provided with a charger to ride through Mold and his men were put in horse brakes to be drawn through the streets. The bands of the Buckley Engineers band and the Clarence Boys were present. Keene's own company, who had stayed behind, joined the parade with their band under Lieutenant Robin Kelly. The Fire Brigade turned out with a four in hand. The procession wended its way through Chester Street, Wrexham Street, Glanrafon and High Street to the Town Hall. Every window and position of advantage had its spectators and while the parade was wending its way the bell-ringers at the parish church rang forth a merry peal. In the Town Hall a good number had attended to give a welcome reception and on the appearance of Captain Keene and his boys they came in for a great ovations. At the town hall they were officially welcomed by the chair of the Mold U.D.C. Tony Keene responded by talking of their service.

Many a time on the lonely South African veldt he had thought of Mold and the friends who were so generous to them 15 months ago, and he and his men wondered what Mold people were thinking of them. But in their wildest dreams they never hoped for such a day as that. It was a day they would remember all the rest of their lives. He had told them at the start they could only do one thing, that was to help to add to the grandeur of the Empire, and he hoped that they had in a small way helped to fulfil that promise. One thing he could say, that as far as the men were concerned they had given him every support. During the whole 15 months of marching and hardships and of toil, they had borne all without murmur, and had supported. They had been put on half rations, their clothes had been worn

Facing: Return of the Volunteers from South Africa; the decorated arches in Chester Street

Above: The parade awaits the arrival of the South African Volunteers at Mold Railway Station. In the foreground is the local fire-engine.

Below: The parade moves off from Mold Railway Station headed by the Buckley Engineers band.

threadbare, yet they had stuck through it all. Mold had done as well as any, and the whole contingent might well be proud of them. It was 15 months since they left. They went from the Cape to Durban, from Durban to Ladysmith. They were the first volunteers to leave, the first to get to the front, and the first to get into the Transavaal, and they were proud of this. From Ladysmith they went to Durban, and from there Kimbereley to take part in the relief of Mafeking. They helped to form the main body under General Hunter which took part in the relief of Mafeking. He said it was his lot again to thank them for what that had done. He could hardly express himself for the way in which the organisation and the reception had been carried out, and in taking a walk round and talking to old friends and from what he could see and hear, he began to realize the amount of work and thought must have been spent upon it all. For what they had done in South Africa they had been amply repaid. He said they had gone through a great deal — they had gone 15,000 miles by water, 3,000 to 4,000 by rail, *etc.*, and 1,000 miles on foot. When they first arrived at Ladysmith it was in a pouring rain. The place itself was reeking with fever. They were too late to take part in the relief, but the inhabitants, horses and dogs, gave indications of the siege, they all looked starved and were skeletons. The buildings with corrugated roofs were in holes, and the whole town gave an indication of the privations and terrible hardships which must have been undergone.

On the Monday a dinner was given for Keene and his men at the Black Lion and Keene spoke again of his experiences.

They afterwards proceeded to Litchenburg, a distance of about thirty miles, and then on to Potchefstroom, the old capital of the Transvaal. It was then that the civilian side of the Volunteer Company came in prominence. In many instances the Volunteers' knowledge of some craft or trade became very useful. There were a great many engines and trains, which the Boers had sent to Potchestroom from Johannesburg, thinking they would be safe there, when Johannesburg was captured by the British. The British secured the whole these trains, but there were no drivers, and volunteers were called for. He (Captain Keene) was able to supply three men out of his company, one an engine driver and the other two stokers. The Yeomanry also supplied an engine-driver. Thus the trains were got into working order. (Applause) The company stayed there some time, and then went to Krugersdorp, where for a little while they had an easy time. Next they went to Heidelberg. They were in contact with the enemy three weeks and finally they got into Frederickstad, where they were surrounded many days and hardly dared to show their heads for fear of being sniped at. Although they had a very anxious time there, the situation was not without its humours. One of their amusements was to watch the water cart going for water. They always used to wonder whether it would be hit or not. Eventually the ammunition they were waiting for came in, and they went out and drove the Boers away, dealing them a severe blow. Just then they got orders for home. An invasion, however, broke out and they were sent to Britstown, where they remained to the end of their sojourn in South Africa. There they met the Yeomanry, whom they last saw in Wrexham. They saw two or three Mold troopers there, including Trooper Evans and Trooper Roberts, son of Dr Roberts of Pontblyddyn. Both were looking very well indeed. While in this place they heard of the death of Queen Victoria. The effect it had on the native mind was perfectly extraordinary. They used to call her the 'Great White Mother', and they looked upon her as a deity who would never die. When she died they seemed quite staggered, and even those who lived in hovels and in the Kaffir kraals put little bits of crape over their doorways to mark their respect. (Applause)

Life for Tony Keene must have seemed quiet and uneventful on his return to Britain. He was promoted Major in June 1903 and in July is presented by Lord Roberts, on behalf of the Law Society, with a Commemorative Medal and Bill of Honour for his South African service, one of only two awarded. He resumed his work at the Practice in Mold with his father and Robin Kelly. He was appointed Clerk to the Buckley Urban District Council in 1902 and held the post until 1914. The Practice had a branch office in Buckley during this time as a result of his presence there. He was chairman of the Mold Cricket Club for many years.

He was deemed unfit on health grounds for service in the Great War. But his involvement with the Territorials, as the Volunteers became, lasted for the rest of his life. He became Secretary of the Territorial Army Association and was instrumental in the building of the headquarters of the Association on land that had formed part of the garden at the Practice headquarters. The Keene's and the Kelly's had never owned the property. He remained a bachelor.

On the death of his father, he became Clerk to the Justices for Mold and Hope Divisions and also served as a school-manager at Gwernymynydd. He was temporarily staying at The Dolphin Hotel when he was taken ill with a stroke and died in October, 1921. It was said of him during the Great War that 'he was probably the most eagerly sought for official in Flintshire for information relative to the Forces and anxious friends will long remember the sympathy and patience with which he received them and his tireless efforts to gain information from Official Sources both at home and abroad'.

During the period of the war he was secretary of the Flintshire Comforts Fund also acting for a time as military representative and those best qualified to judge his war time activities can realize how well he merited the tribute to his memory paid at Flintshire Quarter sessions by Lord Justice Bankes.

He was an active churchman like all his family, and a Conservative but took little active interest in politics. He served on the committee of the Mold Savings Bank. Whilst he would provide leadership if it was required he could play second fiddle as when he was stage manager for the Dramatic Society in 1899.

Tony Keene possessed an attractive personality. Blessed with a keen perception he was quick to realize a position and was happy in the lucidity with which he could convey his conception to others. He worked as he thought, with great rapidity and the precision that was a guiding factor in his contact with 'the daily round' was doubtless in part derived from years of military training.

In the Magistrates Court the chairman said 'as long as they had a worthy cause no-one would help them more heartily than Colonel Keene'. J. B. Marston, a local solicitor who had been articled to the Practice, added:

> He felt that all through his life Colonel Keene behaved like a very honourable gentleman like his father had done before him and like the firm with which he was associated had always conducted their business.

He was undoubtedly a natural leader of men. The *Chester Courant* in reporting his death said:

> Colonel Keene apart from his interest in the Volunteers and subsequently the Territorials took a keen interest in Engineering in which he was a skilled mechanic. He was a man who in business matters had a very clear perception and having a masterly grasp for detail he was able to clearly communicate the result of his impressions to others. His business life was marked throughout by promptitude and precision and he enjoyed the complete confidence of all with whom he was brought in contact whether socially or professionally.

The *County Herald* tells us that the funeral with full military honours took place amidst unprecedented scenes of public mourning. During the funeral practically all business was suspended in the town. To the military they were certainly burying one of their own that day. The pall bearers comprised of nine Colonels including the later lord lieutenant, Watkin Mainwaring, and Colonel Crawshaw of rugby football fame. The Order of procession was the firing party from the 5th Battalion, R.W.F., all ex-servicemen and their band and officers and men from many different units. The police had twenty men under the direction of the Chief Constable and his deputy.

Two lords lieutenant and others too numerable to mention attended, all the Keene & Kelly staff were there including Misses Ellis and Edwards who, other than direct family members, were the only ladies present. They must

T. M. Keene's medals as displayed at the Royal Welch Fusiliers Museum, Caernarfon Castle

have been amongst the first typists employed by the Practice.

The church was crowded and the hymns were from the military 'On the resurrection morning' and 'Abide with Me'.

The *County Herald* again tells us,

> Colonel Keene was a real gentleman held in high esteem by a wide circle of friends. He was a gentleman of quiet disposition and ever ready to do a kindly act and would go out of his way to assist any worthy object.

The *Observer* says:

> Immensely liked and highly respected, a man of distinguished ability and charming disposition.

Tony Keene would have appreciated the support of the town and his brother officers for this. In the R.W.F. Museum in Caernarfon are his medals:

> Military O.B.E. for his First World War Service
> Territorial Army Decoration TD
> South Africa Medal (with four clasps for service in
> Orange Free State, Natal, Transvaal and South Africa)

He was laid to rest in the grave of his father and mother in Mold churchyard, a much-revered man in his time but now, unfortunately, forgotten.

Chapter 15
Robin Kelly and the Office of Sheriff

Robert Stewart Kelly (named after his grandfather and known as 'Robin'), was born on 12th June, 1875, the eldest of the nine sons of Thomas Thelwell Kelly. He was sent to Shrewsbury School (Bennett's House) with several of his brothers. He arrived in May 1889 with his younger brother Thelwell, and left in April 1892 just before he was seventeen. He had progressed to the Lower IV and was 6/15 in French, 8/15 in maths, 3/15 in English and 14/15 in classics. He did not leave behind him any memories of sporting prowess. He has been described to me academically as 'I guess he was making heavy weather of the curriculum'. But his place in history is assured because he was the first under-sheriff in England and Wales to become high sheriff of his county.

What is the office of sheriff? It has changed in emphasis over the centuries and is now administrative and an honour to be appointed. The office goes back to Saxon times. The shire reeve was corrupted to sheriff and immediately before the Norman conquest he held office at the King's pleasure and

a) collected revenue

b) proclaimed the King's Peace

c) was responsible for apprehending criminals with the help of the hue and cry if appropriate. He was the executive Officer of the Court.

After the Norman conquest he supplied the balance between the Crown and the barons. William the Conqueror indeed left in post all Saxon sheriffs who had not actively opposed him.

The sheriff became supreme in the shire courts at the head of every department of county administration and it was a post so valued that some families wanted it to be hereditary. In Westmoreland in 1275 a stranger was appointed to the office but was regarded as merely acting for the two heiress daughters of Robert de Vipont. When these two ladies disagreed over the appointment of an under-sheriff, the King nominated someone to act until the sisters agreed. A woman, Anne, Countess of Pembroke, held the office around this time and sat with the judge at Appleby.

The thirteenth century was the hey-day of the power of the sheriff. When a strong king was on the throne he kept the office jealously under control but in time of anarchy such as Stephen's reign all control was lost and such men as the notoriously corrupt Geoffrey de Manderville — the most notoriously corrupt of all barons held the shrievalty of one, two or even three counties.

Henry II, who created the basis of our legal system, reduced the sheriffs to order and the Inquest of Sheriffs in 1170 dismissed very nearly all of them.

In Saxon times the trial by ordeal, such as — carrying red hot iron for nine steps — hand in boiling water — sinking in cold water — morsels of bread sticking in the throat — and later trial by battle, was the responsibility of the sheriff. Ordeal was submitting to judgement of God. The Normans introduced trial by jury but it took a long time to catch on.

Then came the advent of the Assize with travelling judges and justice became centrally administered. The power of the sheriff was greatly diminished but his responsibilities increased and were well defined. The sheriff was the personal agent of the Crown in the county with no limit on the duties he might be called upon to perform.

Twice a year at Easter and Michaelmas the sheriff had to appear at the Exchequer (under a fine of 100 shillings for every day he was late) to account for the revenue due from his county. The money then paid was receipted by means of tallies. These tallies were sticks usually of hazelwood bored near one end so they could be filed on rods. The sums paid being denoted by incisions ranging in width according to the magnitude of the sums. After being marked in this way the stick was split into two parts — one part (the tally) was kept by the sheriff, the other part (the counter tally) being retained by the Exchequer. The system of receipt was undisturbed until 1826 when a more up to date method of accounting was introduced. The origins of the fire that destroyed the Houses of Parliament some years later was attributed to the overheating of the flues used for warming the House of Lords consequent upon the excessive heat engendered by the burning of the old Exchequer tallies.

The sheriff became the county's returning officer for elections a duty which he continues to carry out today. He was responsible for sending the knights to the Great Council that became the House of Commons. Elections to House of Commons are now run by the Clerk to the County Council as Deputy Returning Officer but the returning officer is the sheriff who receives the writ from the Queen for the election to be held. Generally the sheriff declares at least one result. The sheriff now covers the old county of Clwyd with about seven parliamentary constituencies. They generally choose a known close contest or that in which they live to declare.

When going about his duties in medieval times the sheriff was entitled to claim hospitality but this did lead to abuses.

The sheriff's chief officer was his under-sheriff who by special permission of the exchequer might answer for such duties as the sheriff chose to entrust to him.

The sheriff's responsibility for the peace of the shire included, in early times, the oversight of the system of compulsory suretyship known as 'Frank Pledge' by which as a precaution against crime, freeman were granted in tens or tithings within each was answerable for the good behaviour of the whole. This system was obsolete by 1500 but he remained Keeper of the Peace.

The sheriff originally exercised all the military authority in the county but the lord lieutenant took over in 1557. The sheriff, although he ceased to be military commander, still had the power to call on a *posse comitatus* to assist him. England and Wales had sheriffs and posse's long before Hollywood thought about them.

When the Riot Act was passed in 1714 the sheriff and under-sheriff were two of the persons authorised to read it. Robin Kelly's father, Thomas Thelwell Kelly, was under-sheriff at the time of the Mold riots but this is dealt with elsewhere.

The care of prisoners gradually passed to the justices.

From the start of Assizes the sheriff was responsible for the care and safety of the judges. He would collect the judge at the county boundary and deliver him to the next county sheriff at the boundary. Javelin men were employed for protection until 1859. The sheriff is still responsible but the local police force provide the protection. The wand carried by the under-sheriff to and from court is the modern representation of that tradition of protection. The thought of Hugh Gough using the wand to protect the judge has exercised our minds for years.

The appointments of under-sheriff is the sole choice of the sheriff and even before the Sheriffs Act of 1887 the appointments had become annual, Hugh Roberts and Arthur Troughton Roberts had preceded the two Kellys and the two Keenes. The sheriff has to have 'sufficient' land but the term 'sufficient' is not defined. In my time a nominee was found to have all his freehold property in his company's name and before nomination had to buy part of the garden adjoining his own house and garden to qualify.

When I started in the office the most important date in November was never the 5th — it was the 12th. The day the Privy Council pricked the sheriffs list. The choice was always known — the first on the list — but the under-sheriff was always relieved there was no hitch — followed by the formal publication in the *London Gazette*. Procedure included appointment of bailiffs, London agents and the entering into of the bonds within a month.

When I started in 1955 one of my first tasks on behalf of the under-sheriff was to summon the jury for the Quarter Sessions and Assizes. The court does this itself now — imagine the range of excuses of those who did not wish to do the duty!

How should a sheriff dress on formal occasions? For ex-military men it is fairly straight forward. They wear their military dress uniform. For the lay-man, there is a form of court dress prescribed as worn by Robin Kelly in 1953. The problem was discovered when Miss Marigold Graham was appointed High Sheriff of Clwyd. Negotiations with the Lord Chancellor and Privy Council produced a compromise form of dress appropriate to Miss Graham and the post she held. The entertainment provided by a high sheriff when savouring of an official character is an occasion on which orders, military decorations and medals should be worn with evening dress. The word 'decorations' on the invitations card will be the intimation that the entertainment is an official one. The under-sheriff wears morning dress or court dress or other uniform. Did Colonel Keene when under-sheriff in 1904 and 1915 wear military uniform? I do not know.

Another of the functions of the high sheriff is to read the proclamation of a new monarch. This has not always gone smoothly. In 1727 one William Wynne of Holywell was sheriff. Two of the justices went to take him the proclamation, He was playing bowls and, like Sir Francis Drake, refused to leave his game. After three hours Roger Mostyn and Peter Pennant failed to convince him. The under-sheriff eventually arrived and read the proclamation at the Holywell town cross. William Wynne was a known Jacobite and there is no record he was ever punished for his refusal.

The sheriff is responsible for seeing to the carrying out of any death penalty imposed by the courts. Robin Kelly first became under-sheriff in 1902 and was last under-sheriff in 1952. In the intervening years the title was held by outsiders for two years but Robin Kelly carried out the administration. When interviewed in 1951 he told the *Chronicle* he had never had to attend an execution although he had had several near shaves. The closest call he ever had was when he ordered the hangman's rope for Pierrepoint (the public executioner) but the convicted person was reprieved at the last moment. A death warrant for a lady reprieved in the 1920s is amongst Keene & Kellys deposits in the County Archives. Hugh Gough at a later date shared a railway journey with Pierpoint.

But Robin Kelly spoke too soon and in 1952 a Rhyl man, H. R. Harris, was sentenced to death and not reprieved. The high sheriff of the time was Gladstone of Hawarden Castle who told Robin Kelly 'I know this is a duty I can delegate to you but we will both go.' They did. The execution was to took place at Strangeways. When talking of it in later years Kelly remarked how 'very interesting he found it'. It was a bit like witnessing a will. You had to be present and able to see but not necessarily looking when it happened. This bond with Gladstone was to remain. He would always ask

County of } To the High Sheriff of the County.
to wit.

Whereas at the Session of Oyer and Terminer and General Gaol Delivery, holden at **Mold** in and for the County of Flint on Tuesday the First day of February in the eleventh year of the Reign of our Sovereign Lord George the Fifth by the Grace of God of the United Kingdom of Great Britain and Ireland, King, Defender of the Faith. Ellen Jane Jones was duly convicted of **Murder** and was thereupon sentenced to be taken to the place from whence she came and thence to a place of execution and there to be hanged by the neck until her body should be dead and that her body when dead should be taken down and buried within the precincts of the Prison in which she should have last been confined after her said conviction **Now,** I, the undersigned, The Hon: Sir Charles Montague Lush knight being one of the Justices of His Majesty's High Court of Justice named in the Commission of Oyer and Terminer and General Gaol Delivery issued and now in force, for the said County **Do hereby Order** and **Direct** you to cause execution to be done on the body of the said Ellen Jane Jones according to law.

Given under my hand and seal this first day of February in the year of our Lord one thousand nine hundred and Twenty one.

Death Warrant in the name of Ellen Jane Jones, 1921   [FRO D/KK/1536]

Letter to R. S. Kelly
of Mold. Under sheriff.

303 Manchester Rd
Hollinwood
Nr Manchester
Feb 13. 1752

Dear Sir,

re H. R. Harris

I beg to acknowledge the receipt of your letter of the 12th instant. I now wish to confirm, that, I shall be at liberty to carry out the execution of the above named, at H. of Prison, Manchester, on Tuesday the 26th instant. If I do not hear to the contrary I shall report for duty in good time, on Monday the 25th instant.

Yours Faithfully
A Pierrepoint

Letter from Albert Pierrepoint confirming his availablity, 1952

after Kelly when I saw him in the Magistrates Court.

His experience of arranging an execution was easier than that of his predecessor in 1769 who petitioned the Right Honourable Lord Commissioners of His Majesties Treasury.

The Humble petition of Ralph Griffiths High Sheriff of the county of Flint for the present year 1769 concerning the execution of Edward Edwards for Burglary SHEWETH that your petitioner was at great difficulty and expense by himself, his clerks, and other messengers and agents he employed on journeys to Liverpool and Shrewsbury to hire an executioner the convict being of Wales it was almost impossible to procure any of that country to undertake the execution.

	£	s	d
Travelling and other expenses on that occasion	15	10	0
A man at Salop engaged to do this business gave him inpart	5	5	0
Two men for conducting him	4	10	0
After much trouble and expense John Babington gave to the wife	6	6	0
and to Babington	6	6	0
Paid for erecting a gallows. A business very difficult to be done in this county	4	12	0
For hire of a cart-coffin and burial	2	10	0
And for other expenses	5	0	0
Total	49	19	0

Which humbly hope your Lordship will please to allow for your petitioner, who *etc.*

The sheriff was responsible for providing the judge with his lodgings during an Assize. Many a time Hugh Gough was out of the office looking at alternatives when a change was necessary.

The under-sheriff is now responsible for the enforcement of High Court judgements. He seizes goods for sale. If another claims ownership an Interpleader is issued to determine who owns the goods. He charges poundage — a percentage on what is recovered. The bailiff charges fees also. He keeps the money fourteen days to avoid bankruptcy of the debtor but has to complete his work within six months. Under-sheriffs generally have a reputation for doing the job very successfully. This is a writ of *fiere facias*.

There was a celebrated incident in 1909. A socialite by the name of Violet Charlesworth from St Asaph had faked her own death in a road accident at the headland at Penmaenmawr still known as 'Violet's Leap'. Eventually the force of the law caught up with her. She was greatly in debt and her position attracted much national publicity. There is a photograph from the *Daily Dispatch* from this time of Robin Kelly and T. S. Adams (Charlie Adams' father and Sheriff's Officer) in mackintoshs and flat caps furtively going around her property to see if they could obtain access as they were not allowed to break in to levy on Miss Charlesworth's goods.

Before 1967 the sheriff through his under-sheriff would hold courts. One such court would fix damages for a breach of promise case. Another would make a report of *capias ad satisfaciendum*. An M.P. could not be made to pay a debt within forty days of leaving the House of Commons. They would

Daily Dispatch *photograph of Adams and Kelly at Violet Charlesworth's house, 1911*

enforce *habeas corpus*. They could issue a certificate of *languidus* (certifying someone could not be moved).

A writ of *elegit* was when a judgement creditor desires to proceed against the lands of the debtor. In Hugh Gough's time such a writ was issued and sent to him. Hugh Gough telephoned to fix a convenient date for a hearing. The solicitor had believed if he waited twelve months he took automatic possession. A hearing was the last thing he wanted. It died a natural death.

They could also enforce decrees from the church courts: *Fiere Facias de Bonus Ecclesiasticus*. They collected fines imposed at the Assize Court. Thomas Thelwell Kelly and Alfred Thomas Keene's experiences are chronicled elsewhere.

On leaving school Robin Kelly entered immediate articles and was admitted as a solicitor in 1897. In 1884, Keene & Kelly had agreed a son of each could come into partnership at the expense of father's share and this happened for Robin Kelly in 1898. He had no prowess at games at school but enjoyed participating in exercise, walking, tennis, golf and cricket. He was a formidable walker. In between the two world wars he was a familiar sight walking or cycling through local byways collecting insurance premiums for the firm's insurance agency with Sun Insurance Limited. He mounted his bicycle unusually by placing his foot on the back.

On another occasion, when Major Godsall from the Maelor was sheriff, who had his own cricket ground and the Sheriff's XI played the Under-Sheriff's XI.

In 1903, he entered, with many others, a 25-mile walking match. It was open to residents within an 8-mile radius of Mold. It left the town via Padeswood, Penymynydd, Broughton, Hawarden, Ewloe, Queensferry, Connah's Quay, Flint and Northop. A cash prize of £15 was to be awarded to four competitors and there were other prizes. The first Volunteer covering the round distance received a prize from Mrs Robin Kelly — that was Robin Kelly himself.

Phillip Tatton Davies-Cooke started it at 2.02p.m. and the winner's time was 4 hours 23¹/2 minutes as he came back to the packed High Street. Kelly had moved from 4th to 3rd going through Sychdyn. He gave his prize to his sergeant the next Volunteer home. Needless to say, Rutter Thomas was on the organising committee of which William Bayne was the secretary and Thomas Mann Keene (Tony) the treasurer (all Keene & Kelly).

Like his father before him he was a church-goer and Tory and worshipped at St Mary's Parish Church for many years.

Public office was to be as much a feature of his life like his fathers. At a meeting of the Police Committee on 23rd February 1901 he failed to be appointed clerk by one vote. The successful applicant for the £500 a year post was the coroner who had to give up the coronership to take it.

His father had been Clerk to Hawarden and Hope Magistrates and he succeeded him and, on the death of Colonel Keene in 1921, added the Mold and Northop Petty Sessional Divisions to his responsibilities. He served part-time until his retirement on becoming High Sheriff in 1953.

Kelly was rarely successful in his pursuit of public appointments. Tom Ollive, after he was appointed County Council Clerk, moved sideways to be Treasurer and in 1911 his successor, Bromley, retired.

There was a Councillor called Tibby whom the Conservatives (who were in control at the time) wanted as clerk because he knew about educational law but he was not a solicitor. The Liberals were quite happy to accept an appointment by the Conservatives if he was a qualified lawyer. If not, they wanted Robin Kelly. The *Flintshire Observer* of 16th June, 1911, has five long columns on a full house debate on the matter. What a change from the behind closed doors approach to local government now. Tibby would have to pay for legal advice. Tibby, having being promised the job by the Conservatives, resigned his seat and Robin Kelly was unlucky again. The fact that the wording of the advertisement had prevented other non-lawyers applying mattered not. Who has heard of H. A. Tibby today?

Robin Kelly was a very shy, unambitious man (except with the ladies) and this led to his being bullied when sitting as Clerk. The period between the two wars was a time when the Marshall Hall style of advocacy was at its peak and was to be found in the Magistrates Court. He would be harangued and verbally abused in open court by certain solicitors because his advice to the magistrates did not suit the solicitor. He would not fight back. I saw one of the assailants, Kerfoot Roberts, in action in Flint Magistrates Court in later years and when the case was not going his way he turned on the Chairman of the Bench haranguing him for not taking action to stop trains on the nearby Chester–Holyhead railway line shaking the Flint Town Hall where the court was being held.

A further example of court exchanges was published in the early 1900s. Under the heading 'Remarkable scene in Flintshire' it was reported 'A Case of Northop Petty Sessions on Thursday gave rise to some warm altercations.' A man, Henry Jones, a carpenter of Connah's Quay was summoned for drunkenness. The defence was raised by Mr J. B. Marsden of Mold, (he had been articled to Thomas Thelwell Kelly), that this man was on his own premises and attempting to get into his own house when the police constable came on the scene. The bench dismissed the case on the ground that defendant was on private property. During the hearing many angry scenes were witnessed and towards the end the Chairman (Mr T. Bate) said the magistrates could not be there all day on one case. They had been very patient.

MR MARSDEN: You have not been patient.

MR J. WATKINSON (another magistrate): Don't contradict. Go on with your case.

MR W. H. CHURTON (solicitor, Chester), who was present in court, made a remark

MR MARSDEN: Go on Mr Churton. Why don't you go on the bench? That's where you ought to be. (To the bench) I gave him the opportunity of going in front but he is always the same. (To Mr Churton) Go on now. I'd like to hear your oratory. It's better than mine!

When I first met him I thought him austere but I realize now it was shyness to me as a stranger. He was very short-sighted and this could give him the appearance of scowling. About 1934, Bob Roberts' daughter Vera went to see her father at his office. She saw Kelly and, thinking him scowling as he looked over his spectacles, scowled back and got into trouble for it. Kelly referred to her father as 'Roberts' but she corrected him saying he was 'Mr Roberts' as she had been taught and got into more trouble and caused embarrassment for her father. He was very careful financially. He would not have approved of the statutory minimum wage. After he had returned from practice and was still Clerk to the Magistrates he shared Dyffryn House in Wrexham Street with Cwyfan Hughes and Hugh Gough who ran the legal practice. When a defendant was sent for trial to quarter session or Assize, depositions were typed in open court by one of his clerks. Instead of obtaining his own mat for the typewriter he always went upstairs to borrow one to deaden the noise of the typewriter in court. He did not believe records should be kept — you should destroy all your mistakes.

But Robin Kelly could be very kind and considerate. He received a writ of *fiere facias* one day (to enforce a debt) against William Pilgrim Morris a Mold solicitor personally. He should have passed it to his sheriff's officer incurring fees for the officer and poundage for himself. But he kept it back and wrote to Pilgrim Morris explaining he had received this writ and he was sure they could come to some satisfactory arrangement over this and sent the letter round by hand.

He received a reply the next morning in the post which said 'Dear Kelly, by the time you receive this I shall be with his Satanic Majesty.' Kelly sent the police around and Pilgrim Morris had committed suicide by drinking a cup of Lysol a well known disinfectant. His second marriage had been entered into by both parties believing the other had money.

One of his executors, his next-door neighbour, told me that Robin Kelly would sit in his lounge window looking at his garden and catch the windfalls as they hit the ground.

Like all young men of his time, he joined the local Volunteers but not with the success of his partner Colonel Keene. They were gazetted second lieutenants together on the same day in 1892 but Kelly remained at that rank for many years. He was 2nd Lieutenant, 2nd Volunteer Bn., R.W.F., in 1900 and Temporary Captain, 16th (Service) Bn., R.W.F., in 1914. He loved the outdoors, indeed on his first marriage the bandsmen of the company of 2nd Battalion presented him with silver mounted walking stick.

Being a very private man he enjoyed a varying relationship with the press. In June 1901 it was reported that he and Wilfred Trubshaw (another solicitor and the local doctor's son) had a remarkable escape. As they were

Robin Kelly (with his second wife, Ethel) at the 'Wedding of the Year', 1953
— that of his successor Hugh Gough

about to enter Fron Haul where Kelly was living, a huge beech tree fell within a few feet of them. Happily, beyond a shock, they escaped injury but considerable damage was some to fruit trees and shrubbery in the garden.

'Penman' (the *Chronicle* editor and author of *Mold Gleanings*) was always profuse in acknowledging his help on the matter such as the lords of Mold or shrieval history, but when he advised the Mold Urban District Council to meet in committee (as would have been the advice anywhere at the time) it was a heinous crime on his part.

On another occasion 'Penman' writes,

> I cannot refrain from mentioning the kindness of Mr R. S. Kelly who so freely placed at my disposal such town records (mostly modern unfortunately) which are in his custody as Clerk to the Urban District Council and whose readiness to help was a model of what a public official should be.

He had become part-time clerk to the Mold Urban District Council in 1902 on the death of another Mold solicitor, G. H. Simon, at the early age of 42. When I came to Mold his plate was still in place in Church Lane though the practice had long ceased to exist. He held the post until 1938 when he was succeeded by Bob Roberts a long time employee of his who was the Council's financial officer but more of this again.

He was married in 1900 to Lizzie Stewart Collinge at All Saints Church, Kinnerton, and they had two daughters and one grand-daughter, now living in California. The honeymoon, after the fashion of the time, was spent in London. The staff gave them four framed photographs — one wonders what of. After her death in 1924 he did marry a second time, to Ethel, who survived him. He had always had a very real interest in agriculture and ran a small farm.

In 1905, Robin Kelly presided over a representative attendance of agriculturalists at the Town Hall. The object of the meeting being to consider the invitation of the University College of North Wales to apply for a course of extensive lectures in agriculture. The Secretary (D. Rutter Thomas inevitably) reported the result of his communication with the Local Education Authority and Local Government Board as to the expenses. The Chairman (Robin Kelly) said in his opinion the lectures were so valuable the question of expenses ought not to be permitted to arise. The secretary's suggestion that the lectures should be delivered second Wednesday in November, December, January and February the next year was adopted and he was told to apply for the free use of the Town Hall anti-rooms for the lectures and committee meetings and to arrange for P. Tatton Davies-Cooke to preside at the first.

He had horses, cattle, chickens and sheep and his granddaughter remembers him explaining to her the various breeds. His interest prompted 'Penman' to write in March 1927,

> Mr R. Stewart Kelly the clerk to the Mold Magistrates and also Clerk to the Mold Urban District Council and Under Sheriff for the County is not only as good lawyer but a good farmer as well. There is nothing like back to the land for the hard-working professional man and in this dictum I have no doubt Mr Kelly's distinguished legal neighbours will agree. Needless to say our Magistrates Clerk us pretty keen as an agriculturalist and just now he is proud of two ewes on his farm for in one day they both gave birth to nine lambs. Mr Kelly thinks this may be a lambing record.

Penman invites comment.

Robin Kelly, High Sheriff of Flintshire, 1953–4

It is this type of incident that, in examining his career, I have to ask 'did God choose that Robin Kelly be a solicitor or Thomas Thelwell Kelly?'

1926 introduced many major changes in the law of property including the abandonment of the doctrine of heir at law. Twenty years later Robin Kelly still referred to it as 'the new law' — showing how he had never adjusted comfortably to the changes. But his place is secure because of his unique achievement at that date of serving as both under-sheriff and high sheriff. He gave a lunch on the first day of the Assize as was the practice for the legal profession attending and his own guests. There was usually a short service on the first day of the Assize unless the judge was a Roman Catholic. The Grand Jury used to go to the lunch.

Some of the more active judges would walk down the street in procession from the church to the old law courts on Hall Fields. It is not all pomp. The position of under-sheriff can attract real as well as theoretical danger. In 1927, at the winter Assize, the judge came out of church and it was blowing a gale. The judge and the high sheriff got into the car to be driven to the court a few minutes before eleven. The under-sheriff had to walk alongside the car with his wand 'giving protection'. The press reported:

> The wind tore through the church yard till a man could hardly stand on

his feet. The wind tossed about the ermine roles in a most daring and impudent fashion and even the judicial wig was not safe. Two stalwart policemen closed in upon his lordship and helped him to maintain something like his dignity, which we expect from a judge while he walked the short distance to his waiting car. The Under Sheriff (Robin Kelly) screwed his tall hat on and held firmly to his white wand as the procession set off on its winding journey to County Hall. In a spirit of wanton delight, the wind howled down the main street and gave to all and sundry — the brave pedestrians the fierce challenge of battle. Chimney pots came tumbling down. Aerial masts were destroyed and slates were flying in all directions. The marvel is no one was hurt.

With hindsight, all incidents have interest. A judge on circuit as an Assize has a marshal in attendance — a young barrister newly admitted learning the ropes. In 1937, this post was filled at one of the Assizes for Mr Justice Lewis by Joe Grimond, later leader of the Liberal Party. The Mold Assize was uneventful, but at Caernarfon, they had the trial of three Welsh Nationalists who had burnt down an aerodrome built, as Joe Grimond said [incorrectly], with some lack of tact, on Owain Glyndŵr's birthplace.

When Robin Kelly's appointment was accelerated twelve months so he served as high sheriff in Coronation year it was well earned. Hugh Gough asked him when Kelly appointed him as his under-sheriff what did he do about a deputy — 'I never needed one, I was never ill'. Ironically he was taken ill just before his first Assize but he was recovered in time to take his seat with his wife in Westminster Abbey for the Coronation and a later garden party and be presented to the Queen on her post-Coronation visit to

Coronation Invitation to Robin Kelly as High Sheriff of Flintshire

Flintshire at the National Eisteddfod in Rhyl. His illness had caused his morning suit not to fit so he borrowed Hugh Gough's to go to the Abbey and it was with this suit that was the nearest Hugh Gough ever got to the Queen.

He died at the age of 90 on 21st October 1971, after a long enjoyed retirement.

Chapter 16
Clan Kelly

Life did not treat Margaret Agnes Kelly all that kindly. It is true that at the age of twenty-five she attracted a widower of forty-four who was charismatic, well-off and splendid, cheerful, company. They married in 1874 and their home at Bryn Coch was a splendid home, well staffed and with everything she could want. For eleven years everything went very well. She gave Thomas Thelwell Kelly six strong sons to create the dynasty which all Victorian men wanted. Then, after a business trip to London, he came back with typhoid fever and according to the press reports only just survived. Then he went out too early and caught a cold. As a result of this he was, for the next sixteen years, a shadow of his previous self. Now I know that Kelly on half power was more than a match for many mere mortals on full power but he was ill many times. The press regularly reported his convalence and in 1897, the saying of prayers for his recovery in Mold church featured in the press. Many courses of treatment were tried but it was not possible to re-instate him to his former energy. This constant nursing fell on Margaret. Help was available but the worry and strain were all hers. It is little wonder, therefore, that her involvement in Mold activities were very minimal. She did attend a lecture in 1892 for the Sunday Evening Lecture Fund. She had four more children, two boys and two girls, and four were under fourteen years of age on her husband's death.

It was said in the *Flintshire Observer* that 'although occupying an honoured position in the district she eschewed participation in public affairs holding that in the domestic virtues there was to be found a woman's sphere of activity and usefulness. Amongst those privileged to claim her friendship or acquaintance she was known to be possessed of an intensely sympathetic nature, feeling keenly the sorrows and lassitude's of her family. When her husband died she had tremendous support from her two children Robin, and later Hugh Kelly in Rhyl but, as we shall see, three of her sons pre-deceased her.

After the death of her husband Bryn Coch had to be sold and it was put up for auction in May 1901. It was described as 'an exceptionally desirable and delightfully situated and imposing commodious Modern Residence with ample outbuildings, charming grounds with Gardeners Cottage together with 85^1/2 acres.'

Bryn Coch Hall, 1901 [FRO D/DM/355/32]

The 'Modern Residence' had ten bed and dressing rooms, four entertaining rooms, a servants hall, kitchens, housemaid's pantry, stores, offices, dairy, cellars, *etc.* The outbuildings included a work-house, harness room, three stall stable with liftover, wood and iron open cart shed, tool, fowl, and implement houses and garage. In addition commodious motor garage, shippen with loft above, loose boxes, riggeries, *etc.*

What about the garden? — '2^1/2 acres are beautifully laid out, with wooded slopes, ornamental shrubberies and shady pleasant paths. Tennis and Croquet Lawns also excellent Kitchen gardens, greenhouse, *etc.*' The adjoining land was sold in separate lots.

It is not in anyway surprising that it had to be sold. Robin by now was living on his own with his new wife and Thelwell was abroad. No way could Margaret Kelly hope to keep the estate and it was sold and she moved to live in Rhyl, returning to live in Mold in 1924 at Tŷ Bryn in Bank Villas.

The present owners allowed me around the house. Focussed as it is around a large hall it is not difficult to imagine it and its gardens as a wonderful home for a large boisterous Victorian family. We were able to identify exactly where the photograph of the young Kellys was taken.

The new home could not of course take all the contents of the old home and there had to be a contents sale. T. S. Adams was the auctioneer for the house but the contents were to be sold by J. E. Davies the uncle of J. Bradburne Price and to whom my own grandfather had been articled at the end of the nineteenth century. The sale took place on the premises on 2nd and 3rd December, 1901. This suggests that the property had failed to find a buyer at the auction. Let us look at the first paragraph in the sale particulars:

Beautiful Old Chippendale Arm and Single Chairs and Settees; richly carved dark and brown oak settees; arm and single chairs; occasional and other tables, exceedingly fine brown Oak Panel Chest, exquisitely carved with flowers and conventional ornamentation dated 1570; elaborately carved dark Oak cabinet Desk; very rare and exceedingly fine old French Empire Clock with Allegorical Figures and Marqueterie Ornamental in Relief; Elegant Mantel Clock in brass gothic pattern embossed case; Bronze figures in lovely design and other articles of virtu; set of old pewter plates and dishes; old grandfather clocks in carved and plain oak cases, having brass dials; rich ornamental carpets and rugs *etc.*

Fine Oil Paintings, Watercolours and Engravings by eminent artists carefully selected library of well-bound books all in good condition.

This is only a third of the description. There were 444 lots in all.

Margaret Kelly needed all the funds she could raise to complete the education of her children. She had two clerks to the justices in her family — her brother Charles Jones, Clerk to Caernarfon Magistrates and a brother-in-law John Charles Hughes, Clerk to Dolgellau Magistrates, and therefore plenty of advice. She died in 1932 at the age of 83 years having been a widow for 30 years. Her eldest son Robert Stewart Kelly (Robin) is featured separately but he always remained in Mold and was a great support to her.

The second son was Thomas Thelwell Kelly, born 28th May, 1876. He entered Shrewsbury School with his brother Robin in May 1889 both being members of F. E. Bennett's house. He left at the end of the summer term in 1893 when he was just 17. He was at the bottom of the Lower Division of the Special Science Form and was technically in the Shell. The forms were 3/4/Shell V/Remove/VI. So he had progressed further than his brother but had had only one term in the Shell.

Notwithstanding his apparent weakness in science, he decided to become a doctor. He features three times in the *Chester Chronicle* in 1902 confirming the continuing magnetism of the Kelly name.

1/2/1902 MEDICAL SUCCESS. Amongst the students of Guy's Hospital who have passed their final examinations and qualified as medical practitioners is Mr Thelwell Kelly second son of the late T. T. Kelly of Bryn Coch, Clerk of the Peace for Flintshire.

8/3/1902 MEDICAL APPOINTMENT for Mr Thelwall Kelly. This gentleman, late of Guys Hospital and second son late of Mr T. T. Kelly, Clerk of the Peace has received a government appointment as civil surgeon to the field forces in South Africa for which place he sails from England next week. This is a third son of Mr Kelly who has offered his services to his country. One is now serving with the Cape Mounted Rifles.

Seven of the Kelly children, 1891

29/3/1902
DEPARTURE OF
MR THELWELL
KELLY
This gentleman who has accepted a post as civil surgeon with the field forces in South Africa sailed on Wednesday in the Steamship *Sicilian*.

He returned to England in June 1903 having served with the Royal Irish Fusiliers, married and was in general practice in Grantham (another coincidence as Alfred Keene had practiced there).

I should pause at this point and refer to the intrepid nature of this generation for travel. The Keene's love affair for the most part was with India while the Kelly's were attracted by South Africa. Our generation, with their 'year out' and back-packing to Australia, *etc.* make out they are trailblazers and original. They have e-mails, good telephones and an air service that can get them home in twenty-four hours. Our travellers of one hundred years ago had none of these and no inoculations they could have before they left, and as we shall see it was not only the men who ventured into the unknown.

Charles Edward Kelly is an example of all of this. He was the third son and born on 1st August 1878. He was educated at Arnold House School, Llandulas, and Queenmore House School, Bromley, in Kent. He then chose the law as his career. It is unclear if he served his articles with his father or a firm in Chester with which his father had started his legal career. He was a youth of undoubted ability and passed his final examination with flying colours in June 1900.

The dull routine of office life was not acceptable to the high spirited and adventurous youngster and he therefore did not apply for admission as a solicitor. We are told thanks to influence in high places he was accepted as a private in the South Africa Constabulary (Baden Powell's force) and sailed for South Africa on 8th January, 1901, in the S.S. *Canada* only a week before his father's death. Private C. E. Kelly (N° 362), died of enteric fever (dysentery) at Klerksdorp, South Africa on 14th April, 1901. There is a simple memorial to him in Mold Parish Church close to that of his father.

Arthur Turner Kelly, the fourth son, was born 20th May, 1880, and died at Bromley, Kent where he was in school, on 2nd June, 1893. His body was brought back to Mold and is buried in the family grave immediately adjoining the car park at Mold cemetery.

Kenneth William Kelly was born 17th February, 1882, and was the third son to go to South Africa. He also went in 1901 and served in the local armed forces. At the time of his mother's death he was in East Griqualand, South Africa. I am told by Hugh Kelly's family that he had to go out to Canada to fetch back the black sheep of the family. While I do not know, I assume it must have been Kenneth and we know nothing more. He can clearly be described as an adventurer.

The sixth son was Cecil Tudor Kelly, born 5th October, 1883. His education was at Sywell House under the Rev Hayward Browne and then at Oswestry School. He was destined for banking and joined the Capital & Counties Bank, serving at Frome and then at Bath. He visited his mother at her home in Rhyl in October 1907 and his brother in Mold. He was tempted by a day's cubbing on the Monday with the Flint and Denbigh Hounds which meant he had to travel back to Bath overnight on the Monday. Hugh Kelly saw him off at Rhyl Station at 10p.m. and he changed at Crewe joining the 1.20a.m. for Bristol via Shrewsbury which had carriages from Glasgow, York and Hull. The train apparently approached Shrewsbury too fast and was badly derailed. Nineteen people were killed or died of their injuries. One of these was Cecil Tudor Kelly who was so badly mutilated that he was wrongly identified at first.

The first the family knew was when the bank in Bath rang to ask why he had not reported for work. He was brought back to Mold for burial. He was the third son who died in Margaret Kelly's lifetime and it was an enormous blow to her. We must remember it was Cecil Kelly who when driving his father back to work after lunch in September 1899 had the pony stumble on a stone and both Kelly's were thrown out onto the road. Tom Kelly had slight injuries to the face while Cecil was practically unhurt.

The seventh son, Hugh Kelly, was the first born after Tom Kelly's attack of typhoid. He was four years younger than Cecil. He went to Llandovery College and was the third son to qualify as a solicitor. But he did it away from the Practice. He commenced in practice in Rhyl in 1911 and was able to be involved in advocacy to a great extent and made a reputation for himself. As seems inevitable for a member of the Kelly family he became the part-time Clerk to the Magistrates in Rhyl and Prestatyn in 1930 a position he held until his retirement in 1959. One particular success occurred in 1912 in defending a client who gave a false name and address and then argued successfully he was a *bonefide* traveller to obtain a drink on a Sunday having travelled to Dyserth from Prestatyn a mile and a quarter away.

At last, in June 1890, Tom Kelly had a daughter Margaret Gwynfryd

Gaynor Kelly to be followed by another Mildred Myfanwy Kelly sixteen months later (note Margaret Kelly's influence over the choice of names). They were only ten or eleven when their father died. Their education was by a German governess, Fraulein Schmidt (later Frau Suiren). Their father was very strict with them and they were told not to go into the vegetable garden. They did and then swore they had not, even though they had raspberry juice on their pinafores. They were stopped from going to a party. They were subject to much teasing from their brothers. The boys carried ferrets around and the invited the girls to put their hands in their pockets.

The death of Tom Kelly produced a more liberal regime with Margaret Agnes Kelly. Mildred became engaged to be married around 1910 to an Englishman living in Argentina called Tidswell. She was of course under age. However, Margaret agreed that the marriage could take place and while in Argentina Margaret (junior) was sent out with her to chaperone. The wedding took place and while there Margaret also met another man in the English community — Jacobs — whom she married and her descendents still live there. Some of Mildred's family live in the Mold area again. Both daughters were visiting Mold at the time of Margaret's death and were able to be at the funeral.

The last of Tom and Margaret's children was Harold Turner Kelly, born 5th August, 1893. Before the First World War there was an apprentice scheme in place for emigrants to New Zealand to be engaged in agriculture. Keene's nephew Arthur benefited from this because we have the indentures to inspect. Harold went to New Zealand to farm although some of the family thought he had been sent there to keep him out of trouble. He may have been an exuberant young man, but I think he went there on a farm apprenticeship and he was still there at his mother's death.

Tom Kelly's children varied from the staid to the exuberant and adventurous. But they were all interesting people as a result.

Chapter 17
1947 — Forward

The end of the Second World War brought many changes to the United Kingdom and to Wales and the Practice was not exempt.

Robin Kelly, the sole partner, was over 70 years of age and decided he had had enough of general practice. He was to continue as part-time Clerk to the Justices and Under-Sheriff until 1953. He transferred the Practice to Walker, Smith & Way who Thomas Thelwell Kelly had asked to help over fifty years before when he and Keene were overwhelmed with the amount of work they had to do. Robin Kelly had moved the practice in 1943/44 to Dyffryn House in Wrexham Street and he continued to occupy the ground floor while the Practice remained on the first floor.

Two new personalities arrived in the town — John Cwyfan Hughes and Hugh Gough.

John Cwyfan Hughes had not been fit enough to serve in the war because of major problems with his eyesight which were to affect him all his life.

For the first time the Practice was served by solicitors who were not politically Conservative — Cwyfan was a Welsh radical and the son of a very famous Welsh Calvinistic minster. He had been University College, Aberystwyth at the same time as many of the best Welsh legal brains that dominated the Welsh law for the next thirty years or so. He was the first who had not qualified after five years articles, having only to serve three with his having a law degree. He had been articled to Lloyd-Jones, a Bangor solicitor — very convenient for a man of Anglesey.

At the outbreak of the war Lloyd-Jones told John Cwyfan 'I am off to the war. Look after things until I get back', and went. John Cwyfan was in at the deep end and swam beautifully. When Lloyd-Jones came back at the end of the war, John Cwyfan moved on to Walker, Smith & Way and started to work in Mold from 1st January 1947, the take-over date.

He approached the law with deeply entrenched values which he taught to all who worked with him. I can never remember his indulging in any sharp practice with any other solicitor. To see Armon Ellis (from the main rivals in the town) and Cwyfan Hughes dealing with each other was a real education. The clients were always put first and the arguments were hard and fair.

After more than sixty years the Practice was headed by a solicitor who had the energy of Thomas Thelwell Kelly. Some of you who read this will have memories of trying to keep up with Cwyfan Hughes in his social life. He changed his car in the early days with great regularity and it was not unknown for John and Menna Cwyfan to come in from going out and go to work. Life was a challenge to be met head on.

Cwyfan Hughes had an early break for a young solicitor coming to a new town. Manufacturers of agricultural equipment locally had a major problem with one of their models. The machine was a baler which picked up the hay and straw on the fields and packed it into bales before dropping the bale onto the fields again. It was essential that it tied knots which held. Very many machines had been sold and the knots on the bales kept coming undone. Thousands and thousands of pounds were claimed by the customers of the manufacturers. All Cwyfan Hughes' legal skills were brought into play. All claims were settled for a very low sum and the firm survived to be a major employer in the area for a great many years. His reputation was made.

It was Cwyfan Hughes who offered me a partnership after only three years qualification and I had neither asked for nor expected one. I will always be grateful for this and the gift of a debenture for the National Stadium in Cardiff.

He was accompanied to Mold by Hugh Gough who was a victim of the outbreak of the war. He had started his articles before the war travelling into Chester by train from his home in Nannerch. He was called up before he had completed and passed his finals. Like many returning from the war

Robin Steele-Mortimer of Golden Grove, Llanasa, signs his declaration of office in the presence of his predecessor, Colonel Jones-Mortimer, the Deputy Lieutenant, Colonel Davies-Cooke, and Hugh Gough.

a return to study was difficult but, with John Cwyfan's help, support and encouragement, he made it and was admitted in March 1948.

After six years, having bosses did not suit and the Practice resumed the name of Keene & Kelly and was, by now, settled in The Limes, a former dame school, at the top of the High Street, with Cwyfan Hughes and Hugh Gough as the only partners. There has never been a suggestion the name should be changed.

'Partnership is like marriage — for life' was one of Cwyfan Hughes maxims and the result was harmony all the time. The fracturing and new partnerships that went on elsewhere, particularly in Wrexham, earned many adverse comments from him. When Robin Kelly was accelerated to become high sheriff it was only Hugh Gough who could succeed him as under-sheriff. Cwyfan Hughes would have emigrated rather than carry the wand, a view that I shared and which helped to cement our relationship.

The solemnity and tradition of the post suited Hugh Gough down to the ground. He could converse with the landed gentry or the giants of local manufacturing with great ease as they occupied the office of high sheriff and he valued its history. He led the high sheriff and the judge with all the importance that the occasion demanded; Robin Kelly, as his first sheriff, gave directions and advice to him which, if he followed, invariably meant he would not go wrong. However we had no doubt that if an attack was made on Her Majesty's Assize Judge it would be the police who would effectively defend him — not Hugh Gough.

The sheriffs who are appointed do have an enormous pride in their achievement but not all go as far as Charles Davison of Connah's Quay who presented his parish church with a full peal of bells to commemorate his service as sheriff.

Many mark their year of office in different ways. 'Cass' Jones-Mortimer served as sheriff for Flintshire and Denbighshire, qualifying for both. He researched the previous appointees going back hundreds of years. He also published the speeches he made at the Assize luncheons. In one he quoted the words of a minor bard from south Wales who published this stanza in his entry for an Eisteddfod prize poem on the set theme of the 'County Towns of Cambria'.

> If Penyffordd and Penycae
> and others I should fill in
> mean what they say pray tell me why
> Mold's not called Penicillin.

When Hugh Gough was under-sheriff of Flintshire only, he sent his officer Charlie Adams to distrain on the goods of a farmer. It turned out that part of his land was in Flintshire and part in Denbighshire. The verbal report received said 'he had driven a sufficient number of cattle from Denbighshire into Flintshire and levied on them.'

Not long after Hugh Gough became under-sheriff, it was announced that the Lord Chief Justice, Lord Goddard, was to retire after about thirty years in the post. Since he had been a judge, he had never been the Assize judge on the Wales and Chester circuit. So he decided to come for his swansong. He had gained a fearful reputation and threw the whole area into panic. Senior police officers hardened with service became jelly at the mention of his name. All arrangements for the Assize were checked, re-checked and then checked again. The Clerk of the Peace responsible for the administration of justice at Quarter Sessions quivered at the thought of Goddard's possible inquiries. After all the apprehensions, the visit passed normally but the sighs of relief could have been heard miles away. This is the only occasion the lord lieutenant shared the bench with the judge and the high sheriff.

Major changes started from 1947. After over two hundred years women became the main employees and Maglona Jones became the first to be employed by Cwyfan soon to be followed by her sister Glenys who later became my first secretary after qualifying, after having her children — others followed. The First World War had brought women into the office such as the Misses Ellis, but men still predominated.

The mining leases that had been the mainstay with appointments for Alfred Keene and Tom Kelly were no more. The legal work of the landed estates and the lords of Mold had long gone and the rapid expansion of the property owning democracy was under way.

Good title for thirty years had to be produced by a purchaser's solicitor. The Gwysaney estate as an example had been subjected to an entail for many years. This was a device which ensured successions and prevented an impecunious heir raising excessive mortgages or selling. As soon as the heir was twenty one it was entailed again. It did mean that the title started with a vesting deed of 1851. The title was well known locally but must have been a shock to an outsider. Newly qualified solicitors think an entail is what you put on a donkey!

The Law Society in its anxiety to prevent unfair competition had brought in a minimum scale to regulate the fees for conveyancing. Law Society officials were always locally and nationally claiming that there were so many different steps in a conveyance to justify the scale. Cwyfan would never have broken the scale unilaterally but was not worried by the threat to its existence. 'The Lord will provide' was his eternal optimism but he would explain that there were so many lawyers in Parliament we need not worry.

Cwyfan Hughes somewhere met Haydn Roberts from Holywell whose

Hugh Gough (carrying the top hat) leads the Sheriff's Chaplain, the High Sheriff (Tom Hibbert), Lord Chief Justice Goddard, the Lord Lieutenant Brigadier Watkin Mainwaring and other dignitaries in the walk to and from the Parish Church before the commencement of the Mold Assizes, 1956.

Lord Chief Justice Goddard and the Lord Lieutenant Brigadier Watkin Mainwaring, en route to the Mold Assizes, 1956.

official description was public relations officer for the Road Haulage Association. He was a father confessor for every road haulier in north Wales.

In the post war years, it was possible to buy an army surplus vehicle and secure a contract to do work. To avoid open conflict the licensing system was introduced for 'A', 'B' and 'C' licences. On an 'A' licence you could carry another's goods on certain terms and on a 'C' licence you could carry your own. A 'B' licence was a bit of both but with clearly defined terms and definitions.

To supervise the system a licensing authority was created and split up for several parts of the country and north Wales was included in the north west. If you wished to obtain or to change the terms of your license you applied to the licensing authority for permission. Your proposal was advertised and other haulers or objectors and notably British Road Services and British Railways were given the opportunity to object. The licensing authority held a public hearing to consider the matter.

There was a belief that these matters should be resolved locally and about once a quarter as required the licensing authority would sit in both Welshpool or Newtown and Caernarfon. All the interested parties, other than the licensing authority, would gather the night before at the Elephant & Castle in Newtown or the Royal Goat Hotel, Beddgelert.

Cwyfan Hughes chose to instruct counsel, which was the start of a very long friendship with Edward Jones and Gerald Crowe, (both later judges), who were at the Liverpool bar. After dinner, Haydn Roberts would marshal the hauliers whose cases were listed for the next day to have final conferences. Reg Milner the shorthand writer, Bob Beames and Arthur Hill for British Railways and Arthur Jolly for B.R.S. would have gone to their rooms to prepare their cases for the next day. The party would then reassemble about 9.30p.m. for a very convivial evening. Gerald Crowe was even known to go fishing at night for sea trout in the Glaslyn whatever the hour or light.

The haulage agreement became as important as the mining lease had been in earlier times. This was the document when a haulier sold his business to another. There were no word processors or photographic machines so everything had to be checked by two people although it was following a general form.

Bob Beames was a very good specialist lawyer and a real gentleman. On his retirement from British Railways he joined the Practice as a consultant to do licensing work and some advocacy. He may have been poacher turned gamekeeper but the haulage industry were very pleased to have him on their side. He would telephone me and say I have some papers to bring back, do you fancy a spot of lunch. He was such good company the answer was always yes.

When Bob joined as a consultant, Hugh Gough was summoned by the judge at the Assize suddenly one day. It was Mr Justice Daniel Brabin who wanted to know how Bob had been persuaded to join us. 'You are not so soft are you?' — they had met together in the war in foreign parts.

There was no tradition of advocacy when Cwyfan Hughes arrived. Robin Kelly had been Clerk to the Magistrates and so could not appear in his own courts. Thomas Kelly did attend inquests and appear in the County Court but this was limited as were the cases in the High Court. Some liquor licenses came to Cwyfan Hughes but not a lot more. Haulage cases, with many hauliers, such as Edgar Williams of Williams Brothers, who in turn became powerful figures in the industry, became very important.

Road hauliers inevitably came into conflict with the police and this led to their being prosecuted in all parts of the county. They wanted an insurance scheme to cover their representation before the courts. Cwyfan Hughes negotiated a lump sum on an annual basis to cover such a scheme. It covered all cases in Magistrates Courts arising out of the operations of their vehicles. This association continues in a different form today. On qualifying I was called upon to go all over the North West Licensing Authority area and beyond and John Gregory has continued this involvement since qualifying.

In the early, 1960s *Stones Justices Manual* which had been the bible for Magistrates Court work was supplanted for road traffic work by *Wilkinson on Road Traffic*. He was clerk to East Anglian Justices. It is now the 'bible' of today.

A haulier client was charged with 'causing' the commission of an offence before Lichfield magistrates and I was asked to represent and plead not guilty. We attended the court and, probably because I was a visiting advocate, I was put into the court with the Clerk to the Magistrates himself a man of considerable experience acting as clerk. I had taken the view that in his book Wilkinson had in fact advanced arguments, which were wrong and, in addressing the court, was having to make it clear that I disagreed with the 'oracle' Wilkinson. At the end of my address the Clerk stood up and indicated that he knew Mr Wilkinson well, very well indeed in fact (my heart stopped) and he disagreed with him as well on this. Relief!

On another occasion, a haulier was referred to me with a charge of using a defective motor vehicle, which had left a trail of diesel through the Mersey Tunnel. The summons said the fuel pipe was defective. All the evidence the prosecution required was that it was the hauliers vehicle and the defect existed. No knowledge was required. Hauliers always wanted to plead not guilty — their representation was being paid for — I advised them to plead guilty to having a defective fuel pipe. But my instructions were to fight.

The evidence given was that it was the haulier's vehicle and the return fuel pipe that was defective. At the end of the prosecution case the Clerk immediately stood up and said to the magistrate before I could move 'wrong part specified, please dismiss' — humiliation after the advice.

Advocacy is the presentation of the client's case in the best possible light whether he has pleaded guilty or not guilty. I was once presenting a plea in mitigation for a man who was drunk when he committed offences. He had been drinking a well-known proprietary brand of a French drink. His instructions to me were that this particular drink had the effect that you could be sober one minute and very drunk the next. I presented his explanation to the magistrates and named the product concerned. I think the national press had been in court for another case that did not realize their hopes. So they seized on my case and gave it very wide publicity. The result was that I drew down upon myself the wrath of the product manufacturers who were going to sue me left right and centre if I did not detract my comments. I had an uncomfortable fortnight when I had done nothing wrong. But my comments were protected having being made in an open court.

Appearing in a strange court meant that you were often listened to with greater attention than in your own local court. The Practice is still one of the leading firms in the country for haulage law — driving hours, records and the condition of vehicles. A charge of a dangerous load was endorsable, whereas an insecure load was not and to the haulier, trading in his own name, this was important with regard to maintaining a clean driving licence.

London solicitors tend to regard a country solicitor as a country bumpkin. Alfred Keene and Thomas Kelly were a match for anyone, as was Cwyfan Hughes. I remember a client of ours proposing to sell out and London solicitors were instructed for the proposed purchaser and suggested we all meet in London to finalize the arrangements.

Cwyfan Hughes wanted me to go with him, not for my expertise, but for moral support. Cwyfan was dealing with all aspects of the case whilst if a different point was raised the London solicitors had to call some one else in. Their lawyers were coming in and out like yo-yos and, because of the limited specialized knowledge they had, Cwyfan Hughes was running out rings around them. The deal fell through because the purchasers solicitors had met their match.

On another occasion I remember a London barrister at a public inquiry into a new road being very boorish and objectionable to many of the local solicitors. That was before he clashed with Armon Ellis who figuratively put his foot on him and then turned his heel to squash him into the ground — you could almost hear the cheering from the locals. He learnt the hard way that out in the provinces there are some very able men.

The fact that he practiced in Wales was very important to Cwyfan Hughes and the Welsh language was a priority. In the 1960s the Mold Urban District Council decided it was time to name the extension to Lon Bryn Coch. They resolved to name it Upper Bryn Coch. A sixth former at Ysgol Maes Garmon, without her parents' knowledge, responded to the public advertisement by exercising her statutory right of objection which meant that the issue had to come before the Magistrates Court. The girl's father who was a chief officer with the county council was very alarmed and consulted Cwyfan Hughes. He fully supported her views but felt he was in a difficult position.

Cwyfan Hughes also agreed with her views and the Practice agreed without hesitation that she should be represented before the magistrates free of charge by me.

She objected to the hybrid English and Welsh and wanted to argue for Bryn Coch Uchaf. This was the time before the position of the Welsh language was strengthened by an Act of Parliament. The case attracted national publicity. Now she would have had her own way and I never understood why her objection was not allowed by the council or upheld by the magistrates.

Cwyfan Hughes was never afraid of something new. Roger Prys was in private practice in Pwllheli and had extensive industrial connections with people such as the Industrial Association of Wales, He came and joined the Practice in about 1958 as a partner and did some court work as well. Roger Prys was a partner for about three years but it did not succeed and he went off to practice on his own in Rhyl.

Whether the employment of so many women was a shock to the Practice I do not know but, by the time I arrived in 1955, they were well in place. Ray Houghton a fine old character who had been a commercial traveller for years was part-time cashier but the staff were all women. The Practice would have had cleaning ladies but I think Victorian solicitors preferred the layers of dust as they could see if anything had been moved.

These were the days before photocopiers and word processors and central heating. The partners secretaries first job was to light the coal fires in the partners' rooms and I never ceased to be surprised at the timing of the partners arrival just as the fire started to give out heat. I am assured that the partners were still there after the fire had ceased to emit heat!

These were the hey-day of the short-hand typist. A cylinder dictaphone did exist but it was not successful. Shorthand was essential and all the girls of that era cultivated it and were very successful and speedy at receiving dictation. Wills that were drafted had to be re-typed to be engrossed with extra clauses and then every document checked.

It was the day of the abstract of title, a form of legal shorthand whereby the contents of document of title could be reduced from the original. Producing an abstract of title was an art form and I have checked many with Stella Thomas, later to be the wife of a high sheriff. Nobody could make them shorter.

The advent of the photocopier machine produced the 'Epitome of Title' and a skill was lost. For a building estate the abstract was printed. Alfred Keene's clerks wrote an abstract out by hand using the same skills.

With all the talk now of vocational training, the Daniel Owen School in Mold, under Ceriog Williams, produced quality highly motivated girls to work in offices and the Practice reaped the full benefit.

Cwyfan Hughes recognized the skills available from the 'clerks' and two attempts were made for young men to train to become old-fashioned clerks. The experiment failed and both went on to higher things and it was no fault of theirs. Time had moved on and any male unqualified staff are few and far between.

Deeds still turn up locally relevant with the name Keene & Kelly written in the handwriting of J. T. Jones, the last of the clerks and a lifelong member of the Mold Parish Church choir.

Cwyfan had the idea of opening a branch office in Connah's Quay in anticipation of a client building an estate that never materialized. We were there for over 35 years until Law Society supervision regulations made it almost impossible to retain. Cwyfan thought it was a first branch office for the practice, but did not know of Thomas Mann Keene's Buckley office before the First World War.

While Cwyfan Hughes blazed new trails, Hugh Gough was left to deal with the old ladies inherited from Robin Kelly. When nephew Johnny in Canada wrote and nephew Bill in Australia did not, wills were changed every six months. By this time Cwyfan Hughes no longer lived in the flat over the office but had moved to Pantymwyn. Part of the flat was occupied by his parents-in-law whilst the office expanded into the rest. They became very familiar sights around the office and, even after her death, Mrs Jones was seen around the office kitchen by people who did not know her in her lifetime.

It would be wrong to regard Hugh Gough's legal experience as dull or uneventful. It has been long established that any alleged deal affecting land has to be the subject of some record in writing signed by the person against whom it is sought to enforce a deal. This also relates to options that affect land. A client of Hugh Gough's had negotiated with another without solicitor involvement just such an option that was evidenced in writing. He refused to honour the agreement. A meeting was then arranged to discuss the matter between the two clients and the solicitors they had appointed including Hugh Gough. The negotiations were getting nowhere when

Hugh Gough's client who had signed the option suddenly grabbed the piece of paper (the option) off the table and ate it. There were not any photostatic copies and I think this was the end of the matter.

It became necessary for Cwyfan Hughes to move back into town for his children's social life. Where did he choose? The Cottage in Hendy Road where Alfred Thomas Keene had brought up his family. Only one of his children qualified as a solicitor — two of Cwyfan Hughes's children qualified — Rhys and Eleri both now practice in Anglesey with their uncle Dafydd.

The saying a cobbler is worst shod is so true. I learnt when I went to the office in 1955 that Cwyfan Hughes was on the Rolls as John Lewis Hughes but he also had an old family name Cwyfan. It took ten to fifteen years to get round to making the statutory declaration to change the name on the Roll to John Lewis Cwyfan Hughes.

Bob Roberts must have left half of himself with Keene & Kelly when he became full-time clerk at the Mold U.D.C. His interest in his grandson led him to his prevailing upon Cwyfan Hughes to accept John Gregory as the last five-year articled pupil. Cwyfan took his responsibilities for articled clerks very seriously and because of this turned many down. He viewed this duty to educate and instruct as paramount. He gave into pressure three times for which John and I will always be grateful. John stayed and is now the senior partner.

The under-sheriff of Denbighshire, Ivan Edwardes-Evan, was elderly and often asked for help from Hugh Gough. Eventually, John became Under-Sheriff of Denbighshire alongside Hugh Gough as Under-Sheriff for Flintshire (but Hugh Gough had been under-sheriff for both since 1974), and on the latter's retirement became Under-Sheriff for Clwyd — a post he holds today and also serves on the Under-Sheriff's Association. This association would have been unknown in Tom Kelly's day, but it is now important and John Gregory serves on its committee. He is currently vice-president and takes over the presidency of the association in May 2003. The former counties became baliwicks within the Clwyd Sheriffwick.

This led to John serving on the committee of the Sheriffs Officers Association and their Complaints Advisory Board. How would he have dealt with Hugh Gough moving livestock?

He has served on the I.T.C. Board (ITV Complaints) not available to Tom Kelly! — the Practice continually breaks new ground. Sheriffs, with John's encouragement, now visit prisons and the local services, such as probation and police, that are involved in the administration of justice.

There had always been an Assize service at Mold church on the first day of the Assize although the direction from the Lord Chancellor was for cessation. On the abolition of Assizes, Hugh Gough was determined the

Swearing in the first High Sheriff of Clwyd, Philip Warburton Lee. Seated in front are two under-sheriffs, Ivan Edwards-Evans and Hugh Gough. The two lords lieutenant are on the bench, to the right of the High Sheriff

service would be saved and the judges have supported this. It became the Crown Court Service, and after Hugh Gough's retirement, John Gregory has ensured the service continued. Only one other county — Cornwall — initially kept it and one of the judges told Hugh Gough that in Cornwall you would not know that the Assizes had been abolished.

Support for the local Law Society continued and both Cwyfan Hughes and Hugh Gough served a two-year stint on the committee, but no-one aspired to be the second president (after Thomas Thelwell Kelly).

Legal Aid came in after the war and made a tremendous change. Local solicitors were part of the self-regulatory system that was introduced. The Practice was held in sufficient esteem and respect for both John and myself to be asked to serve for over twenty years each on the local committee. A service which was designed to help the less well off to obtain access to justice was eventually overwhelmed by those in the profession who thought it was a ticket to print money. The bills that had to be firmly taxed on appeal always featured the same firms.

The County Court had become the means of enforcing debt by means of the judgment summons. For those recalling the scene in the film *Brothers in Law* when the hero goes into court to deal with one of these can be told how true to life it was. Only on the second time would the judge support a committal order (to prison). It was the short straw drawn by all the young solicitors in the town to have to deal with agency Judgement Summonses!

Divorce jurisdiction was sought for Mold but never obtained but the Practice developed an extensive practice in this field that would not have been acceptable to Alfred Keene. In those days hearings were in public and the law has become more complicated. Parliament has looked after its own again.

Government refused to fund indefinitely and the present emaciated Legal Aid scheme is no substitute for what the creators intended.

With the aftermath of the war and the advent of Cwyfan Hughes the nature of the Practice changed. Not only did we appear in the Magistrates Court, in the Lands Tribunal Court, the County and High Courts, but also in the Tribunals.

What a new world opened up with the industrial tribunal. The case law built up and all sacked employees felt they had leave to seek legal or union advice. The Practice soon established an expertise and involvement in this. New doors opened as old ones closed.

The day of the bookies runner was over when the Betting and Gaming Act came into force — we did not have to defend them. Now cash bets could be placed off the race course. But solicitors had to apply for bookmakers permits and licenses for betting offices.

The public appointments, so important to the legal profession, became fewer. Clerks to the Magistrates, County Court Registrars and even some coroners, became full-time. But do not worry, the solicitors had other opportunities. Solicitors could become part-time judges. All sorts of appeals tribunals became established — a Mental Health, Social Security and deputy district judges for the County Court and many others.

The Practice appeared in Quarter Sessions and Assizes both for the defence and the prosecution. All the evidence in committal proceedings was typed before the many accelerations of today's procedure.

The Practice started to appear in the Law Reports where cases of sufficient legal interest are reported. Cwyfan Hughes had Goldsack v Shore. Hugh Gough had Bartley and Bartley. I had Roberts and Evans and L. Rowlands & Co. before the V.A.T. Appeal Tribunal and in all cases the Practice was successful.

Crime began to figure more and more and several murders and attempted murders were successfully handled.

The Limes was no longer big enough on its own and 93 High Street was bought and incorporated to be followed some years later by the acquisition of Winston House.

Exactly one hundred years after Thomas Thelwell Kelly was agent for the Conservatives in the General Election in 1874, John Gregory was agent for the Liberal candidate. Both their candidates were unsuccessful.

Cwyfan Hughes retired to his beloved Anglesey and Gareth Morris Jones from Anglesey joined the team shortly afterwards. Hugh Gough followed him into retirement and now lives in his mother's old house. Who sold her the house? — why Robin Kelly when he moved to Mynydd Isa in 1950, another of this story's coincidences.

The records are full of Alfred Thomas Keene taking instructions and asking counsel to advise or settle documents. This style and tradition was continued by Cwyfan Hughes in his relationships with Professor Joseph Turner (Uncle Jo) a Liverpool chancery specialist. His speed of turn around of his papers was legendary. Unfortunately he was one of the first to have a dictating machine and as the papers bounced on his desk from the postman, the microphone was in his hand. The advice was always sound but if the papers had bounced once or twice more the written opinion might have been shorter.

Hugh Gough continued to be the establishment figure dealing with the incoming, outgoing and would-be sheriffs. At the time of General Elections, Mrs Kathleen Davies-Cooke would call to give him Conservative literature not realizing that he was the first subscriber to the *Liberal News* that I ever knew. Robin Guest and I have both served as county councillors.

The Practice did try to move with the times and the first word processor in a legal practice in Mold was installed and the ability to change a document without retyping the whole was such an improvement.

From being a general practice, the changes that were occurring made it very difficult for one solicitor to advise his client on all matters. This was something the client found difficult to understand. Even in a county town specialization had to come. There were enough solicitors for this to be done. Cwyfan Hughes once said that all we did not deal with was shipwrecks and patents. The last fifteen years has rectified these omissions.

The Law Society was moving towards giving solicitors specific recognitions in certain areas. The Legal Aid Franchise Family Law Panel: Accident Line.

As other doors closed, the Children Act created the need for specialist knowledge and understanding. All had to know about the Act, but the experts had to implement it and Gareth Jones is the acknowledged partner specialist.

This meant that the accounts had to become computerized a Law Society requirement and the Practice was the last in Mold to go down this road. The human based and operated system had to be jettisoned for one less efficient. Access to required information became more difficult. The existing staff had been too good and the machine took a long time to be accepted.

The Practice moved forward so much that now, not only did women make up the mainstay of the staff, but it was the first practice in Mold to take on a female articled clerk. I was never allowed to forget taking her to a site meeting on a muddy farm.

The Practice is a very real and living entity and has been joined by Robin Guest since my retirement. It will go on and it is indestructible and has served the town and the area well for over three hundred years. Cwyfan Hughes was proud of its history and would tell anybody who would listen of its importance and history. I am sure that those that come after me will be able to say the same and justify it.

The Practice is about vocation, people, real people and how and why they do things. It is about professional service for the community. It will go on.